此专著获得了下列课题的资助：

1.粤港澳大湾区旅游产业发展促进乡村振兴社科研究基地（KY202108），广东科学技术职业学院 2021 年度校级科研与社会服务平台项目。

2.广东省"十三五"教育科学规划课题（德育专项）"珠海市大中小学运用本土抗战资源打造红色思政教育品牌研究"，编号 2020JKDY071。

世界旅游组织教学质量认证在中国的实践探析

杨义德　朱瀚　魏微　著

天津出版传媒集团

天津科学技术出版社

图书在版编目（CIP）数据

世界旅游组织教学质量认证在中国的实践探析 / 杨义德, 朱瀚, 魏微著. -- 天津：天津科学技术出版社，2023.3

ISBN 978-7-5742-0949-7

Ⅰ.①世… Ⅱ.①杨… ②朱… ③魏… Ⅲ.①旅游教育 – 教学质量 – 研究 – 中国 Ⅳ.①F590-05

中国国家版本馆CIP数据核字(2023)第045096号

世界旅游组织教学质量认证在中国的实践探析
SHIJIE LÜYOU ZUZHI JIAOXUE ZHILIANG RENZHENG
ZAI ZHONGGUO DE SHIJIAN TANXI

责任编辑：马　悦

责任印制：兰　毅

出　　版：天津出版传媒集团
　　　　　天津科学技术出版社

地　　址：天津市西康路35号

邮　　编：300051

电　　话：（022）23332490

网　　址：www.tjkjcbs.com.cn

发　　行：新华书店经销

印　　刷：定州启航印刷有限公司

开本 710×1000　1/16　印张 17.25　字数 262 000

2023年3月第1版第1次印刷

定价：98.00元

序　言

　　姜大源曾说："中国高等职业教育是世界教育百花园里的一朵奇葩。这是以 1300 所高职院校的体量生存于中国广袤国土上的一种教育，是与中国改革开放同步发展起来的一种教育。"如今，高水平学校和高水平专业群建设正在中国大地上如火如荼地进行着。

　　杨义德团队善于学习和大胆创新，在没有多少先例可循的条件下，杨义德和他的同事们不畏艰难、不惧繁杂，在中山大学有关专家的鼓励下，积极主动地探索联合国世界旅游组织教育质量认证的理论和规律，勇于创新、大胆实践，历经两年时光顺利获得联合国世界旅游组织教育质量认证！

　　本书从质量认证的六个维度（雇主、学生、教师、课程、管理以及旅游道德规范等）进行了深入细致的阐述，为其他兄弟院校参与类似认证提供了良好的范本，对其他院校旅游大类专业参与国际组织认证具有较好的借鉴意义和指导价值。

教育部全国高职高专旅游管理教学指导委员会委员、教授　吴肖淮

2022 年 10 月 10 日

♀ 前 言 ♀

　　教育部在《教育部 2018 年工作要点》启动中国特色高水平高职学校和专业建设计划，即"双高建设计划"。坚持扶优扶强和提升整体保障相结合，建设一批当地离不开、业内都认可、国际可交流的优质高职院校。近年来，各大高职院校都在为入选中国双高院校而快马加鞭地进行院校建设，其中旅游大类专业群建设格外抢眼，各大旅游院校除了加强自身建设之外，还积极参与世界旅游组织教学质量认证。

　　世界旅游组织教学质量认证（UNWTO TedQual）是由联合国的专门机构世界旅游组织主持进行的项目，旨在对全球范围内从事旅游教育、研究和培训的机构进行全方位、多维度、立体式的人才培养质量评估，对符合其质量标准并采取行之有效措施实施全球旅游道德规范的机构颁发认证证书。

　　笔者曾于 2018 年主持广东科学技术职业学院旅游管理专业接受该组织的教学质量认证的会议。广东科学技术职业学院成为广东省第一所通过该项认证的高职院校。

　　在有关方面的关心和支持下，项目主持者将其参与认证的理论与实践进行梳理，终以书稿形式面世。本书将是国内最早系统探讨世界旅游组织教学质量认证理论与实践的专著之一，既有通俗易懂的理论，又有操作具体的实践。既可以作为旅游院校专业和课程改革的参考用书，也可以作为应用型本科和高职院校参与认证的指导用书。

　　由于作者水平有限，书中难免存在不足之处，敬请读者朋友批评指正！

杨义德 朱瀚 魏微

2022 年 10 月

目 录

第一章 联合国世界旅游组织质量认证概要

第一节 世界旅游组织教学质量认证体系的概念阐释

联合国世界旅游组织（United Nations World Tourism Organization，UNWTO）是联合国的政府间国际组织，是旅游领域的领导性国际组织，其总部设在西班牙马德里。最早由国际官方旅游宣传组织联盟(IUOTPO)发展而来。2003年11月成为联合国的专门机构。其宗旨是促进和发展全球旅游事业，使之有利于经济发展、国际相互了解、和平与繁荣。

A quality assurance certificate awarded by UNWTO to those Education Institutions who have met the quality requirements established by UNWTO and who can prove that they have taken steps towards implementing the Global Code of Ethics for Tourism.

由联合国世界旅游组织（UNWTO）向符合该组织制定的质量标准和要求，并证明已采取适当的措施执行全球旅游业道德守则的教育机构颁发质量认证证书。

联合国世界旅游组织教育质量认证（简称"教育质量认证"）是联合国世界旅游组织Themis基金会（UNWTO Themis Foundation）支持下开展的全球性旅游教育质量认证项目，主要评估全世界范围内的旅游院校

能否在专业领域中为学生提供高标准的专业教育和实践训练，并致力于提升旅游教育质量水平。通过该质量认证已成为打造和培育全球一流旅游教育机构的必经之路。

联合国世界旅游组织教育质量认证主要从五个维度进行：办学定位和人才培养目标与社会需求的适应度、人才培养目标与培养效果的达成度、教学资源对人才培养的保障度、教学质量保障机制运行的有效度以及学生和用人单位的满意度。

图 1-1　办学定位、培养目标与社会需求的适应性框架

第二节　项目认证的意义

联合国世界旅游组织教育质量认证具有以下 6 个方面的意义：

（1）TedQual 教育质量认证是由联合国世界旅游组织颁发的唯一具有国际标准的旅游教育、培训及研究项目的质量认证。

（2）通过认证的项目可以在其官方文件、宣传材料和认证文件上使用联合国世界旅游组织 TedQual 认证的标志图案。

（3）通过认证的项目及相关机构可以拥有更多的交流手段，获得国际性的推广与促进。

（4）有机会参加由联合国世界旅游组织举办的各种旅游教育、培训活动。为获得认证的机构提供与政府部门和私营企业进行沟通合作的机会。

（5）有机会申请加入联合国世界旅游组织教育与科学委员会（UNWTO Education and Science Council）。

（6）认证机构将成为由联合国世界旅游组织 Themis 基金会领导的 TedQual 认证 Network 系统的成员。该网络系统旨在促进成员机构之间以及与联合国世界旅游组织之间的合作，并且进行知识、实践和技术方面的资源共享。

第三节　目前国际国内通过此项认证的机构数量

根据世界旅游组织官方网站的统计，从全球已通过认证的学校分布来看，目前非洲国家 1 所，美洲国家 23 所，中东国家 4 所，亚太国家 25 所，美洲国家 23 所。

中国是通过认证高校最多的国家，共有 24 所高校的不同旅游相关专业获得了认证。中国获得认证的学校有中山大学、暨南大学、华南理工大学、华南师范大学、华侨大学、上海对外经贸大学、北京第二外国语学院、黄山学院、桂林理工大学、青岛大学、香港理工大学、香港中文大学、香港职业训练局、澳门科技大学、澳门城市大学、澳门旅游学院、珠海科技学院、西安欧亚学院等 18 所本科高校和浙江旅游职业学院、成都职业技术学院、山东旅游职业学院、南京旅游职业学院、广东科学技术职业学院、宁波城市职业技术学院等 6 所高职学院。

第四节　项目认证的主要维度

图 1-2 为质量认证的五个维度。

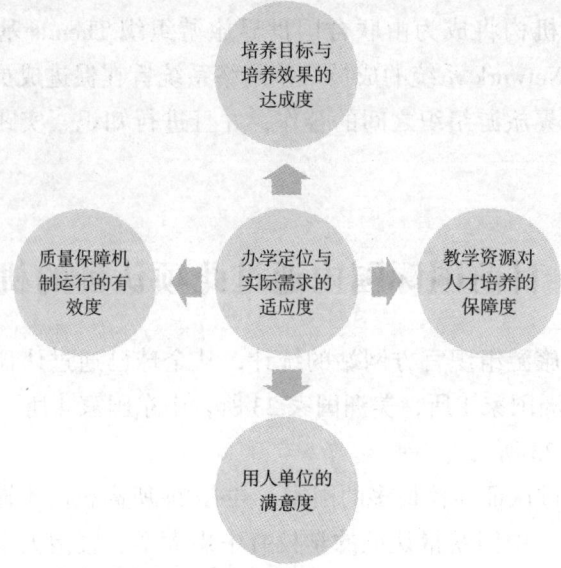

图 1-2　质量认证的五个维度

世界旅游组织教学质量认证各单项的比重如表所示（总分 845 分）。

表1-1

单项	雇主	学生	教师	课程	管理	全球旅游道德规范执行
分值	100	100	100	100	100	345

注：760 分以上为 Grade A（优秀）；630～759 分为 Grade B（良好）；
　　510～629 分为 Grade C（合格）；　510 分以下为 Grade D（未通过）。

第五节　认证的基本程序

一、申请认证的主体

凡从事旅游教育、研究或培训的机构，无论公立或私立，只要具有明确而规范的章程，在培养和教育学生方面有较好的经验与声誉，至少拥有一届以上的毕业生，拥护并执行全球旅游道德规范，皆可申请认证。

二、申请认证的流程

首先，教学机构（旅游院校）向世界旅游组织提出认证申请，世界旅游组织 Themis 基金会通过官方电子邮箱发回登记表；其次，教育机构（旅游院校）反馈登记表，基金会发送进行教学质量自评的邀请；再次，教育机构（旅游院校）反馈自评报告的中英文版本，由世界旅游组织专家进行初评，如通过初评，则缴纳评估费用；最后，基金会与旅游院校协商确定现场（或网络）评估的日程表。评估结束之后三个月内由世界旅游组织 themis 基金会颁发认证证书。

第六节 全球旅游道德规范的执行

世界旅游组织自诞生之日起，便致力于促进全球旅游业的高质量发展，并与 1999 年 9 月通过了全球旅游道德规范。该规范共有以下十条。

Article 1：Tourism's contribution to mutual understanding and respect between peoples and societies.

第一条：

旅游业对促进人民与社会之间相互理解与尊重的贡献。

Article 2：Tourism as a vehicle for individual and collective fulfillment.

第二条：

旅游作为个人与集体满足的工具。

Article 3：Tourism, a factor of sustainable development.

第三条：

旅游是可持续发展的一个因素。

Article 4：Tourism, a user of cultural heritage of mankind and contributor to its enhancement.

第四条：

旅游业：人类文化遗产的利用者及改善这些遗产的贡献者。

Article 5：Tourism, a beneficial activity for host countries and communities.

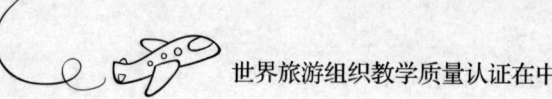

第五条：

旅游业是一项对东道国家和社区有益的活动。

Article 6 : Obligations of stakeholders in tourism development.

第六条：

旅游发展中利益相关者的义务。

Article 7 : Right to tourism.

第七条：

旅游的权利。

Article 8 : Liberty of tourist movements.

第八条：

旅游者活动的自由。

Article 9 : Rights of the workers and entrepreneurs in the tourism industry.

第九条：

旅游业从业人员和企业家的权利。

Article 10 : Implementation of the principles of the Global Code of Ethics for Tourism.

第十条：

全球旅游道德规范原则的实施。

第二章 认证维度中的核心问题

第一节 雇主

一、开设本专业的 SWOT 分析

要开办一个专业通常需要进行多方面的论证，包括师资队伍、教学资源、招生来源、市场需求等，从管理学角度来说，要进行 SWOT 分析。

现以 G 学院为例，运用 SWOT 分析方法详细说明该校旅游管理专业设置的必要性，具体如下：

（一）优势（Strengths）

1.硬件方面优势

G 学院图书馆全馆入藏文献总量达 236 万册，其中包括纸质图书 144 万册（包含过刊合订本 18 239 册，光盘 28 313 张），电子图书 78 万册，电子期刊折合图书 14 万册。引进了知网数据库、读秀数据库、超星电子图书数据库、方正 Apabi 电子图书、新东方多媒体学习库等 10 余种数据库。

G 学院面向本专业学生建立了校内外实训基地。校内建立了中餐实训室、西餐实训室、调酒实训室、茶艺实训室、导游实训室、形体礼仪实训室以及化妆实训室。计算机机房安装了金棕榈旅行社管理软件、云

驴通智慧旅游软件、酒店管理软件等，为学生提供智慧旅游实操平台。校外与广东省拱北口岸中国旅行社、珠海长隆国际海洋度假区、珠海海泉湾度假区、珠海圆明新园旅游有限公司、珠海进出口商会、珠海海湾大酒店、珠海航展公司、珠海华发喜来登酒店、珠海瑞吉酒店、深圳万豪国际酒店等 20 多家旅游景区、企业建立了稳定的实习基地关系。

2. 软件方面优势

G 学院旅游管理专业具有一支结构合理的专兼职教师队伍。专任教师 22 人，其中教授 3 人，副教授 4 人，博士 4 人，双师素质教师 12 人，具有高级茶艺师、高级导游、高级旅游咨询师、高级会展策划师等职业资格证书者多人，旅游酒店总经理、旅行社部门经理、行业协会兼职教师 27 人。在 2013—2018 年由教育部举办的全国职业院校技能大赛广东省选拔赛中，连续 6 年获得一等奖，并获得导游服务、中餐主题宴会设计等赛项国赛一、二等奖。2016 年本专业毕业生在广东省导游职业技能大赛中获得全省冠军，荣获"广东省五一劳动奖章"。

3. 办学模式优势

G 学院旅游管理专业在传统培养模式的基础上积极探索，开展了中高职衔接三二分段培养模式。深入开展校企合作，在广东省内率先实施现代学徒制人才培养方案，并与全国知名企业长隆投资有限公司联合组建广科长隆旅游产业学院，校企共建，共同培养企业真正需要的技能型人才。

4. 专业自身优势

（1）旅游管理专业高度符合珠海市的产业发展的优势、特色和总体趋势。1991 年，珠海旅游城被国家旅游局评为"全国风景名胜 40 佳"。多年来旅游业一直是珠海市的支柱产业。加强城市宣传，加快建设滨海国际休闲旅游目的地和国家全域旅游示范区，推动珠海旅游产品品牌设计，发挥横琴长隆等龙头项目作用，带动旅游消费。① 珠海拥有的五星级酒店、国际旅行社、高尔夫球场的数量居全国前列，珠海城市旅游在全国有相当高的知名度、美誉度和影响力。珠海正在打造的"三高一特"产业体系中的"高端服务业"及"特色海洋经济和生态农业"均与旅游

---

① 姚奕生.2018 年珠海市人民政府工作报告 [EB/OL].（2018-01-30）[2022-10-15]. http://www.zhuhai.gov.cn/gkmlpt/content/1/1839/post_1839265.html#1640.

业有紧密关系。珠海市每次公布的《珠海市产业发展导向目录》，均将旅游业列为优先发展的产业。

（2）G学院旅游管理专业高度符合学校的发展规划。学校"十二五"规划指出，重点发展对现代服务业有重要支撑作用的旅游类和物流类专业。学校"创新强校工程"也将旅游、酒店专业列为重点发展专业。

（3）G学院旅游管理专业已具备明显的优势和特色。旅游管理专业自成立以来，一直设在外国语学院，师资集旅游与外语于一体，是"校级重点专业"，多年来，本专业与珠港澳旅游行业企业合作的深度、本专业学生的 CET-4 和英语导游资格证的通过率、在全国职业院校技能大赛的成绩等方面在全省同类专业中有明显的优势和特色。2018 年 7 月，外国语学院更名为外贸与旅游学院，加强对旅游管理专业的支撑与扶持。

（二）劣势（Weaknesses）

（1）G学院旅游管理专业学科带头人、后备带头人队伍建设有待进一步加强。

（2）G学院旅游管理专业师资年龄、学历、学缘结构有待进一步优化。

（3）G学院旅游管理专业国际合作与交流有待进一步加强。

（三）机会（Opportunities）

旅游行业被称为无烟产业和朝阳产业，是第三产业的重要组成部分，早在 2012 年全国已有 28 个省份将旅游业定位为支柱产业。我国旅游业发展迅猛，2017 年旅游总收入超过 5.3 万亿元，在全球旅游总收入排名中位居第二。连续多年保持世界第一大出境旅游客源国和全球第四大入境旅游接待国。广东省作为旅游大省旅游收入连续多年保持国内领先。珠海市曾以整个城市景观（珠海旅游城）被原国家旅游局授予"全国旅游胜地 40 佳"的称号，2017 年被授予"中国休闲旅游示范城市"荣誉称号。国家"十三五"旅游业发展规划明确表示旅游产业要成为国家支柱产业。《珠海市旅游发展总体规划修编（2016—2030）》提出珠海将"与港澳共建滨海国际休闲旅游目的地"。

广东省是中国经济总量最大和发展最快的省份之一，2017 年广东省实现地区生产总值 89 879.23 亿元，具有较强的消费能力。旅游业发展较早，主要旅游经济指标在全国名列前茅，现已形成工业旅游、农业旅游、乡村旅游、滨海旅游、温泉旅游、休闲旅游等十多个旅游项目。广东省旅游业发展一直处于全国领先水平。根据《广东省旅游业发展"十三五"规划》，"十二五"期间，广东省全省旅游总收入由 2010 年的 3 804 亿元增长到 2015 年的 10 365 亿元，增长 172.5%；旅游业增加值由 2 373 亿元增长到 4 663 亿元，增长 96.5%，占 GDP 比重由 5.2% 增长到 6.4%。入境过夜旅游者从 3 140.93 万人次增长到 3 446.94 万人次，增长 9.7%。国内过夜旅游者从 2.11 亿人次增长到 3.28 亿人次，增长 55.45%。2015 年，全省旅游业直接就业人数约为 190 万人，旅游投资规模达到 1 030 亿元。全省旅游总收入、过夜游客总人数、国内过夜游客人数、旅游业增加值占全省 GDP 和第三产业的比重等主要指标均超额完成任务，分别超出规划目标 19.5%、19%、27.1%、51% 和 55.6%。"十二五"期间，广东省旅行社由 1 292 家增加到 2 128 家，其中出境游组团社由 151 家增加到 332 家；国家旅游星级饭店由 1 204 家降至 936 家，其中五星级饭店由 93 家增至 116 家；国家 A 级旅游景区由 139 家增加到 293 家，其中 5A 级景区由 2 家增至 11 家。目前广东有世界遗产 2 个，国家级旅游度假区 1 家，国家生态旅游示范区 3 家。

（四）威胁（Threats）

根据《中国大学及学科专业评价报告（2020—2021）》，截至 2020 年 1 月，全国高职院校开设旅游管理职业的院校数量达到 834 所。

Now SWOT analysis method is used to explain the necessity of setting up the tourism management program in detail, as follows：

（一）Strengths

1.Advantages in Hardware

The polytechnic library has a total volume of 2.36 million books, among which 1.44 million paper books（including 18,239 volumes of printed bound

books and 28,313 disks), 780,000 electronic books and 140,000 books of electronic journals. More than 10 kinds of databases including CNKI database, duxiu database, super star e-book database, founder Apabi e-book and new Oriental multimedia were introduced.

To cultivate students' vocational skills, the school established more than 10 different training rooms used for Chinese-style canteen service, western canteen service, bartender service, tea art training, tour guide training, shape-up training and cosmetics training. Some rooms installed heavy-hitters include travel agencies operating software, cloud donkey wisdom tourism software, hotel management software to provide students with the wisdom tourism field platform. The school has established a stable practice base with more than 20 tourist attractions and enterprises, including Guangdong Gongbei Port China Travel Service, Zhuhai Chimelong International Marine Resort, Zhuhai Ocean Spring Resort, Zhuhai New Yuanming Park, Zhuhai Import and Export Chamber of Commerce, Zhuhai Marriot Hotel, Zhuhai Airshow Company and Shenzhen Sheraton Hotel.

2. Advantages in Software

This major has a reasonable proportion of professional and part-time teachers. There are 22 full-time teachers, including 3 professors, 4 associate professors and 4 doctors. Among them, there are 12 double-qualified teachers, who have professional qualifications such as tea art technician, tea critic technician, guestroom manager and exhibition planner. Hotel managers, travel agency managers, 27 part-time teachers of industry association. In 2013-2018 vocational skills competitions of Guangdong province, the first prize medalists come out during six consecutive years, and moreover, students from this college won the first prize in the national tour guide service competition and second prize in the Chinese -style banquet design contest in 2018. Also some graduates took part in Guangdong Workers Vocational Skills Contest, won the provincial title of "Guangdong May 1 Labor Medal".

3. Advantages of School-Running Mode

On the basis of the traditional training mode, the tourism management program actively explores the mode of connecting the middle and higher vocational colleges and developing the third-stage training mode. They carry out in-depth school-enterprise cooperation, actively prepare for the establishment of the Guangke Chimelong Modern Service industry College jointly with Chimelong investment and development co., LTD., a well-known enterprise in China, and co-cultivate skilled talents that meet the needs of enterprises.

4. Professional Advantages

Tourism management is highly in line with the advantages, characteristics and development trend of Zhuhai industry. Zhuhai is a good example to be included on the list of the first national excellent tourism cities. For many years, Zhuhai is on the top list of inbound tourism in the whole country and has got third place in Guangdong province, its tourism revenues accounted for more than 16% of the GDP (far higher than that of Shenzhen, Guangzhou and other cities). With a large amount of five-star hotels, international travel agencies and golf courses, Zhuhai city tourism has a high degree of visibility and reputation and influence in the country. The "high-end service industry" and "featured Marine economy and ecological agriculture" in the "three high and one special" industrial system of Zhuhai are closely related to the tourism industry. Every time Zhuhai Government publishes the industrial development oriented catalogue, among which tourism as a priority industry.

The program is in line with the development plan of the school. According to the 12th five-year plan of the polytechnic, tourism and logistics programs, which play an important role in supporting modern service industry, should be developed. The school's "innovation and strengthening project" also lists tourism and hotel majors as key development majors.

This major has obvious advantages and features. Since the establishment over 15 years ago, the tourism management program has been under the supervision of school of foreign languages.As "the key program", over the years, it has widened the professional cooperation with enterprises from Hong Kong and Macao tourism industry.As students wonderful excellence in

CET-4, English tour guide qualification, national and local vocational skills contest the school has demonstrated obviously its professional advantages and characteristics. In July 2018, the school of foreign languages was renamed the school of foreign trade and tourism, which further strengthened the support for the program of tourism management.

（二）Weaknesses

The cultivation of academic leaders of tourism management specialty needs to be further strengthened.

The age, educational background and academic structure of tourism management teachers need to be further strengthened.

The international exchange with tourism management program needs to be further strengthened.

（三）Opportunities

As an important part of the tertiary industry, the tourism industry has become a smoke-free industry and a sunrise industry. As early as 2012, 28 provinces in China have positioned tourism as a pillar industry. China's tourism industry has witnessed rapid development, with total tourism revenue exceeding 5.3 trillion *yuan* in 2017, ranking second in the global total tourism revenue list. For many years, China has been the world's largest source of outbound tourists and the world's fourth largest inbound tourism host country. Guangdong, as a major tourism province, has maintained the highest tourism income in China for many years. In 2017, Zhuhai city was awarded the honorary title of "China's demonstration city of leisure tourism" which is the only one case in Guangdong province. The 13th five-year plan for the development of tourism industry clearly indicates that the tourism industry will become the pillar industry of the country. By 2020, the total tourism market will reach 6.7 billion person-times and the revenue will reach 7 trillion *yuan*. Guangdong plans the tourism revenue reaches 1.6 trillion *yuan* by 2020.

Zhuhai's plan for tourism development（2016–2030）proposes that Zhuhai accomplishes an international leisure tourism destination together with Hong Kong and Macao.

Guangdong is one of the largest and fastest growing provinces in China. In 2017, Guangdong achieved a regional GDP of 89,879.23 billion *yuan*, with strong consumption capacity. And the main tourism economic indicators among the top in the country. The tourism industry has increasingly developed, and more than 10 tourism projects have been formed, including industrial tourism, agricultural tourism, rural tourism, coastal tourism, hot spring tourism and leisure tourism. Guangdong province is located in the southeast coast of China and has a good geographical advantage. With Guangdong–Hong Kong–Macao Greater Bay Area being one of the four major bay areas in the world. The mainland coastline is 4,114km long, ranking first in the country. Guangdong province is the largest tourist source in China, with a permanent population of over 100 million and a high consumption capacity, and a large number of domestic and foreign tourists, forming a stable basic market. A large number of compatriots from Hong Kong, Macao and overseas Chinese, as well as famous overseas Chinese homes such as Shantou and Jiangmen, are also potential tourist markets. According to the data, by 2017, there were 2,345 different kinds of travel agencies in Guangdong（419 outbound travel agencies and 19 foreign travel agencies), 65,348 employees, 1,210 scenic spots across the province（314 rated and 896 unrated), and 21,6012 people. The huge tourism market and tourism enterprises provide good employment prospects for relevantstudents. The rapid tourism development brings a large number of job opportunities. At present, there are about 6 million staff working in the tourism industry, and the actual demand in the industry is about 8 million, with vacancies of nearly 2 million. Moreover, the vacancies are still increasing at a rate of about 200,000 per year.

（四）Threats

By the end of 2017, China had 1,690 higher education institutions and

ordinary institutions of higher learning that offer tourism departments (majors), with 444,400 students, 924 secondary vocational schools and 232,000 students. The increasing number of colleges of the same type will inevitably lead to increased competition for quality students, training, internship and even employment.

二、本专业的使命（Mission）

一所学校的存在自有它的担当与责任，一个专业的开设也有它的使命所在。这一点，国际组织非常重视。

现以 G 学院旅游管理专业为例，阐明其人才培养的使命。

G 学院是国家示范性骨干高职院校，学校的发展目标是成为国内一流、世界知名的高等职业学校。同时，学院是广东省唯一的"互联网+"创新创业示范学校，具有极强的科技特色。旅游管理专业作为首批广东省品牌专业建设点和广东科学技术职业学院十三个省级二类品牌专业之一，是学校办学特色的具体体现。

G 学院旅游管理专业的人才培养使命为培养具有熟练的旅游实践能力和英语应用能力、适应广东省和粤港澳大湾区旅游业需要的高素质涉外旅游技能型人才。本专业就业岗位群：①旅行社岗位群，包括旅行社导游、计调、销售、会议等部门中高级服务员和经营管理人员；②酒店岗位群，包括前厅、客房、餐厅、销售、康体、娱乐、会议等部门的中高级服务员和经营管理人员；③其他旅游企业岗位群，包括国际邮轮公司、旅游运输公司、景区景点、餐饮企业、度假区、会展公司及其他旅游相关企业的从事服务、策划、销售、经营管理的中高级服务员和经营管理人员。

Guangdong Polytechnic of Science and Technology is one of national demonstration vocational colleges, whose target is to develop into a famous vocational college in the world. It is also the only one internet plus entrepreneurship demonstration college in Guangdong. Tourism management major is one of brand major construction sites and one of thirteen provincial brand majors, which is the specific example of school running characteristic.

The mission of professional cultivation in tourism management major are :

to cultivate the students with proficient tourism practical ability and English application ability and tourism management skill needed in Guangdong –Hong Kong– Macao Greater Bay Area tourism.

The Employment posts include： ① travel agency-related（tour guide, operator, salesman, conference attendant, manager）. ② hotel-related（middle to high end waiters or managers of lobby, guest room, restaurant, sales, entertainment, MICE）. ③ other job positions (cruise lines, transport company, tourism sites, catering, holiday resort, exhibition company and other management related to tourism).

三、本专业对学生能力的培养

（一）职业核心能力的培养（Core Professional Ability）

1. 专业知识习得（Professional Knowledge）

（1）了解我国政策法规（包括旅游政策法规）和旅游业发展动态。

To realize the laws and legislation including tourism law in our country and the development of tourism.

（2）掌握4000词左右英语词汇，熟悉旅游业专用英语，掌握基本语法。

To master about 4000 English words, tourism English and basic grammar.

（3）掌握计算机和旅游电子商务的基础知识和操作方法。

To master the usage of computer and the basic knowledge of e-business on tourism.

（4）熟悉旅游客源地和目的地的旅游文化、民俗风情和景点景区概况，熟悉旅游礼仪常识。

To familiarize the culture and folk custom of tourists sites and tourism destination.

（5）掌握导游、计调、外联、餐饮、前厅、客房、康体、会展等旅游服务的基本流程、规范、标准、方法和技巧。

To master the procedures, standards, methods and skills of guide,tour guide, operator, external connection, catering, lobby, guest room, gymnasium, exhibition.

（6）熟悉旅行社、酒店等旅游企业的主要业务及其流程，掌握旅游企业经营与管理的基础知识、基本理论和方法。

To familiarize the major business and procedures of tourism agency and hotel, master the basic operation knowledge, theory and ways of tourism companies.

2. 面向社会公众的旅游服务能力养成（Service Ability for the Public）

（1）具有导游、计调、外联、餐饮、前厅、客房、康体等旅游服务的操作能力。

To have the operational capacity of tour guide, operator, external connection, catering, lobby, guest room, gymnasium.

（2）具有旅游市场调研和开拓能力，并具有旅游、会展产品的开发、设计、策划、营销、创新的能力。

To have abilities of market research and market developing, capable of developing, designing, planing and innovating tourism products and exhibition.

（3）具有较强的组织、沟通、协调能力和现场控制、特殊问题的应变处理能力，具备旅游企业督导管理、人力资源管理和财务管理能力。

To have the management ability of organization, communication and coordination. To have the ability to control and handle the emergency situation and to master the management ability of tourism company superior, human resources and finance.

（4）在旅游企业的主要岗位上，能够熟练运用英语等外语进行交流与沟通的能力。

To have the ability to communicate with guests in some job positions in English.

（二）适应社会的综合素质培养（Comprehensive Quality）

（1）思想道德素质：能够遵纪守法，具备良好的思想品德、社会公德和职业道德，树立正确的世界观、人生观和价值观，具有较强的敬业精神和社会责任感。

To obey the law and have social moral and professional ethics.

（2）文化素质：具有较高的文学艺术素养、人文科学素养和审美素养，具备适应职业变化的终身学习能力。

To have art, humanity, aesthetic quality and learning ability to adjust to the vocational change.

（3）身心素质：拥有健康的体魄，养成良好的体育锻炼和卫生习惯，具备健全的心理和乐观的人生态度，具有良好的心理承受能力和社会适应能力。

To have a healthy body and sound psychology and optimistic attitude.

（4）职业素质：具有严谨务实、深入细致的工作作风和爱岗敬业、团结协作、勇于开拓创新的精神风貌。

To have the carefulness working attitude, team work spirit and innovation spirit.

四、本专业的人才需求报告

2019 年旅游管理专业人才需求调研报告。

The investigation report on the need of professional talents graduating from tourism management program in 2019.

G 学院旅游管理专业于 2004 年开始招生，现有在校生近 700 人，迄今为止，已为旅游企业和社会输送了近 3 200 名高端技能型人才。为完善 2019 级旅游管理专业专业人才培养方案，培养受旅游企业和社会更加欢迎的高素质高端旅游技能型人才，促进本专业持续健康发展，在 2019 年 5-8 月，本专业教师完成了为期四个月的人才需求调研。

This major enrolled students from 2004. Today, there are totally 700 students studying in the major. We have cultivated nearly 3，200 students with proficient skill for the tourism enterprises. The teachers in the major have made investigation on the need of professional talents for four months to improve the talents training program in this major, cultivate more popular skilled talents for society and put forward the development of the major.

（一）调研形式和方法（The ways of investigation）

本次调研采用了调查问卷、文献检索等多种方法。调查问卷和访谈的对象主要是珠三角地区特别是珠海市的旅行社、酒店、景点景区等旅游企业的管理人员以及本专业毕业生，调研内容包括旅游企业的岗位需求数量、职业能力和素质要求；文献检索调研的内容包括旅游企业的招

聘信息、区域旅游市场发展的动态和对人才需求的动态，并调研了对本专业人才培养方案的意见。

Questionnaire, interview and literature search are adopted in this investigation. The interviewees are the staff and graduates working in tourism agencies, hotels, tourism sites. The content of this investigation includes the job position of tourism companies, the number in need, vocational ability; the content of literature search includes the recruitment information, the dynamic development of tourism market and talents needs and the suggestions on the talents training program in this major.

区域旅游发展动态及其人才需求分析。

The Dynamic Development and Demand Analysis on Regional Tourism.

世界旅游组织预测，到 2015 年，中国将成为世界第一大旅游接待国和第四大旅游出境国。

The world tourism organization predicts, China will be the greatest tourism received country and the fourth largest departure country by 2015.

《国务院关于加快发展旅游业的意见》（国发〔2009〕41 号）指出：要把旅游业培育成国民经济的战略性支柱产业和人民群众更加满意的现代服务业。*Suggestions of state council on promoting tourism industry states*, tourism should be developed into a strategic pillar industry of the nation's economy which is more popular in people's mind.

The outline of the Twelfth Five-year Plan on tourism states that there will be 1,525 people working in the job related to tourism and there will be newly increased 0.7million people in the industry.

广东省是中国旅游强省，多年来，广东省入境旅游人数和旅游外汇收入等指标均居全国首位。《珠江三角洲地区改革发展规划纲要》提出广东省将建设全国旅游综合改革示范区，建成亚太地区具有重要影响力的国际旅游目的地和游客集散地。

Tourism is one of the strengths of Guangdong Province. Inbound tourist number and foreign exchange earning from tourism of Guangdong Province are listed on the top in the country. *The reformation and development outline of the Pearl River Delta Region* proposed that tourism reform demonstration region will be built in Guangdong. Guangdong will become the influential international tourism destination and distributing center.

多年来，学校所在地广州市入境旅游收入等主要旅游经济指标居全国第3位，学校主校区所在地珠海市入境旅游人数和入境旅游收入居全国第5位（或第6位）和广东省第3位，珠海拥有的五星级酒店、国际旅行社、高尔夫球场的数量居全国前列。长期以来，珠海市均将旅游业作为优先发展的产业和第三产业的龙头。

For many years, the tourism income of Guangzhou, the city which our school is located in,is listed on the third place in the country. For many years, the tourism income of Zhuhai, the city which our major campus is located in, is listed on the five place in the country and the third place in the country. The number of five-start hotel, tourism agency, golf course in Zhuhai are on the top in the country. Tourism is the prior industry to develop in Zhuhai.

随着珠海国际商务休闲旅游度假区的建设和发展，珠海旅游企业对旅游人才需求的数量和质量都将提出更高的要求。但目前，珠海市旅游部门的从业人员素质不尽如人意。

With the development of international business and leisure holiday resort, tourism enterprises in Zhuhai put higher requirement on tourism talents. However, the quality of most employees working in tourism companies are not so well.

根据珠海市首次经济普查资料显示：珠海旅游部门从业人员中，本科及本科以上学历的仅有2.8%，大专占10.4%，中专与高中的比例最大，占54.5%，初中及以下文化程度的职工占32.3%。

The data of economic research of Zhuhai shows that the staff with bachelor degree or further higher degree occupies only 2.8%, with junior college degree accounts for 10.4%, with high school degree 54.5% and with middle school degree 32.3%.

珠海旅游部门的人才队伍基本上以中专及高中学历为主，高层次的人才相对缺乏，导游素质参差不齐，高素质的会议策划人才和酒店专业管理人才也相对偏少。据调查，目前珠海市有星级酒店近100家，旅行社90家，按平均每家酒店每年需要10位、每家旅行社需要2位高技能

人才和基层管理人才计算，珠海市每年星级酒店和旅行社需要近 1 200 人的高技能服务人才和基层管理人才。

Most of the employees are with high school degree. Employees with bachelor degree are rare. The quality of tourism guide are irregular and the talents majoring in meeting plan and hotel management are rare. According to some researches, there are nearly 100 start hotels, 90 tourism agencies. According to the standard that 10 talents are needed in one hotel and 2 talents are needed in one agency for one year, there will be nearly 1,200 talents needed in Zhuhai for every year.

表1-1　珠海旅游部门从业人员文化程度一览表

项目	初中及以下	中专／高中	大专	本科	研究生	总计
人数（人）	4 515	7 611	1 449	376	17	13 968
比重（%）	32.3	54.5	10.4	2.7	0.1	100

资料来源：珠海市经济普查汇总资料

Chart1-1　the education of staff in tourism industry

Item	Middle school or below	High school	Associate degree	Bachelor	Master degree or above	total
persons	4 515	7 611	1 449	376	17	13 968
Proportion(%)	32.3	54.5	10.4	2.7	0.1	100

Sources from economic census in Zhuhai.

表1-2　珠海旅游部门从业人员技术职称一览表

项目	高级	中级	初级	高级技师	技师	高级工	中级工	总计
人数（人）	57	388	590	34	66	60	314	1 509
比重（%）	3.8	25.7	39.1	2.3	4.4	4	20.7	100

资料来源：珠海市经济普查汇总资料

Chart1-2　professional title of staff in tourism industry

Item	senior	Medium	primary	senior technician	technician	Senior worker	Secondary worker	total
person	57	388	590	34	66	60	314	1 509
proportion (%)	3.8	25.7	39.1	2.3	4.4	4	20.7	100

Sources from economic census in Zhuhai.

（二）本专业岗位群（Major Job Positions）

（1）旅行社岗位群：英语导游、出国领队、前台咨询、计调。

（2）酒店岗位群：前厅、销售代表、西餐厅、客房部、康乐部、采购部。

（3）其他旅游企业岗位群：景点景区、旅游航空、车船企业对外销售代表。

Job positions in travel agency : guides, guides for travel abroad, receptionists, operator.

Job positions in hotel : waiters in lobby, sales representative, western style dinning restaurant, room attendants, entertainment department attendants, purchase department attendants.

Other job positions : jobs in tourism sites, air liner, sales representatives for leasing cars and boats.

（三）主要岗位工作任务、技能要求、核心能力、关键职业素质和对应课程分析（Analysis on the Job Tasks, Requirements, Core Skills, Qualities and Corresponding Courses）

1.导游（Tour Guide）

（1）工作任务：实施与安排旅游活动、联络与接待、讲解服务、维护安全、处理问题。

Job tasks : to arrange activities, connect and receive guests,have a good introduction to tourism sites, maintain security and deal with the emergency.

（2）技能要求：熟悉导游服务规范，对特殊问题反应敏捷、处理措施得当，导游讲解流畅生动，注意仪容仪表。

Skills requirements : familiarize the standards of guide service, deal with emergency feasibly, have a good introduction to the tourism sites.

（3）核心能力：语言表达能力，讲解能力，组织协调能力，应变能力和特殊问题处理能力，跨文化交际能力。

Core skills : language ability, introduction ability, coordination ability, the ability to deal with emergency and cross-cultural communication ability.

（4）关键职业素质：高尚的品德，广博的知识，健康的身心，扎实的英语基础。

Core qualities : good morality, extensive knowledge, healthy body and English communication ability.

（5）对应课程：导游业务、旅游英语口语、导游基础知识、旅游法规。

Corresponding courses : guide business, tourist oral English, basic knowledge of tour guide, tourist regulations.

2. 海外领队（Tour Leader for Travelling Abroad）

（1）工作任务：介绍情况、全程陪同、落实旅游合同、联络工作、组织协调工作。

Job duties : introduce the situation, accompany the guest for the whole journey, implement the travel contract, contact work, organize and coordinate the work.

（2）技能要求：熟悉接待计划，办理和保管好票证，搞好团结工作。

Skill requirement : familiarize reception plan, handle and keep ticket certificate, do a good job of unity.

（3）核心能力：跨文化交际能力，英语口头表达能力，组织协调能力，应变能力和特殊问题处理能力。

Core competence : intercultural communication, oral English, organization and coordination, adaptability and special problem solving skills.

（4）关键职业素质：高尚的品德，广博的知识特别是客源国知识，健康的身心，扎实的英语基础。

Key occupational quality : high moral character, extensive knowledge, especially knowledge of the country of origin, healthy body and mind, solid English foundation.

（5）对应课程：导游业务、旅游英语听说、旅游英语口语、旅游英语、基础英语、导游基础知识、旅游法规、客源国概况。

Corresponding courses : guide business, tourism English listening and speaking, tourism English oral English, tourism English, basic English, basic knowledge of tour guide, tourism laws and regulations, general situation of source country.

3. 计调（Operator）

（1）工作任务：采购、客流调度、统计。

Work tasks : procurement, passenger flow scheduling, statistics.

（2）技能要求：搜集与对比旅游产品基本信息，设置游览行程，采购旅游产品，核算成本，制定外联营销计划，确定外联营销策略。

Skill requirements : collect and compare the basic information of tourism products, set up tour itinerary, purchase tourism products, calculate costs, make outreach marketing plans, and determine outreach marketing strategies.

（3）核心能力：策划能力、沟通协调能力、分析核算能力、计算机应用能力。

Core competence : planning, communication and coordination, analysis and accounting, and computer application.

（4）关键职业素质：掌握一定统计分析方法，创新意识强。

Key occupational quality : certain statistical analysis methods, strong sense of innovation.

（5）对应课程：旅游经营与管理，旅游市场营销，旅行社计调实务，应用文写作。

Corresponding courses : tourism management and management, tourism marketing, travel agency planning and adjustment practice, practical writing.

4. 前厅接待：以酒店前台主管为例（Lobby receptionist: Take the Hotel Lobby supervisor as an Example）

（1）工作任务：督导问讯迎接服务，督导前台领班和接待员的仪容仪表和劳动纪律，参与前台接待，安排班次，掌握客房预订情况，制定培训计划。

Job duties : supervise the reception service, supervise the appearance and labor discipline of the front desk foreman and the receptionist, participate in the reception, arrange the shift, master the room reservation and make the training plan.

（2）技能要求：搞好协调及联系，有效处理投诉，最大程度销售客房。

Skill requirement : coordinate and contact the guests and colleagues well,

handle complaints effectively and sell guest rooms to the maximum extent.

（3）核心能力：组织协调能力，处理应变能力，语言和文字表达能力。

Core competence : organization, coordination, adaptability, language and written communication.

（4）关键职业素质：懂得外事接待的礼仪礼节知识，掌握总台运行和管理的业务知识，掌握1门外语。

Key professional quality : understand the etiquette and etiquette knowledge of foreign affairs reception, master the operational and management knowledge of the headquarters, master a foreign language.

（5）对应课程：饭店前厅与客房管理、旅游英语、日语、旅游市场营销。

Corresponding courses : hotel lobby and guest room management, tourism English, Japanese, tourism marketing.

5. 西餐厅服务：以迎领员为例（western restaurant service：take the receptionist as an example）

（1）工作任务：餐厅入口处问候客人，安排就座。

Job duties : greet guests at the entrance of the restaurant and arrange seating.

（2）技能要求：要微笑问候，尊重客人桌位选择，妥善处理引领过程中出现的问题。

Skill requirements : smile and greet, respect the guests' table selection, and properly handle the problems in the process of leading.

（3）核心能力：具有一定语言和文字表达能力，能写工作记录，讲话口齿清楚。能用流利的外语为客人服务。

Core competence : write work records and speak clearly and serve guests in a fluent foreign language.

（4）关键职业素质：饭店菜肴、饮料、酒水的品种、风味、价格知识，外事礼节、礼貌知识，饭店各部门的服务设施、项目及营业时间，服务心理、食品营养卫生常识、食品卫生法、饭店规章制度。热爱本职工作，有较强的服务意识。

Key professional quality : hotel dishes, drinks, wine varieties, flavor, price knowledge, foreign affairs etiquette, courtesy knowledge, hotel service facilities, projects and business hours, service psychology, food nutrition hygiene common sense, food hygiene law, hotel rules and regulations. The person who work in the job position should love his job and have a strong sense of service.

（5）对应课程：旅游英语、餐饮服务与管理、餐饮服务技能实训。

Corresponding courses : tourism English, catering service and management, catering service skills training.

（四）珠海旅游企业对旅游管理专业人才的职业能力和素质要求（Vocational Capacity and Quality Requirements Zhuhai Tourism Enterprises Set on Professionals）

1. 对学历层次的要求（Requirements on Education level）

珠海市的国际旅行社和高星级酒店的部门经理以上管理者学历以大专为主，本科学历极少，并且科班出身的较少。部门经理职位以下的人员中85%左右为大专以下学历。被调研的各个旅游企业均特别青睐和欢迎高职高专旅游专业毕业生。

Department managers of international travel agencies and high star hotels in Zhuhai have a college degree or above. About 85 percent of those below the department manager position have a college degree or less. All the tourism enterprises that have been investigated especially favor and welcome the graduates of tourism major in higher vocational colleges.

2. 对基本素质的要求（Requirements on Quality）

（1）思想道德素质：遵纪守法，热爱旅游工作，服务意识和敬业意识强，能吃苦耐劳。

Ideological and moral quality : abide by the law and discipline, love tourism work, strong sense of service and professionalism, able to bear hardships and stand hard work.

（2）文化素质：具有良好的文化素养，具有适应职业变化的终身学习能力。

Cultural quality : good cultural quality, lifelong learning ability to adapt

to career adjustment.

（3）身心素质：具有健康的体魄、良好的适应能力，具有较好的心理调节能力和心理承受能力。

Physical and mental quality : have healthy body and mind, good adaptability, good ability of psychological adjustment and psychological endurance.

3. 对知识结构的要求（Requirements on knowledge Structure）

旅游政策法规知识；公共关系和礼节礼仪知识；英语和小语种知识；计算机应用知识；史地文化知识；心理学知识；旅游营销和管理知识；多种旅行常识；职业岗位的操作规范知识。

Knowledge of tourism policies and regulations; knowledge of public relations and etiquette; knowledge of English and minor languages; computer application knowledge; historical and cultural knowledge; knowledge of psychology; knowledge of tourism marketing and management; a variety of travel knowledge; knowledge of operational norms for professional positions.

4. 对能力结构的要求（Requirements on Capability Structure）

（1）通用能力：具有较强的文字和口头表达能力；具有较强的计算机应用能力；具有较强的社会适应能力和社交能力；具有较强的沟通、协调和协作能力；具有较强观察能力、分析判断能力、自学能力、独立工作能力和创新能力。

General ability : strong verbal and written skills; strong computer skills; strong social adaptability and social skills; strong communication, coordination and collaboration skills; strong observation ability, analysis and judgment ability, self-study ability, independent working ability and innovation ability.

（2）专业能力：具有跨文化交际能力；具有较强的英语导游讲解与服务能力，胜任地陪、全陪和出境领队工作；具有较强的旅游服务接待能力和旅游产品的开发、设计、策划、营销能力；具有旅游市场的调查、分析、预测、开拓和组织客源的能力。

Professional competence : intercultural communication skills; strong English guide interpretation and service skills, competent for local, all accompanying and outbound tour guide work; strong ability of tourism service

reception and tourism product development, design, planning and marketing; ability to investigate, analyze, forecast, explore and organize tourist sources in tourism market.

5.对核心职业技能的要求（Core Occupational Skill Requirements）

具有较强的旅游服务规范操作能力；具有较强的沟通、协调、应变能力；具有较强的英语口头交际能力；旅游市场营销能力；利用网络获取、处理旅游信息的能力。

Strong operation ability of tourism service standard; strong communication, coordination and adaptability; strong English oral communication skills; tourism marketing ability; ability to access and process travel information over the Internet.

（五）用人单位对现有人才培养方案的意见（Employer's opinion on the Existing Talent Training Program）

用人单位高度认可现有的旅游管理专业人才培养方案，特别认可旅游英语口语、旅行社计调实务、会展实务和有关实训等课程的开设及其课程标准。但旅游企业认为本专业应新增旅游策划、旅游会展、旅游文化、职业规划等课程，需加大实训课程教学的力度，提高学生的规范操作能力和应变处理能力，应让学生参加更多的校内外文体活动和社会实践活动，应进一步加强旅游职业意识、态度的教育。

The employers highly recognize the existing talent training programs for tourism management professionals, and in particular recognizes the establishment and curriculum standards of such courses as tourism oral English, travel agency planning and adjustment practice, exhibition practice and relevant practical training. But they hold that this professional tourism enterprises should be the new tourism planning, tourism exhibition, tourism culture, career planning, such as curriculum, should be more efforts to practice teaching, improve students' ability of standard operation and strain capacity, should let the students to be more stylistic face-to-face activities and social practice, should further strengthen vocational awareness, attitude of tourism education.

第二节　学生

毕业生就业情况直接反映了某学校某专业的人才培养质量和水平，同时为人才培养方案的制定（修订）提供了良好的依据。不以就业为导向的职业教育形同坐井观天、缘木求鱼。因此，毕业生的就业状况历来成为世界旅游组织评估学校教学质量的一个重要指标。

一、近三年的毕业生就业报告

（一）2015届旅游管理专业毕业生跟踪调查报告

1. 调查的基本情况

为了解2015届旅游管理专业毕业生的就业和工作状况，为进一步完善本专业工学结合人才培养模式和推动本专业教学改革提供借鉴和参考，外国语学院对2015届旅游管理专业毕业生进行了跟踪调查。

此次跟踪调查采用问卷调查方法，其具体方式和过程是：以邮寄、发电子邮件等形式向2015届旅游管理专业全体毕业生共127人发放了共127份调查问卷，毕业生填写问卷后，以邮寄或发电子邮件等形式返回我院。共回收调查问卷121份，约占本专业应调查人数的95.28%；有效调查表83份，约占回收调查表的68.60%，约占应调查人数的65.35%。

2. 调查结果与分析

毕业生跟踪调查表中涉及12个方面的问题：①毕业生所在用人单位性质；②毕业生工作岗位与所学专业是否对口；③毕业生跳槽次数情况；④毕业生起薪情况；⑤毕业生目前月收入情况；⑥毕业生确定最初工作单位的途径；⑦毕业生择业时看重工作单位情况；⑧毕业生对目前工作的满意度情况；⑨毕业生认为自己在单位受重用的程度；⑩毕业生认为在校学习过程中哪些能力最有利于就业后发展；⑪毕业生认为用人单位对大学生素养方面的重视情况；⑫毕业生对母校的评价情况。12个问题全部为选择题。以上主要问题的调查结果及其分析如下。

（1）毕业生所在用人单位性质。

表2-1　毕业生所在用人单位性质的调查结果

单位：个

选项	人数	选项	人数
1. 行政机关	0	6. 私营企业	62
2. 国有企业	5	7. 集体企业	1
3. 事业单位	3	8. 自主创业	3
4. 社会组织	0	9. 其他	8
5. 三资企业	1		

由表 2-1 可知，毕业生就业的单位绝大部分集中在私营企业，其比例达到 74.50% 左右，并且绝大部分单位位于珠三角地区。进入珠三角私营企业的毕业生最多的原因：一方面珠三角是中国市场化程度较高和改革开放最早的地区之一，私营企业较多，特别是旅游企业中私营企业更多。另一方面，这些企业特别是中小型私营企业选人用人的机制较为灵活，一般对毕业生的学历要求不太高，非常欢迎具有动手能力和吃苦耐劳精神的高技能型人才。另有少部分毕业生在国有企业、事业单位、三资企业、集体企业就业和属于自主创业、其他情况，毕业生就业的企业呈现多样化的特点，反映了毕业生不断进取的精神以及创新创业能力和意识的增强。

（2）毕业生工作岗位与所学专业是否对口。

表2-2　毕业生工作岗位与所学专业对口情况的调查结果

选项	人数／个	比例／%
1. 对口	62	74.50
2. 不对口	21	25.30

由表 2-2 可知，第 2 个问题的调查结果只有对口和不对口两种情况，其中，对口的人数比例约为 74.50%；不对口的人数比例约为 25.30%。对口的人数比例高于往年，就业情况比全国旅游专业毕业生的平均情况，反映了我院在不断加强旅游专业学生的专业思想和职业意识方面取得了明显的成效。但不对口的人数仍然占有一定比例，其原因是目前毕业生自主择业，工作岗位与所学专业不对口是较为常见的现象，特别是从全

国来看，旅游专业毕业生工作岗位与所学专业不对口的情况更为普遍。旅游行业需要从最基层干起，工作辛苦，并且开始阶段工资较低，部分毕业生不乐于干，或者干一段时间后就离开了旅游行业。这可能是少部分毕业生缺少吃苦耐劳精神、没有长远职业生涯规划的反映，这种情况要求我院需要进一步加强学生的职业意识教育，做好学生的职业生涯规划。

（3）毕业生跳槽次数情况。

表2-3　毕业生跳槽次数情况的调查结果

单位：个

选项	人数	选项	人数
1. 1 次	67	4. 4 次	1
2. 2 次	14	5. 4 次以上	0
3. 3 次	1		

根据表2-3可知，80.72%左右的毕业生只跳槽1次，一方面是因为毕业生实习和毕业的时间尚短，另一方面，也是旅游专业毕业生追求稳定和"干一行，爱一行"思想的反映。

（4）毕业生的起薪与当前月收入情况。

表2-4　毕业生起薪情况的调查结果

单位：个

选项	人数	选项	人数
1. 2 500 元以下	69	4. 3 501～4 000 元	0
2. 2 501～3 000 元	12	5. 4 000 元以上	1
3. 3 001～3 500 元	1		

表2-5　毕业生目前月收入情况的调查结果

选项	人数	选项	人数
1. 2 500 元以下	62	4. 3 501～4 000 元	1
2. 2 501～3 000 元	18	5. 4 000 元以上	1
3. 3 001～3 500 元	1		

毕业生的起薪与当前月收入情况见表2-4和表2-5。毕业生起薪主要集中在2 500元以下的，比例为83.13%，这是因为本专业毕业生主要

集中在酒店实习，毕业生一般将在企业实习的工资填写为起薪工资，而旅游专业实习生一般从最基层的工作干起，因而工资较低。但实际上，由于在酒店实习是包吃包住的，如果包括实习期间的吃、住消费，从严格意义上讲，毕业生的起薪工资高于2 500元。起薪较高的毕业生主要在珠三角地区三资企业工作或在珠三角地区的旅行社从事导游工作。从表2-5可知，毕业生实习结束后，即毕业后，工资有一定上涨，但涨幅不大，这是因为学生刚毕业，仍然从事基层工作。实际上，根据对我院往届旅游专业毕业生的长期跟踪调查，旅游专业毕业生在旅游企业坚持2年以上的，均能晋升为基层管理者以上的职位，相应地，工资会有较大幅度的提升。

（5）毕业生确定最初工作单位的途径和择业时着重工作单位情况。

表2-6　毕业生确定最初工作单位的途径

单位：个

选项	人数	选项	人数
1. 校园招聘会	29	5. 社会招聘	5
2. 网上招聘	19	6. 新闻媒体	0
3. 亲友介绍	14	7. 其他	10
4. 自我推荐	6		

表2-7　毕业生择业时看重工作单位情况

2- 单位：个

选项	人数	选项	人数
1. 个人发展空间大小	62	4. 培训、提高机会	24
2. 行业及其发展前景	46	5. 经济收入及福利待遇	45
3. 公司环境及企业文化	33	6. 工作地点	10

根据调查结果，旅游管理专业毕业生选择最初工作的途径按人数由多到少的顺序分别是校园招聘会、网上招聘、亲友介绍、其他、自我推荐、社会招聘。在这个市场经济和资讯业发达的时代，毕业生确定最初工作的途径呈现多样化的特点。其中，通过校园招聘会确定最初工作单位的毕业生人数最多，其比例达到34.94%，说明外国语学院于2013年10月下旬举办的旅游专业实习生和毕业生专场招聘会和学校于2013年12月举办的招聘会取得了一定的成效，学生对校园招聘会有较多和较高的期待，今后可邀请地区更广和数量更多的旅行社企业参加校园招聘会。

虽然有较多毕业生看重单位给予自己的经济收入和福利待遇，但有更多的人看重个人发展空间大小和行业企业的发展前景，也有很多毕业生关心企业环境和企业文化、培训与提高机会，这反映毕业生找工作时更加理性，较为考虑自己的长远发展。

（6）毕业生对目前工作的满意度情况和认为自己在单位受重用的程度。

表2-8　毕业生对目前工作的满意度情况

单位：个

选项	人数	选项	人数
1. 非常满意	3	3. 不太满意	18
2. 比较满意	62	4. 很不满意	0

表2-9　毕业生认为自己在单位受重用的程度

单位：个

选项	人数	选项	人数
1. 很受重用	31	3. 程度一般	18
2. 较受重用	33	4. 不受重用	1

根据调查结果，旅游管理专业对目前工作的满意度情况和认为自己在单位受重用的程度具有一定的正相关性。有78.31%左右的毕业生对目前工作比较满意和非常满意，有约22.69%的毕业生对目前工作不太满意，没有对目前工作很不满意的毕业生，总体上说明毕业生有较好的工作心态和不断进取的精神。77.11%左右的毕业生认为自己在单位很受重用和较受重用，约21.69%的毕业生认为自己在单位的受重用程度一般，只有1人认为自己在单位不受重用，这在一定程度上反映了旅游管理专业毕业生具有吃苦耐劳的品质、较强的工作能力和较好的职业发展前景。

（7）毕业生认为在校学习过程中最有利于就业后发展的能力和认为用人单位对大学生素养方面的重视情况。

表2-10　毕业生认为在校学习过程中最有利于就业后发展的能力

单位：个

选项	人数	选项	人数
1. 专业知识	12	4. 组织、工作能力	24
2. 学习、分析问题的能力	38	5. 人际交往能力	47
3. 实操、动手能力	23	6. 其他	5

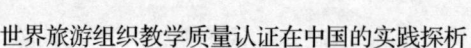

表2-11 毕业生认为用人单位对大学生素养方面的重视情况

单位：个

选项	人数	选项	人数
1. 良好的沟通技巧	38	6. 开拓、创新能力	14
2. 良好的职业道德	36	7. 持久的学习能力	16
3. 实践应用能力	34	8. 诚实守信	13
4. 正确积极的态度	47	9. 责任心	30
5. 领导与管理能力	8		

　　毕业生认为在校学习过程中最有利于就业发展的能力按选择的人数由多到少分别为人际交往能力、学习和分析问题的能力、组织和工作能力、实操和动手能力、专业知识、其他。其选择比较符合实际，其中，较多的毕业生认为人际交往能力对今后工作最重要，我们认为这只是毕业生在初入职场时一定阶段内的认识，有一定的正确性，但从全局和长远看，则不尽然。毕业生认为用人单位最重视的大学生素质主要有正确积极的态度、良好的沟通技巧、良好的职业道德、实践应用能力、责任心等，这启示我们今后要进一步加强学生职业意识、职业道德和心态教育，培养学生的沟通能力和实操能力。

　　（8）毕业生对母校的评价情况。

表2-12 毕业生对母校的评价情况

项目	好	比例/%	一般	比例/%	差	比例/%
1. 办学条件	49	59.04	34	40.96		
2. 教学质量	44	53.01	39	46.99		
3. 课程设置	30	36.14	52	62.65	1	1.20
4. 教学内容	45	54.22	37	44.58	1	1.20
5. 师资水平	62	74.70	21	25.30		
6. 实操实训	35	42.17	44	53.01	3	3.61
7. 人文教育	60	72.29	23	27.71		
8. 品德教育	59	71.08	22	26.51	2	2.41
9. 专业与职业的衔接	49	59.04	33	39.76	1	1.20
10. 学校管理	53	63.86	30	36.14		
11. 总体评价	53	63.86	30	36.14		

总体而言，毕业生对母校的评价较好，在11个项目中，选择"好"超过一半人数的有师资水平、人文教育、品德教育、学校管理等9个项目，只有课程设置、实操实训2个项目选择"好"的人数比例在50%以下，这说明要进一步完善课程设置和加强实训教学。

3. 对专业建设的几点建议

第一，切实加强实践教学。

大部分毕业生反映实践能力、动手操作能力、沟通能力是最有利于毕业生就业后发展的能力和素质，也是用人单位特别看重的素养，部分毕业生也对母校提出了加强对学生技能训练、外语口头交际能力培养的建议，同时，实践能力的培养也是高职院校人才培养的重点。其具体措施有以下内容：

（1）建立认知性实习、校内实训、第二课堂、校外顶岗实习的完整的、立体化的实践课程体系。

（2）进一步改善导游实训室、餐饮实训室、前厅与客房实训室等校内实训室的条件，建立生产性实训基地和教学企业。

（3）结合课堂教学内容，组织学生到旅游企业参观考察，组织学生进行旅游市场调查或其他实践活动，组织第二课堂，全面提高学生的沟通能力、组织能力、语言表达能力。

（4）完善本专业的毕业顶岗实习管理和考核制度，切实提高实习的成效。

（5）提高教师的实践能力。

第二，进一步推动人才培养模式改革。

广泛和深入地开展教研教改活动，搞好师资培训，鼓励教学改革，并加强教学督导管理，以进一步提高课堂教学质量。

第三，进一步加强旅游职业规划指导。

很多毕业生在旅游企业以外的单位工作，或者在旅游企业工作一段时间后自动离开，这是毕业生职业意识不强的表现，因此，要自始至终搞好在校生的专业思想教育和旅游职业意识教育。主要包括使学生了解旅游企业发展前景，训练和培养学生的职业习惯和行为，邀请在旅游企业工作的优秀毕业生来校与在校生沟通和交流。

（二）2016届旅游管理专业毕业生跟踪调查报告

1. 基本情况

为了解2016届旅游管理专业毕业生毕业一年的就业和工作状况，以便不断完善、优化和创新本专业人才培养模式，提高本专业教育教学改革的成效，2016年9月1日至10月31日，学院对2016届旅游管理专业毕业生进行了为期2个多月的跟踪调查。

此次跟踪调查采用问卷调查和网络调查相结合的形式，其中，问卷调查的具体过程如下：2016年9月以邮寄、发电子邮件等形式，向2016届旅游管理专业全体毕业生共121人，发放了共121份调查问卷，毕业生填写问卷后，以邮寄或发电子邮件等形式寄回学校。截至10月31日为止，共回收调查问卷117份，占本专业应调查人数的96.69%；有效调查表97份，占回收调查表份数的82.91%，占应调查人数的80.17%。

2. 调查结果与分析

毕业生跟踪调查表中涉及12个方面的问题，全为封闭性问题：①毕业生所在用人单位性质；②毕业生工作岗位与所学专业是否对口；③毕业生跳槽次数情况；④毕业生起薪情况；⑤毕业生目前月收入情况；⑥毕业生确定最初工作单位的途径；⑦毕业生择业时看重工作单位情况；⑧毕业生对目前工作的满意度情况；⑨毕业生认为本专业学习期间最大的收获；⑩毕业生认为在校学习过程中哪些能力最有利于就业后发展；⑪毕业生认为用人单位对大学生素养方面的重视情况；⑫毕业生对母校的评价情况。以上主要问题的调查结果及分析如下。

（1）毕业生所在用人单位性质。

表2-13　毕业生所在用人单位性质的调查结果

单位：个

选项	人数	选项	人数
1. 行政机关	0	6. 私营企业	64
2. 国有企业	9	7. 集体企业	0
3. 事业单位	7	8. 自主创业	3
4. 社会组织	1	9. 其他	11
5. 三资企业	2		

据表 2-13 可知，毕业生就业的单位绝大部分集中在私营企业，占比约为 65.98%，但这一比例比 2015 届毕业生相应比例有所降低。进入私营企业的毕业生最多的原因：一是广东省和珠三角地区是中国市场化程度较高和改革开放最早的地区之一，私营企业较多，特别是旅行社、酒店等旅游企业中私营企业更多；二是这些企业特别是中小型私营企业选人用人的机制较为灵活，一般对毕业生的学历要求不太高，非常欢迎具有较高的职业素养、综合素质、动手能力和吃苦耐劳精神的高职毕业生。另有少部分毕业生在国有企业、事业单位、三资企业就业和属于自主创业、其他情况，毕业生就业的企业呈现多样化的特点，反映了毕业生不断进取的精神以及一定的创新创业能力和意识。与往年不同的是，本届毕业生到国有企业和事业单位的人数有所增加，反映了毕业生求稳的心态。

（2）毕业生工作岗位与所学专业是否对口。

表2-14　毕业生工作岗位与所学专业对口情况的调查结果

选项	人数／个	比例／%
1. 对口	62	63.92%
2. 自主创业	3	3.09%
3. 其他	32	32.99%

由表 2-14 可知，专业对口的人数比例约为 63.92%；自主创业的人数比例约为 3.09%，其他情况的人数比例为 32.99%。对口人数的比例比往年有所下降，但比全国旅游专业毕业生的平均情况要好，这从侧面说明珠三角的旅游企业较多，对专业人才的需求量较大，也反映了本专业毕业生的专业思想较为稳定。但不对口的人数仍然占有一定比例，其原因是目前毕业生自主择业，工作岗位与所学专业不对口是较为常见的现象，特别是从全国来看，旅游专业毕业生不对口的情况更为普遍。旅游行业需要从最基层干起，工作辛苦，并且开始阶段工资较低，部分毕业生不乐于干，或者干一段时间后就离开了旅游行业。这可能是少部分毕业生缺少吃苦耐劳精神、没有长远职业生涯规划的反映，这种情况要求我院进一步加强学生的职业意识教育，搞好学生的职业生涯规划。

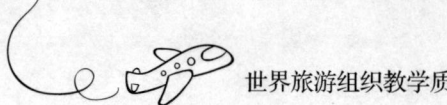

（3）毕业生跳槽次数情况。

表2-15　毕业生跳槽次数情况的调查结果

单位：个

选项	人数	选项	人数
1.1 次	73	4.4 次	
2.2 次	19	5.4 次以上	
3.3 次	5		

根据表2-15，每位毕业生至少跳槽1次，是旅游企业人员流动率高的一般特点的反映。但本专业毕业生以跳槽1次居多，最多只跳槽3次，一方面是因为毕业生实习和毕业的时间尚短，另一方面，也是旅游专业毕业生追求稳定和"干一行，爱一行"思想的反映。

（4）毕业生的起薪与当前月收入情况。

表2-16　毕业生起薪情况的调查结果

单位：个

选项	人数	选项	人数
1.2 500 元以下	70	4.3 501~4 000 元	1
2.2 501～3 000 元	20	5.4 000 元以上	0
3.3 001～3 500 元	6		

表2-17　毕业生目前月收入情况的调查结果

单位：个

选项	人数	选项	人数
1.2 500 元以下	49	4.3 501～4 000 元	2
2.2 501～3 000 元	42	5.4 000 元以上	0
3.3 001～3 500 元	4		

毕业生的起薪与当前月收入情况如表2-16和表2-17所示。毕业生起薪主要集中在2 500元以下，比例为72.16%，这是因为本专业毕业生主要集中在酒店实习，毕业生一般将在企业实习的工资填写为起薪工资，而旅游专业实习生一般从最基层的工作干起，因而工资较低。但另一方面，实际上，由于在酒店实习是包吃包住的，如果包括实习期间的吃、住消费，从严格意义上来说，绝大部分毕业生的起薪工资在2 800以上。起薪较高的毕业生主要在珠三角地区三资企业工作或在珠三角地区的旅行社从事导游工作。从表2-17可知，毕业生实习结束后，即毕业后，工

资有一定上涨，但涨幅不大，这是因为学生刚毕业，仍然从事基层工作。实际上，根据对我院往届旅游专业毕业生的长期跟踪调查，旅游专业毕业生在旅游企业坚持 2 年以上，均能晋升为基层管理者以上的职位，相应地，工资会有较大幅度的提升。

（5）毕业生确定最初工作单位的途径。

表2-18　毕业生确定最初工作单位途径的调查结果

单位：个

选项	人数	选项	人数
1. 校园招聘会	26	5. 社会招聘	9
2. 网上招聘	43	6. 新闻媒体	0
3. 亲友介绍	14	7. 其他	4
4. 自我推荐	1		

如表 2-18 所示，毕业生最初确定工作单位的最重要的途径是网上招聘，占有效调查人数比例为 44.33%，说明用人单位从网上招聘已成为最重要的招聘渠道，这种方式既迎合信息时代和受众（即求职者）的需求，也节省招聘成本，说明网上求职已成为当代年轻人求职手段的新常态。其次是校园招聘会，占有效调查人数比例为 26.80%，说明学校举办的招聘会和本专业举办的专场招聘会发挥了重要作用，也反映了很多毕业生的第一份工作就是当时实习的单位。其他依次是亲友介绍、社会招聘、其他和自我推荐。

（6）毕业生择业时看重工作单位情况和目前对工作的满意度。

表2-19　毕业生择业时看重工作单位情况的调查结果

单位：个

选项	人数	选项	人数
1. 个人发展空间大小	75	4. 培训、提高机会	35
2. 行业及其发展前景	54	5. 经济收入及福利待遇	61
3. 公司环境及企业文化	51	6. 工作地点	21

表2-20　毕业生对目前工作满意度情况的调查结果

单位：个

选项	人数	选项	人数
1. 非常满意	7	3. 不太满意	7
2. 比较满意	82	4. 很不满意	1

表2-19是多选题的调查结果，调查结果显示，学生最看重的是个人发展空间大小，另外，也看重公司环境及企业文化、行业及其发展空间、培训、提高机会等，这反映毕业生有一定的长远眼光，求职越来越理性。毕业生把经济收入及福利待遇放在第二重要的位置，这是毕业生尚无"经济基础"，看重现实的必然结果。表2-20反映出绝大多数毕业生对目前工作比较满意，说明本专业毕业生期望值越来越现实。

（7）毕业生认为在校学习期间所获知识和能力的重要性排序。

表2-21　毕业生认为本专业学习期间最大收获的调查结果

单位：个

选项	人数	选项	人数
1. 学到扎实的基础理论和专业知识	25	3. 有较强的动手能力	14
2. 培养了思考、分析、解决问题能力	54	4. 有一定的创新能力	4

表2-22　毕业生认为在校学习期间最有利于就业后发展的能力的调查结果

单位：个

选项	人数	选项	人数
1. 专业知识	26	4. 组织、工作能力	44
2. 学习、分析问题的能力	55	5. 人际交往能力	36
3. 实操、动手能力	31	6. 其他	6

表2-21和表2-22的调查结果有较强的相关性。毕业一年后，毕业生最看重的是学习、分析问题和解决问题的能力，这与刚毕业时绝大部分毕业生认为动手能力最重要有明显的差别。这一调查结果给我们的启示是，作为高职院校，我们既要培养学生的实操和动手能力，又要培养学生分析和解决问题的能力，这对毕业生的可持续发展很重要。

（8）毕业生认为用人单位对大学生素养方面的重视情况。

表2-23　毕业生认为用人单位对大学生素养方面重视情况的调查结果

单位：个

选项	人数	选项	人数
1. 良好的沟通技巧	59	6. 开拓、创新能力	19
2. 良好的职业道德	36	7. 持久的学习能力	15
3. 实践应用能力	46	8. 诚实守信	5
4. 正确积极的态度	58	9. 责任心	45
5. 领导与管理能力	14		

表2-23调查结果显示，用人单位最看重的大学生的素质是"良好的沟通技巧"其人数略多于"正确积极的态度"，原因可能是本专业毕业生主要是从事服务业，服务人员与客人沟通的技巧和能力直接影响单位的客源和收入利润。用人单位把大学生正确积极的态度、责任心、实践应用能力、良好的职业道德等也看得很重要，这从侧面反映当代大学生在这些方面较为欠缺，并需要学校加强这些方面的教育培养。

（9）毕业生对母校的评价情况。

表2-24　毕业生对母校的评价情况调查结果

项目	好 / 个	比例 /%	一般 / 个	比例 /%	差 / 个	比例 /%
1. 办学条件	45	46.39	52	53.61		
2. 教学质量	52	53.61	45	46.39		
3. 课程设置	35	36.08	60	61.86	2	2.06
4. 教学内容	45	46.39	52	53.61		
5. 师资水平	69	71.13	28	28.87		
6. 实操实训	28	28.87	58	59.79	11	11.34
7. 人文教育	47	48.45	49	50.52	1	1.03
8. 品德教育	60	61.86	37	38.14		
9. 专业与职业的衔接	53	54.64	42	43.30	2	2.06
10. 学校管理	47	48.45	47	48.45	3	3.09
11. 总体评价	51	52.58	46	47.42		

毕业生对母校的评价情况见表2-24。总体评价较好，其中，评价相对较高的有师资水平、品德教育、专业与职业的衔接、教学质量、学校管理、人文教育、办学条件等，这反映了本专业的师资队伍建设、课程与教学内容改革、实训条件建设都取得明显成效，也反映了学校层面的管理水平、综合素质课程教学质量较高。

3. 对专业建设的思考

（1）进一步加强对学生的职业意识教育和职业规划指导。很多毕业生在旅游企业以外的单位工作，或者在旅游企业工作一段时间后自动离开，这是部分毕业生急功近利、缺乏长远职业规划的表现。今后，学校除了要大力加强职业规划课程的教学，还要创建旅游企业经理人讲坛、优秀毕业生进课堂等职业教育平台，发挥旅游企业优秀员工榜样的作用和对在校学生的感染力，增强旅游职业意识教育和职业规划指导的针对

性和成效。

（2）进一步提高学生实践能力以及分析问题和解决问题的能力。用人单位和部分毕业生反映实践能力、沟通能力是最有利于毕业生就业后发展的能力和素质，也是用人单位特别看重的素养，部分毕业生也对母校提出了加强对学生的技能训练、外语口头交际能力培养的建议，同时，实践能力的培养也是高职院校培养人才的重点。其具体措施有以下内容：①建立认知性实习、校内实训、第二课堂、校外顶岗实习的完整的、立体化的实践课程体系；②充分利用本专业现有的校内实训基地，提高利用率，组织生产性实训教学；③结合专业特点，组织学生进行旅游市场调查或其他实践活动，组织第二课堂，全面提高学生的沟通能力、组织能力、语言表达能力；④完善本专业的毕业顶岗实习管理和考核制度，切实提高实习的成效；⑤持续组织教师下企业挂职锻炼和搞好教师职业资格培训，进一步提高教师的实践能力。

（3）加强创新创业教育。从调查结果看，创业的毕业生和取得创新性成果的毕业生比例极小，这从一定程度上反映出学校创新创业教育还需加强。其思路和措施主要有以下内容：①加强专任教师自身的创新创业教育意识和能力的培训，鼓励专任教师参加创新创业教育能力提升培训班，以此为基础，将学生的创新意识培养和创新思维养成融入教育教学全过程；②在专业拓展课程模块中，开设"旅游门店的创办与运营"等专门的创新创业课程；③组织开展校内旅游类创新创业比赛，如开展旅游线路的创意设计比赛，并积极组织学生参加省级以上创新创业大赛；④积极申报省级以上大学生创新创业训练计划项目，并组织强大的教师指导团队，加强对此项目的全程指导，同时，聘请有创新创业能力的企业导师和取得创业成绩的优秀毕业生不定期指导学生创业训练和实践。

（三）2017届旅游管理专业毕业生跟踪调查报告

1.基本情况

外国语学院旅游管理专业2017届毕业生共有89人，共调查89人，回收调查表89份，占本专业应调查人数的100%，有效调查表89份，占回收调查表的100%，占应调查人数的100%。

历时3个多月的走访调查，足迹涵盖了珠三角、粤东、粤西和粤北

地区。从学生就业的单位属性来看，私企占绝大部分，人数为86人，比例约为96.63%。毕业生在与本专业相关的行业工作的人数为61人，对口率约为68.54%。毕业生对现工作持基本满意和非常满意的人数为85人，占比约为95.51%。在工作中认为最重要的品质为正确积极的态度和良好的沟通技巧的人数占比，分别约为65.17%和62.92%。该调查报告较好地反映出现代职场对毕业生的基本要求。

2.调查结果

以下为调查问卷统计结果，见表2-25至2-36。

（1）毕业生所在用人单位性质。

表2-25 毕业生所在用人单位性质的调查结果

单位：个

选项	人数	选项	人数
1.行政机关	0	6.私营企业	78
2.国有企业	1	7.集体企业	4
3.事业单位	3	8.自主创业	1
4.社会组织	0	9.其他	6
5.三资企业	2		

（2）毕业生工作岗位与所学专业是否对口。

表2-26 毕业生工作岗位与所学专业对口情况的调查结果

单位：个

选项	人数	选项	人数
1.对口	61		
2.不对口	47		

（3）毕业生跳槽次数情况。

表2-27 别野生跳槽次数情况的调查结果

单位：个

选项	人数	选项	人数
1.1次	50	4.4次	0
2.2次	15	5.4次以上	0
3.3次	3		

（4）毕业生起薪情况。

表2-28　毕业生起薪情况的调查结果

单位：个

选项	人数	选项	人数
1.2 500元以下	47	4.3 501～4 000元	0
2.2 501～3 000元	14	5.4 000元以上	0
3.3 001～3 500元	2		

（5）毕业生目前月收入情况。

表2-29　毕业生目前月收入情况的调查结果

单位：个

选项	人数	选项	人数
1.2 500元以下	29	4.3 501～4 000元	1
2.2 501～3 000元	27	5.4 000元以上	1
3.3 001～3 500元	7		

（6）毕业生确定最初工作单位的途径。

表2-30　毕业生确定最初工作单位途径的调查结果

单位：个

选项	人数	选项	人数
1. 校园招聘会	11	5. 社会招聘	3
2. 网上招聘	28	6. 新闻媒体	0
3. 亲友介绍	13	7. 其他	8
4. 自我推荐	2		

（7）毕业生择业时看重工作单位情况（多选，不超过3项）。

表2-31　毕业生择业时看重工作单位情况的调查结果

单位：个

选项	人数	选项	人数
1.个人发展空间大小	52	4.培训、提高机会	36
2.行业及其发展前景	53	5.经济收入及福利待遇	47
3.公司环境及企业文化	43	6.工作地点	30

（8）毕业生对目前工作的满意度情况。

表2-32　毕业生对目前工作满意度情况的调查结果

单位：个

选项	人数	选项	人数
1. 非常满意	12	3. 不太满意	3
2. 比较满意	73	4. 很不满意	0

（9）毕业生认为自己在单位受重用的程度。

表2-33　毕业生认为自己在单位受重用的程度

单位：个

选项	人数	选项	人数
1. 很受重用	31	3. 程度一般	15
2. 较受重用	60	4. 不受重用	2

（10）毕业生认为在校学习过程中哪些能力最有利于就业后发展（多选，不超过2项）。

表2-34　毕业生认为在校学习期间最有利于就业后发展的能力的调查结果

单位：个

选项	人数	选项	人数
1. 专业知识	22	4. 组织、工作能力	27
2. 学习、分析问题的能力	57	5. 人际交往能力	47
3. 实操、动手能力	38	6. 其他	3

（11）毕业生认为用人单位对大学生素养方面的重视情况（多选，不超过3项）。

表2-35　毕业生认为用人单位大学生素养方面重视情况的调查结果

单位：个

选项	人数	选项	人数
1. 良好的沟通技巧	56	6. 开拓、创新能力	23
2. 良好的职业道德	34	7. 持久的学习能力	23
3. 实践应用能力	29	8. 诚实守信	15
4. 正确积极的态度	58	9. 责任心	42
5. 领导与管理能力	12		

（12）毕业生对母校的评价情况。

表2-36　毕业生对目前的评价情况调查结果

单位：个

项目	好/个	比例/%	一般/个	比例/%	差/个	比例/%
1. 办学条件	78	72.22%	30	27.78%	—	—
2. 教学质量	74	68.52%	34	31.48%	—	—
3. 课程设置	49	45.37%	59	54.63%		
4. 教学内容	59	54.63%	48	44.44%	1	0.93%
5. 师资水平	2	1.85%	26	24.07%	—	—
6. 实操实训	48	44.44%	59	54.63%	1	0.93%
7. 人文教育	75	69.44%	33	30.56%	—	—
8. 品德教育	78	72.22%	30	27.78%	—	—
9. 专业与职业的衔接	64	59.26%	43	39.81%	1	0.93%
10. 学校管理	77	71.30%	31	28.70%		
11. 总体评价	81	75.00%	27	25.00%		

二、学生在省级以上技能大赛中的卓越表现

2013年到2018年，旅游管理专业学生获得各类技能大赛奖项54项，其中全国一等奖4项、全国二等奖5项、全国三等奖7项，广东省一等奖9项、广东省二等奖16项、广东省三等奖10项，广东省五一劳动奖章1项，全国优秀组织奖1项，全国最佳讲解奖1项，全国最佳才艺展示奖1项。

表2-37　2013—2018年旅游管理专业学生获奖统计表

序号	竞赛名称	级别	等级	参赛学生	时间
1	"东科杯"第六届全国职业院校外贸技能竞赛	全国	优秀组织奖	林辉冰	2013
2	广东省五一劳动奖章	广东省	—	丁雅新	2017
3	"千策杯"第五届全国旅游院校服务技能大赛高职组鸡尾酒调制项目	全国	一等奖	林辉冰	2013
4	"东科杯"第六届全国职业院校外贸技能竞赛外贸技能（高职组）	全国	一等奖	宋彩娇	2013
5	"巽震杯"第八届全国旅游院校服务技能（导游服务）大赛（普通话导游）	全国	一等奖	刘笛	2016
6	2018年全国职业院校技能大赛高职组导游服务赛项	全国	一等奖	林淑婷	2018

续　表

序号	竞赛名称	级别	等级	参赛学生	时间
7	2014 年全国职业院校技能大赛高职组广东省选拔赛（中餐主题宴会设计）	广东省	一等奖	翁英红	2014
8	2015 年全国职业院校技能大赛高职组广东省选拔赛（中餐主题宴会设计）	广东省	一等奖	李玉婵	2015
9	2015 年全国职业院校技能大赛高职组广东省选拔赛（英语导游）	广东省	一等奖	曾樱琪	2015
10	2016 年全国职业院校技能大赛高职组广东省选拔赛（英语导游）	广东省	一等奖	吴燕芬	2016
11	2016 年全国职业院校技能大赛高职组广东省选拔赛（普通话导游）	广东省	一等奖	刘笛	2016
12	2016 年全国职业院校技能大赛高职组广东省选拔赛（中餐主题宴会设计）	广东省	一等奖	池曼琴	2016
13	2016 年广东省导游服务技能大赛（英语组）	广东省	一等奖	陈慧敏	2017
14	2017 年全国职业院校技能大赛高职组广东省选拔赛（导游服务）	广东省	一等奖	吴婷婷	2017
15	2018 年全国职业院校技能大赛高职组广东省选拔赛（导游服务）	广东省	一等奖	林淑婷	2018
16	"千策杯"第五届全国旅游院校服务技能大赛高职组西餐宴会摆台项目	全国	二等奖	曾桂有	2013
17	第五届"外研社杯"全国高职高专英语写作大赛全国总决赛	全国	二等奖	王晓红	2014
18	"巽震杯"第八届全国旅游院校服务技能（导游服务）大赛（普通话导游）	全国	二等奖	丁雅新	2016
19	"巽震杯"第八届全国旅游院校服务技能（导游服务）大赛（英语导游）	全国	二等奖	邓华英	2016
20	"神州视景杯"第七届全国旅游院校服务技能（饭店服务）大赛中式铺床及夜床创意	全国	二等奖	蔡美云	2015
21	2014 年全国职业院校技能大赛高职组广东省选拔赛（中餐主题宴会设计）	广东省	二等奖	梁洁媛	2014
22	2015 年全国职业院校技能大赛高职组导游服务赛项比赛	广东省	二等奖	丁雅新	2015
23	2015 全国职业院校技能大赛高职组广东省选拔赛中餐（主题宴会设计）	广东省	二等奖	吕慧玲	2015
24	2015 年全国职业院校技能大赛高职组广东省选拔赛（普通话导游）	广东省	二等奖	黄常炽	2015
25	2015 年全国职业院校技能大赛高职组广东省选拔赛（普通话导游）	广东省	二等奖	董瑞敏	2015

续　表

序号	竞赛名称	级别	等级	参赛学生	时间
26	2015 年全国职业院校技能大赛高职组广东省选拔赛（西餐宴会服务）	广东省	二等奖	林银婷	2015
27	2016 年全国职业院校技能大赛高职组广东省选拔赛（英语导游）	广东省	二等奖	邓华英	2016
28	2016 年全国职业院校技能大赛高职组广东省选拔赛（普通话导游）	广东省	二等奖	喻璐	2016
29	2016 年全国职业院校技能大赛高职组广东省选拔赛（中餐主题宴会设计）	广东省	二等奖	董瑞敏	2016
30	2016 年全国职业院校技能大赛高职组广东省选拔赛（西餐宴会服务）	广东省	二等奖	罗婉怡	2016
31	2016 年全国职业院校技能大赛高职组广东省选拔赛（西餐宴会服务）	广东省	二等奖	许雅婷	2016
32	2017 年全国职业院校技能大赛高职组广东省选拔赛导游服务项目	广东省	二等奖	杨洁	2017
33	2016 年广东省高等职业院校技能大赛暨2017 年全国职业院校技能大赛高职组广东省选拔赛（西餐宴会服务）	广东省	二等奖	谢黄瑶	2017
34	2016 年广东省高等职业院校技能大赛暨2017 年全国职业院校技能大赛高职组广东省选拔赛（西餐宴会服务）	广东省	二等奖	张鹏玲	2017
35	2017—2018 年度广东省职业院校技能大赛西餐宴会服务	广东省	二等奖	何国枝	2018
36	2017—2018 年度广东省职业院校技能大赛中餐主题宴会设计	广东省	二等奖	王瑞蓉、陈家芳、马迪芬	2018
37	"千策杯"第五届全国旅游院校服务技能大赛高职组中餐宴会摆台项目	全国	三等奖	刘心宇	2013
38	"千策杯"第五届全国旅游院校服务技能大赛高职组中式铺床及开夜床项目	全国	三等奖	陈佳琳	2013
39	"神州视景杯"第六届全国旅游院校服务技能（导游服务）大赛（中文组）	全国	三等奖	巫美娟	2014
40	"神州视景杯"第六届全国旅游院校服务技能（导游服务）大赛（中文组）	全国	三等奖	吴爱贤	2014
41	"神州视景杯"第七届全国旅游院校服务技能（饭店服务）大赛中餐宴会摆台	全国	三等奖	林晓婷	2015
42	"神州视景杯"第七届全国旅游院校服务技能（饭店服务）大赛	全国	三等奖	黄萃灵	2015

续 表

序号	竞赛名称	级别	等级	参赛学生	时间
43	"巽震杯"第八届全国旅游院校服务技能（导游服务）大赛（英语导游）	全国	三等奖	曾樱琪	2016
44	"巽震杯"第八届全国旅游院校服务技能（导游服务）大赛（普通话导游）	全国	最佳讲解奖	刘笛	2016
45	"巽震杯"第八届全国旅游院校服务技能（导游服务）大赛（普通话导游）	全国	最佳才艺展示奖	刘笛	2016
46	2013年全国职业院校技能大赛高职组广东省选拔赛（西式宴会服务）	广东省	三等奖	林沛玲	2013
47	2013年全国职业院校技能大赛高职组广东省选拔赛（西式宴会服务）	广东省	三等奖	吴倩婷	2013
48	2013年全国职业院校技能大赛高职组广东省选拔赛（中餐主题宴会设计）	广东省	三等奖	李艳娟	2013
49	2013年全国职业院校技能大赛高职组广东省选拔赛导游服务项目（英语组）	广东省	三等奖	刘洲航	2013
50	2013年全国职业院校技能大赛高职组广东省选拔赛导游服务项目（英语组）	广东省	三等奖	张传猛	2013
51	2013年全国职业院校技能大赛高职组广东省选拔赛导游服务项目（普通话组）	广东省	三等奖	方楚玲	2013
52	2014年全国职业院校技能大赛高职组广东省选拔赛导游服务项目（英语组）	广东省	三等奖	王泳音	2014
53	2015年全国职业院校技能大赛高职组广东省选拔赛（西餐宴会服务）	广东省	三等奖	许雅婷	2015
54	2016年广东高等职业院校技能大赛暨2017年全国职业院校技能大赛高职组广东省选拔赛（中华茶艺）	广东省	三等奖	黄曼丽	2017
55	2013年全国职业院校技能大赛高职组广东省选拔赛导游服务项目（普通话组）	广东省	三等奖	刘岩	2018

第三节 课程

教育部印发的《基础教育课程改革纲要》指出：国家课程标准是教材编写、教学、评估和考试命题的依据，是国家管理和评价课程的基础。应体现国家对不同阶段的学生在知识与技能、过程与方法、情感态度与价值观等方面的基本要求，规定各门课程的性质、目标、内容框架，提出教学和评价建议。从以上规定中可以看出，课程标准包括以下内涵。

（1）它是按门类制定的；

（2）它规定本门课程的性质、目标、内容框架；

（3）它提出了指导性的教学原则和评价建议；

（4）它不包括教学重点、难点、时间分配等具体内容；

（5）它规定了不同阶段学生在知识与技能、过程与方法、情感态度与价值观等方面所应达到的基本要求。

由于课程标准规定的是国家（学校）对学生在某方面或某领域的基本素质要求，因此，它毫无疑问地对教材、教学和评价具有重要指导意义，是教材、教学和评价的出发点与归宿。因为无论教材还是教学，都是为这些方面或领域的基本素质的培养服务的。可以说，课程标准中规定的基本素质要求是教材、教学和评价的灵魂，也是整个职业教育课程的灵魂。这也正是各国极其重视课程改革，尤其是极其重视课程标准研制工作的重要原因。现在英美等国纷纷组织全国最强的力量、投入大量物力经费研制各科课程标准，表现出他们对国家课程标准的日益重视。无论教材怎么编写，无论教学如何设计，无论评价如何开展，都必须围绕着这一基本素质要求服务，都不能脱离这个核心。

课程标准是教材、教学的基本依据，并不等于课程标准是对教材、教学方方面面的具体规定。课程标准对某方面或某领域基本要求的规定主要体现为在课程标准中所确定的课程目标和课程内容。因此，课程标准的指导作用主要体现在它规定了各科教材、教学所要实现的课程目标和各科教材、教学中所要学习的课程内容，规定了所需评价的基本素质以及评价的基本标准。

现以具体课程为例，说明课程标准的基本要求。

一、G 学院研学旅行实务课程标准

表2-38

学院（部门）	旅游学院
适用专业名称	旅游管理
课标编码	17067020
课 程 名 称	研学旅行实务
执笔人	朱瀚
审核人	周梁

（一）课程性质与任务

本课程是三年制高职高专院校旅游管理专业大学二年级阶段必修的专业拓展课程，是针对该专业学生"1+X"研学旅行策划与管理 (EEPM) 职业技能等级证书（中级）的理论与实践课程，属于典型的"课证融通"课程。

本课程对在研学旅行岗位的课程设计、研学团服务等要求，通过设置理论结合实践的教学内容，旨在针对研学旅行岗位的基本技能要求，培养学生研学旅行课程设计、研学旅行课程教学，研学旅行课程实操中交流沟通、突发状况应对等各项综合能力，提升学生社会实习和就业的竞争力。本课程目前是校级"金课"建设课程，符合高职人才培养目标和旅游行业岗位（群）的任职要求，对于学生在校期间实习及毕业后从事研学旅行行业工作有着重要的指导作用。

本课程的先修课程有导游基础知识、旅游电子商务、沟通与口才等，后续课程是专业综合实训（5）、顶岗实习和毕业设计（论文）。

（二）课程目标与要求

依据教育部职业技术教育中心研究所发布的《研学旅行策划与管理（EEPM）职业技能等级标准》（标准代码：540001）要求，本课程目标大致分为三类：一是知识目标，要求学生了解研学旅行的基本概念，并熟悉研学旅行课程设计八大要素的内涵；二是能力目标，要求学生能研制合格的研学旅行课程产品（含《研学手册》）、能从事研学旅行课程讲解工作、能建立研学旅行评价机制、能在研学旅行课程实操中进行有效沟通、能在研学旅行课程实操中处理一般性突发事故；三是素质目标，要求学生能在学习过程中用敬业精神和社会责任感激励自己，并具备一定的创新创业能力开展研学旅行的各项工作。

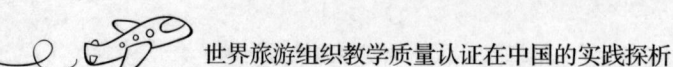

表2-39　课程目标对专业培养规格分解指标的支撑矩阵

目标分类	目标编码	课程目标	Ea1	Ea2	Ea3	Ea4	Ea5	Ea6	Ea7	Ea8
知识	C1	了解研学旅行的基本概念	M	H	H	M	L	H	L	L
	C2	熟悉研学旅行课程设计八大要素的内涵	H	H	M	H	L	M	M	M
能力	C3	能研制合格的研学旅行课程产品（含《研学手册》）	M	H	M	H	H	H	H	H
	C4	能从事研学旅行课程讲解工作	M	H	M	H	H	H	H	M
	C5	能建立研学旅行评价机制，引导学生进行自评和互评	H	M	L	M	L	M	L	H
	C6	能在研学旅行课程实操中进行有效沟通	H	H	H	H	H	H	H	L
	C7	能在研学旅行课程实操中处理一般性突发事故	M	H	L	H	M	H	H	L
素质	C8	能通过设计或实施研学课程感受祖国历史、文化、自然等社会资源，并进行传播	H	H	H	L	L	M	L	L
	C9	具备一定的创新创业能力	M	H	L	H	H	H	H	H

（三）课程结构与内容

1.课程结构

本课程共3学分,56学时，其中理论教学28学时，实践教学28学时，线上教学12学时。

为了达到教学目标，本课程设置了四个模块。

（1）研学旅行基本概念建构：旨在引导学生了解研学旅行的性质、目的和意义，并对国内外中小学生研学旅行有一个初步认知。

（2）研学旅行活动课程设计：旨在通过对研学旅行课程主题、课程目标、课程资源、课程内容、课程实施、课程评价、课程师资、研学手册八大课程要素的学习，让学生掌握研发研学旅行课程的基本技能，设计合格的研学旅行课程。

（3）研学旅行课程实施：重点关注研学旅行过程中的安全管理及法律风险。

（4）研学旅行课程实践：在珠海鹭鸟天下校外实践教学基地开展研学旅行课程实践，对本课程的学习进行总结，并进行成果展示。

表2-40 课程结构与学时建议

模块	主题／课程	授课学期数	学分	建议学时
一	研学旅行基本概念建构	1	0.2	8
二	研学旅行活动课程设计	1	2	32
三	研学旅行课程实施	1	0.3	8
四	研学旅行课程实践	1	0.5	8

2. 课程内容

（1）研学旅行基本概念建构。

【内容要求】

①研学旅行的性质、目的和意义。

②国内、国外中小学生研学旅行概览。

【目标要求】

让学生了解研学旅行的性质、目的和意义，使其对国内外中小学生研学旅行有一个初步认知。

【教学要求】

由于本模块是研学旅行基本概念的建构，故而采取以教师讲授为主、以课堂讨论为辅的教学策略，运用启发式教学和小组讨论的教学方法，注重学生的学习反馈，为下一模块奠定基础。

教学方法	☑讲授 ☑讨论或座谈 □问题导向学习 ☑分组合作学习 ☑案例教学
	□任务驱动 □项目教学 □情景教学 □演示汇报 □实践教学 □参观访问
	□引导文教学 □其他

【场地要求】

多媒体教室。

（2）研学旅行活动课程设计。

【内容要求】

①基于核心素养的研学旅行及主题设计。

②课程目标。

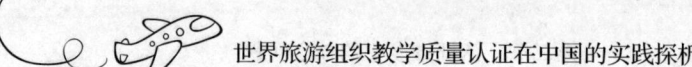
③ 课程内容、课程实施。

④课程评价、学生评价。

⑤研学旅行跨学科融合创新。

⑥研学手册的基本内容及制作。

⑦研学旅行案例评析。

⑧小组作业展示及点评。

【目标要求】

通过对研学旅行课程主题、课程目标、课程资源、课程内容、课程实施、课程评价、课程师资、研学手册八大课程要素的学习，让学生掌握研发研学旅行课程的基本技能，能够设计合格的研学旅行课程。

【教学要求】

用项目教学、启发式教学、自主探究、小组讨论、任务驱动等教学方法，注重理论与实践相结合，用理论结合案例的方法引导学生对研学旅行课程的八大要素逐一进行实操，最终设计出完整、合格、能落地的研学旅行课程。

教学方法	☑ 讲授　☑ 讨论或座谈　☐ 问题导向学习　☑ 分组合作学习　☑ 案例教学
	☑ 任务驱动　☑ 项目教学　☐ 情景教学　☑ 演示汇报　☐ 实践教学　☐ 参观访问
	☐ 引导文教学　☐ 其他

【场地要求】

多媒体教室。

（3）研学旅行课程实施。

【内容要求】

①安全管理与保障。

② 法律风险与防范。

【目标要求】

通过讲解研学旅行实施的相关行业标准，结合研学旅行安全及法律案例，让学生做到在研学旅行过程中保障基本人身、财产安全，防范常见法律风险。

【教学要求】

采用自主探究、小组讨论的教学方法，用研学旅行行业标准结合案

例的方法引导学生了解在研学旅行过程中常见的安全隐患及法律风险，做到保障基本人身、财产安全，防范常见法律风险。

教学方法	☑ 讲授 ☑ 讨论或座谈 ☐ 问题导向学习 ☐ 分组合作学习 ☑ 案例教学 ☐ 任务驱动 ☐ 项目教学 ☑ 情景教学 ☐ 演示汇报 ☐ 实践教学 ☐ 参观访问 ☐ 引导文教学 ☐ 其他

【场地要求】

多媒体教室。

（4）研学旅行课程实践。

【内容要求】

①生态类研学课程设计实操（珠海鹭鸟天下校外实践教学基地）。

②课程考核。

【目标要求】

利用珠海鹭鸟天下校外实践教学基地开展研学旅行课程实践，对本课程的学习进行总结及成果展示。

【教学要求】

学生前往珠海鹭鸟天下校外实践教学基地开展研学旅行课程实践，本课程企业指导教师与校内教师一同指导课程实践。各项目组需要有明确的实践目标和实践任务。采用项目教学、自主探究、小组讨论、任务驱动等教学方法，注重引导学生利用课程资源（如湿地水鸟、湿地植物、有机蔬菜、疍家文化等）设计出合格的生态类研学旅行课程。

教学方法	☑ 讲授 ☑ 讨论或座谈 ☐ 问题导向学习 ☑ 分组合作学习 ☑ 案例教学 ☑ 任务驱动 ☑ 项目教学 ☐ 情景教学 ☑ 演示汇报 ☐ 实践教学 ☐ 参观访问 ☐ 引导文教学 ☐ 其他

【场地要求】

珠海鹭鸟天下校外实践教学基地。

（四）课程内容与课程目标支撑矩阵

表2-41　课程内容与课程目标支撑矩阵

序号	任务单元／知识点章节目录	C1	C2	C3	C4	C5	C6	C7	C8	C9
1	模块一：研学旅行基本概念建构	H							M	
1.1	研学旅行的性质、目的、意义	H							M	
1.2	国内、国外中小学生研学旅行概览	H							M	
2	模块二：研学旅行活动课程设计	M	H	H	L	H			H	
2.1	基于核心素养的研学旅行及主题设计	H	H	H	H				H	M
2.2	课程目标		H	H		H			H	
2.3	课程内容、课程实施		H	H	H	M	H	H	H	
2.4	课程评价、学生评价		H	H		H	H		M	
2.5	研学旅行跨学科融合创新	M	M	H					H	H
2.6	研学手册的基本内容及制作		H	H	H				H	M
2.7	研学旅行案例评析		H	L					H	
2.8	小组作业展示及点评		H							
3	模块三：研学旅行课程实施	M	M		H		M	H	H	L
3.1	安全管理与保障	M		M	H		H	H		
3.2	法律风险与防范	M		M			M	H		
4	模块四：研学旅行课程实践	M	H	H	H	H	H	H	H	M
4.1	生态类研学课程设计实操（珠海鹭鸟天下校外实践教学基地）		H	H	H				H	H
4.2	课程考核									

（五）学生考核与评价

1. 课程考核设计

本课程采取形成性评价和终结性评价并重的方式进行考核，平时成绩和期末成绩各占50%。

平时成绩 100 分，以 50% 计入总评成绩：其中 40% 是平时课堂贡献分数，包括课堂回答问题、课堂启发式提问引导同学思考、课后与教师或小组讨论后形成思考报告或问题等；50% 是小组项目、个人作业及期中测试（线上进行）；10% 是考勤。

期末成绩 100 分，以 50% 计入总评成绩：以小组为单位，选取小组设计的研学旅行活动课程设计方案中的一个教学环节，提交一个不低于十分钟的研学旅行课程讲解视频，或在课堂上进行 5～10 分钟的研学旅行课程教学展示（具体要求及评分标准见相关文件）。

表2-42　课程考核与评价设计

评价维度	过程性考核								终结性考核
分值占比	25%				20%			10%	50%
评价分项	单元测验	期中考试	作业	演示汇报	项目实战	小组讨论	学习总结	专题调研	出勤	期末考试
次数	8	1	36	2	2	12	5	1	28	1

2.学业质量水平

从课程的角度概述学业质量水平的分级及其依据。

表2-43　学业质量水平说明

质量维度 （质量等级）	A（优）	B（良）	C（中）
出勤率	100%	90% 以上	80% 以上
作业质量	均分 90 分以上	均分 80 分以上	均分 70 分以上
单元及期中测试	均分 90 分以上	均分 80 分以上	均分 70 分以上
课程贡献	提出启发式问题 1 个及以上，或回答问题 4 次以上，或与教师讨论、小组讨论后形成思考报告 1 篇	课堂回答问题 2 次以上	课堂回答问题 1 次以上

（六）课程实施保障

1.教学要求

（1）研学旅行基本概念建构模块：让学生了解研学旅行的性质、目的和意义，并对国内外中小学生研学旅行有一个初步认知，具备研学旅行课程设计的初步想法。

（2）研学旅行课程设计模块：让学生掌握研学旅行课程八大基本要素：课程主题、课程目标、课程资源、课程内容、课程实施、课程评价、课程师资、研学手册，整合我国历史、文化、自然、科技等社会资源进行研学旅行课程设计与研发，创造性开发研学旅行课程，如以当地红色资源为背景的研学旅行课程。

（3）研学旅行课程实施模块：让学生具备在研学旅行过程中基本的抵御安全风险及防范法律风险的能力。

（4）研学旅行课程实践模块：利用珠海鹭鸟天下校外实践教学基地开展研学旅行课程实践，让学生以湿地资源为背景，创造性地开发生态类研学旅行课程，践行生态环保，培养环保意识，帮扶乡村振兴。

2. 师资要求

【基本要求】

高校教师应有旅游管理、文学、传播学等相关专业背景，具备硕士以上学位或中级以上职称，拥有研学旅行策划与管理（EEPM）职业资格等级证书（中级或以上）；企业教师应有研学旅行行业两年以上的从业经验，有丰富的研学旅行带团经历或管理经历，或是市级以上研学旅行基地主要负责人，或是研学课程主讲教师。

【团队能力提升】

借助"金课"及实践教学基地建设平台，吸纳更多不同学科背景、年龄层次、工作岗位的学校、政府、企业人员，整合资源，建立一支以培训研学旅行行业人才为主要目的、以开发跨学科融合创新课程为主要手段的研学旅行实务课程师资团队。

（七）教材要求与选择

根据研学旅行策划与管理（EEPM）职业技能等级标准要求，本课程教材需涵盖研学旅行课程设计（中级）及研学旅行课程讲解实操（初级）的相关内容。推荐教材：《研学旅行实操手册》。

（八）参考书籍与网络资源

参考书籍：《研学旅行活动课程开发与实施》《研学旅行课程设计（第2版）》。

网络资源：全国大学生红色旅游创意策划大赛，井冈山青少年教育基地，http：//www.jgsqsnjy.com/。中国研学旅行网，http：//www.tiyan.org.cn/。万里路研学旅行教育网，http：//www.zhongguoyx.com/。

（九）场地与设备要求

（1）场地面积：满足课程人数要求。

（2）场地规格：以正方形或宽敞形为佳，避免狭长形或不规则形状。

（3）场地通风：教室宽敞通风，夏季空调凉爽，冬季室内温暖。

（4）场地灯光：灯光明亮并可分组调节，投影布上方不能有灯光。

（5）分组布置：分成 N 组，每组安排人数 6～8 人为佳。

（6）场地布置：桌面、地面干净卫生，校外实践教学基地有安全保障。

（7）场地设备：多媒体教学设备、校外实践教学基本教学材料（如显微镜、望远镜、手电筒等）。

（8）其他建议：建议增加部分教育学类基础课程作为先导课程，补充学生基础教育学知识。

（十）授课进程与安排

表2-44 课程资源要求和授课安排

序号	任务单元/知识点章节目录	线下教学		课程资源建设						线上教学				
		理论学时	实践学时	视频（个）	虚拟仿真类（个）	非视频（个）	习题（道）	试题（题）	项目/案例（个）	线上学时	课程公告	交流互动	作业次数	单元测验
1	模块一：研学旅行基本概念建构													
1.1	研学旅行的性质、目的、意义	4	0	2		5				1	1	50	1	1
1.2	国内、国外中小学生研学旅行概览	4	0	2		5				1	1	50	1	
2	模块二：研学旅行活动课程设计													
2.1	基于核心素养的研学旅行及主题设计	2	2	2		5				1	1	50	1	
2.2	课程目标	2	2	6		5	1	10		1	1	50	4	1
2.3	课程内容、课程实施	2	2	4		10	1	10		1	1	50	2	1
2.4	课程评价、学生评价	2	2	4		5	1	10		1	1	50	2	1
2.5	研学旅行跨学科融合创新	2	2	2		5	1	10		2	1	50	1	1
2.6	研学手册的基本内容及制作	2	2	6		10	1	10		1	1	50	4	1
2.7	研学旅行案例展示及点评	0	4	4		8			8		1	50	4	1
2.8	小组作业展示及点评	0	4	4		10	1	10	10	1	1	50	4	1
3	模块三：研学旅行课程实施													
3.1	安全管理与保障	4	0	2		5				1	1	50	2	1
3.2	法律风险与防范	4	0	2		5				1	1	50	2	1
4	模块四：研学类研学旅行课程设计实践													
4.1	生态类研学课程设计实操（珠海鹭鸟与天下）校外实践教学基地	0	4					10	10					
4.2	课程考核	0	4				1	10						
	小计：	28	28	40	0	80	8	80	28	12	12	600	28	8

注：一般建设课程资源目的在于辅助学生理解重难点。

（十一）开发团队

表2-45

序号	姓名	部门／企业名称	承担的工作任务	签名
1	朱瀚	旅游学院旅游管理专业	"金课"建设，制定课程标准、教案、教学日历	
2	魏微	旅游学院旅游管理专业	负责"1+X"研学旅行策划与管理职业技能等级证书项目，参与制定课程标准、教案、教学日历	
3	梁华坤	珠海市三板旅游有限公司	校外实践教学	
4	吕君怡	澳门科技大学／湖南游学少年实践教育服务	参与制定课程标准、教案、教学日历	

一、G Polytechnic Study Tour Practice Course Criterion

Table 2-38

Faculty	Tourism College
Major	Tourism Management
Course Code	17067020
Course	Study Tour Practice
Written by	Zhu Han
Reviewed by	Zhou Liang

（一）Course Nature and Tasks

This course is a compulsory professional expansion course for the sophomores of tourism management majors in three-year polytechnic program. It is a course combining theory with practice, aiming at the "1+X" Educational Excursion Planning and Management（EEPM）vocational skill level certificate（intermediate）for students of this major. It is a typical "course-certificate integration" course.

This course is designed to meet the requirements of the course and the service of the study tour service. By combining theory with practical teaching content, it aims to cultivate students' comprehensive abilities in the design of the study tour course, the teaching of the study tour course, communication, and emergency response, and improve students' competitiveness in social practice and employment. This course is currently a school-level "Golden Course" construction course, which meets the training objectives of polytechnic talents and the job requirements of tourism industry posts and plays an important role in guiding students to practice in school and engage in study tour industry after graduation.

The prerequisite courses of this course include Basic Knowledge of Tour Guide, Tourism E-commerce, Communication and Eloquence, etc. The follow-up courses are Professional Comprehensive Training (5), Post Practice and Graduation Design (Thesis).

(二) Course Objectives and Requirements

According to the requirements of the *Vocational Skill Grade Standard for Educational Excursion Planning and Management* (EEPM) (standard code: 540001) issued by the Research Institute of the Vocational and Technical Education Center of the Ministry of Education, the objectives of this course are roughly divided into three categories. First, the knowledge objectives require students to understand the basic concept of study tour and be familiar with the connotation of the eight elements of study tour course design. Second, the ability objectives require students to develop qualified study tour course products (including Research Manual) and be able to explain knowledge in study tour courses, establish evaluation mechanisms for study tour, communicate effectively, and deal with general emergencies in the practical operation of study tour courses. Third, the value objectives require students to motivate themselves with professionalism and social responsibility in the learning process and have certain innovation and entrepreneurship ability to carry out various tasks of study tour.

Table 2-39： Matrix of Course Objectives for Major Training Specification
Decomposition Index

Dimension	Code	Course Objectives	Ea1	Ea2	Ea3	Ea4	Ea5	Ea6	Ea7	Ea8
Knowledge	C1	Understand the basic concept of study tour	M	H	H	M	L	H	L	L
	C2	Be familiar with the connotation of the eight elements of the course design of study tour	H	H	M	H	L	M	M	M
Skills and Abilities	C3	Be able to develop qualified study tour courses	M	H	M	H	H	H	H	H
	C4	Be able to explain knowledge in study tour courses	M	H	M	H	H	H	H	M
	C5	Be able to establish an evaluation mechanism for study tour	H	M	L	M	L	M	L	H
	C6	Be able to communicate effectively in the practical operation of the study tour course	H	H	M	H	H	H	H	L
	C7	Be able to handle general emergencies in the practical operation of the study tour course	M	H	L	H	M	H	H	L
Value	C8	Be able to enjoy the history, culture, nature, and other social resources of the motherland through the design or implementation of study tour and spread them	H	H	H	L	L	M	L	L
	C9	Have certain innovation and entrepreneurship ability	M	H	H	L	H	H	H	H

（三）Course Structure and Content

1. Course Structure

This course has 3 credits with 56 class hours, including 28 theoretical hours, 28 practical hours, and 12 online teaching hours.

In order to meet the requirements of teaching objectives, this course has four modules.

(1) The basic concept of study tour. It aims to guide students to understand the nature, purpose, and significance of study tour, and have a preliminary understanding of study tour for primary and secondary school students at home and abroad.

(2) Course design of study tour activities. It aims to enable students to master the basic skills of research and development of study tour courses and design qualified study tour courses through learning eight course elements, including study tour course theme, course objectives, course resources, course content, course implementation, course evaluation, course teachers, research manuals, etc.

(3) Implementation of study tour course. It focuses on safety management and legal risks during study tour.

(4) Practice of the study tour course. The study tour course practice is carried out in Zhuhai Ardeidae World off-campus teaching base to summarize the learning of this course and display the results.

Table 2-40: Course Structure and Class Hours

Module	Topic	Credit	Class Hours
1	The basic concept of study tour	0.2	8
2	Course design of study tour activities	2	32
3	Implementation of study tour course	0.3	8
4	Practice of the study tour course	0.5	8

2. Course Content

(1) The basic concept of study tour.

【Content】

The nature, purpose, and significance of the study tour; Overview of study tour for primary and secondary school students at home and abroad.

【Objectives】

The students are required to understand the nature, purpose, and significance of study tour, and have a preliminary understanding of study tour for primary and secondary students at home and abroad.

【Teaching Requirements】

As this module is the construction of the basic concept of study tour, the teaching strategy is based on lecturing, supplemented by classroom discussion. The teaching methods of heuristic teaching and group discussion are used, and students' learning feedback is emphasized to lay the foundation for the next module.

【Site Requirements】

Multi-Media Classroom.

(2) Course design of study tour activities.

【Content】

Study tour course theme, course objectives, course resources, course content, course implementation, course evaluation, course teachers, and research manuals.

【Objectives】

The students are required to develop and design quality study tour courses.

【Teaching Requirements】

Project teaching, heuristic teaching, independent inquiry, group discussion, task-driven, and other teaching methods are used to focus on the combination of theory and practice, and the method of combining theory with cases is also used to guide students to practice the eight elements of the study tour course, so as to finally design a complete, qualified and practical study tour course.

【Site Requirements】

Multi-Media Classroom.

(3) Implementation of study tour course.

【Content】

Safety management and legal risk prevention in study tour courses.

【Objectives】

The students are required to ensure the basic personal and property safety and prevent common legal risks during the study tour by explaining the relevant safety standards and legal risks implemented in the study tour.

【Teaching Requirements】

The teaching method of independent inquiry and group discussion is used to guide students to understand the common security and legal risks in the implementation of study tour courses.

【Site Requirements】

Multi-Media Classroom.

(4) Practice of the study tour course.

【Content】

Practical operation of ecological study tour course design, final test.

【Objectives】

Students are required to carry out the practice of the study tour course in Zhuhai Ardeidae World off-campus teaching base, summarize the learning of this course, and display the results.

【Teaching Requirements】

The students went to Zhuhai Ardeidae World off-campus teaching base to carry out the practice of the study tour course in groups. The enterprise instructor and the teachers of the course guided the practice together. Each project team needs to have clear practical objectives and tasks. With project teaching, independent inquiry, group discussion, task driven, and other teaching methods, the students are required to use course resources, including wetland waterfowl, wetland plants, organic vegetables, Danjia culture, etc., to design qualified ecological study tour courses.

【Site Requirements】

Zhuhai Ardeidae World off-campus teaching base.

（四）Course Chapter and Course Objective Support

Table 2-41：Course Content and Course Objective Matrix

Chapter	Tasks/Contents	C1	C2	C3	C4	C5	C6	C7	C8	C9
1	Module 1：The basic concept of study tour	H							M	
1.1	Nature, purpose, and significance	H							M	
1.2	Overview of study tour for primary and secondary school students at home and abroad	H							M	
2	Module 2：Course design of study tour activities	M	H	H	L	H			H	
2.1	Study tour course theme	H	H	H	H				H	M
2.2	Teaching objectives		H	H		H			H	
2.3	Course content & Course implementation		H	H	H	M	H	H	H	
2.4	Course evaluation		H	H		H	H		M	
2.5	Interdisciplinary integration and innovation of study tour	M	M	H					H	H
2.6	Content and production of research manual		H	H	H	H			H	M
2.7	Case analysis		H	L					H	
2.8	Group presentation			H						
3	Module 3：Implementation of study tour course	M	M		H		M	H	H	L
3.1	Safety management	M		M	H		H	H		
3.2	Legal risk prevention	M		M			M	H		
4	Module 4：Practice of the study tour course	M	H	H	H	H	H	H	H	M
4.1	Practical operation of ecological study tour course design		H	H	H				H	H
4.2	Final test									

（五）Student assessment and evaluation

1.Course assessment design

This course is assessed by both formative assessment and summative assessment, with the usual and final scores accounting for 50% respectively.

The usual score is 100 points, 50% of which is included in the total score：40% of which is the usual classroom contribution score, including answering questions in class, guiding students to think with heuristic questions in class, and forming a thinking report or question after discussion with teachers or groups after class; 50% are group projects, individual assignments, and mid-term tests（online）；10% is attendance.

The final score is 100 points, 50% of which will be included in the total score. The students are required to take the group as a unit, select a teaching link in the Program Design of Study tour Activities designed by the group, submit a video of no less than 10 minutes of study tour course explanation, or conduct a 5 ～ 10-minutes teaching demonstration of study tour courses in the classroom（see relevant documents for specific requirements and scoring standards）.

Table 2-42：Course Examination and Evaluation Design

Evaluation Dimension	Formative Assessment									Summative Assessment
Percentage	25%				20%				10%	50%
Evaluation items	Unit test	Mid-termtest	Home-work	Demons-tration	Pro-ject	Group discussion	Sum-mary	Investi-gation	Atten-dance	Final test
Times	8	1	36	2	2	12	5	1	28	1

2. Level of Academic Quality

The grading of academic quality level and its basis are summarized from the perspective of curriculum.

Table 2-43: Academic Quality Level

Quality Dimension/ Grade	A	B	C
Attendance Percentage	100%	90%+	80%+
Homework Quality	90+	80+	70+
Unit test	90+	80+	70+
Course Contribution	Raise at least 1 question in class, or answer the questions 4 times at lease, either with the teacher or a thinking report was formed after group discussion	Answer questions at least 2 times	Answer questions at lease once

（六）Course Implementation

1.Teaching requirements

The students are required to understand the nature, purpose, and significance of study tour, have a preliminary understanding of study tour for primary and secondary students at home and abroad, develop and design quality study tour courses, creatively develop ecological study tour courses, practice ecological environmental protection, cultivate environmental awareness, and help rural revitalization.

2.Teacher requirements

【Basic requirement】

The teachers of the course should have relevant professional backgrounds in tourism management, literature, communications, etc., have a master's degree or above or an intermediate level or above professional title, and have Educational Excursion Planning and Management（EEPM）vocational skill level certificate（intermediate level or above）. Enterprise teachers should have at least two years of working experience in the study tour industry, rich experience in study tour group or management, or have the experience of running a study tour base or working as a lecturer of the research course.

【Team ability improvement】

With the help of the "Golden Course" and practical teaching base construction platform, we will attract more school, government, and enterprise personnel with different academic backgrounds, age levels, and jobs, integrating resources and establishing a teaching team of study tour practical courses with the main purpose of training talents in the study tour industry and the main means of developing interdisciplinary integrated innovative courses.

（七）Textbook selection

According to the requirements of EEPM vocational skill level standard, this course material should cover the relevant contents of the course design （intermediate requirements）and the teaching practice （primary）of the course. Recommended textbooks : *Practical Operation Manual for Study Tour.*

（八）Reference Books and Network Resources

Reference books : *Development And Implementation of Study Tour Activity Curriculum, Study Tour Course Design.*

Network resources:National Undergraduate Red Tourism Creative Planning Competition, Jinggangshan Youth Education Base, China Study tour Net, Wanli Road Study tour Education Net.

（九）Site And Equipment Requirements

The teaching site should meet the requirements for the number of students, and square or rectangle classroom is preferred. The classroom is spacious and ventilated, the air conditioning is cold enough in summer, and the room is warm in winter. The light is bright and can be adjusted in groups. The ground is dry and clean, and the off-campus practice teaching base is safe. Multimedia teaching equipment and basic teaching materials for off-campus practical teaching （such as microscope, telescope, flashlight, etc.）are complete.

Suggestion :

It is suggested to add some basic courses of pedagogy as pilot courses to supplement students' basic pedagogical knowledge.

（十）Teaching Process and Arrangement

Table 2-44: Course Resource Requirements and Teaching Arrangements

Chapter	Tasks/Contents	Offline Teaching		Course Resource						Online Teaching			
		Theory Hour	Practice Hour	Video	Virtual	Non Video	Exercises	Test	Project Hour	Course Announcement	Interaction	Homework	Test
1	Module 1: The basic concept of study tour												
1.1	Nature, purpose, and significance	4	0	2		5			1	1	50	1	1
1.2	Overview of study tour for primary and secondary school students at home and abroad	4	0	2		5			1	1	50	1	
2	Module 2: Course design of study tour activities												
2.1	Study tour course theme	2	2	2		5			1	1	50	1	
2.2	Teaching objectives	2	2	6		5	1	10	1	1	50	4	1
2.3	Course content & Course implementation	2	2	4		10	1	10	1	1	50	2	1
2.4	Course evaluation	2	2	4		5	1	10	2	1	50	2	1

Continued Table

Chapter	Tasks/Contents	Offline Teaching		Course Resource							Online Teaching			
		Theory Hour	Prac-tice Hour	Video	Virtual	Non Video	Exercises	Test	Project	Hour	Course Announcement	Interaction	Homework	Test
2.5	Interdisciplinary integration and innovation of study tour	2	2	2		5	1	10		1	1	50	1	1
2.6	Content and production of research manual	2	2	6		10	1	10		1	1	50	4	1
2.7	Case analysis	0	4	4		8			8	1	1	50	4	
2.8	Group presentation	0	4	4		10	1	10	10		1	50	4	1
3	Module 3 : Implementation of study tour course													
3.1	Safety management	4	0	2		5				1	1	50	2	1
3.2	Legal risk prevention	4	0	2		5				1	1	50	2	1
4	Module 4 : Practice of the study tour course													
4.1	Practical operation of ecological study tour course design	0	4			2	1	10	10					
4.2	Final test	0	4				1	10						
	Total :	28	28	40	0	80	8	80	28	12	12	600	28	8

Note : The purpose of general construction curriculum resources is to help students understand the key and difficult points.

（十一）Development Team

Table 2-45

No.	Name	Department/Company	Tasks	Signature
1	Zhu Han	Tourism Management	curriculum standards, teaching plans and teaching calendars	
2	Wei Wei	Tourism Management	"1+X" Educational Excursion Planning and Management（EEPM）vocational skill level certificate test	
3	Liang Huakun	Zhuhai Sanban Tourism Co., Ltd	Off-campus practical teaching	
4	Lv Junyi	Macau University of Science and Technology	Assistance	

二、G 学院出境领队实务课程标准

表2-46

学院（部门）	旅游学院
适用专业名称	旅游管理
课标编码	17067320
课程名称	出境领队实务
执笔人	魏微
审核人	周梁

（一）课程性质与任务

本课程是高职旅游管理专业学生必修的专业核心课程，属于 B 类理论与实践课程。

本课程对接旅行社出境旅游领队岗位的要求，通过讲授出境游领队应具备的资格与素质、出入境法律法规、工作流程、服务方法与讲解技巧、事故的处理与预防等内容，旨在培养学生掌握出境游带团基础理论知识与实践操作技巧，培养学生诚实、守信、善于沟通、富有爱心、具有责任感和合作能力的品质素养，提高学生海外带团的专业技能与服务意识，以使其应对日益发展的出境旅游行业对旅游人才的需求。

本课程的先修课程有旅游学概论、导游业务，后续课程有服务心理学、宴会设计与管理。

（二）课程目标与要求

1. 知识目标

（1）了解国家对出境旅游领队的有关政策规定。

（2）了解领队在出境旅游整体环节中的作用。

（3）掌握丰富的史地文化知识、政策法规知识、旅行生活知识、海关常识等。

（4）了解旅游客源地与目的地知识。具备旅游客源地和目的地的基本知识，包括客源地和目的地的居民文化传统、风俗禁忌、经济文化等方面的基本知识。

（5）识别不同类型团队的带团规程。

（6）熟悉领队常用表格。

2. 能力目标

（1）能够按接待计划完成旅游团队的接团、送团、协调、衔接工作。

（2）能掌握领队基础理论与带团技能。

（3）能掌握常见的领队讲解方法。

（4）能具备跨文化交际能力。

（5）能处理好领队与游客关系。

（6）能妥善处理各种突发事故。

3. 素质目标

（1）具有良好的职业操守和职业道德。

（2）具有健康的身体素质和心理素质。

（3）具有良好的礼节与礼仪。

（4）具有较强的团队协作精神。

表2-47　课程目标对专业培养规格分解指标的支撑矩阵

目标分类	目标编码	课程目标	Ea1	Ea2	Ea3	Ea4	Ea5	Ea6	Ea7	Ea8
知识	C1	了解国家对出境旅游领队的有关政策规定	M	H	M	L	H	M	H	M
	C2	了解领队在出境旅游整体环节中的作用	L	H	H	M	L	M	L	L
	C3	掌握丰富的史地文化知识、政策法规知识、旅行生活知识、海关常识等	H	L	M	M	L	H	L	M
	C4	了解旅游客源地与目的地知识	L	M	M	L	H	H	L	L
	C5	识别不同类型团队的带团规程	M	H	M	L	H	M	H	M
能力	C6	能够按接待计划，完成旅游团队的接团、送团、协调、衔接工作	M	L	L	M	L	H	M	L
	C7	能掌握领队基础理论与带团技能	M	M	L	L	H	M	M	L
	C8	能掌握常见的领队讲解方法	L	H	H	M	L	M	L	L
	C9	能具备跨文化交际能力	M	M	H	L	H	M	M	L
	C10	能处理好领队与游客关系	L	L	L	M	L	H	M	L
	C11	能妥善处理各种突发事故	M	M	M	L	M	M	H	M
素质	C12	具有良好的职业操守和职业道德	L	H	H	M	L	M	L	L
	C13	具有健康的身体素质和心理素质	M	H	M	L	M	H	M	L
	C14	具有良好的礼节与礼仪	M	L	M	L	M	M	L	L
	C15	具有较强的团队协作精神	L	L	M	M	L	L	L	H

（三）课程结构与内容

1.课程结构

本课程共4学分，64学时，其中理论32学时，实践32学时，线上教学16学时，其余为线下教学。

为了达到教学目标，本课程设置了四个模块。

（1）领队职业素养：让学生了解获取领队资格的基本条件，掌握国家关于领队的法律法规，领队在上岗前需储备的知识与技能，领队的注意事项与行为禁忌。

（2）领队工作流程：旨在通过讲授行前说明会的流程和内容，模拟召开行前说明会，使学生掌握出入境的服务流程，手续办理流程，掌握境外带团工作的流程几个环节，直至掌握整个业务流程。

（3）领队服务技能：学习填报各种出入境相关表格，具备带团讲解能力，处理出入境突发状况。

（4）领队特殊问题处理：掌握机场及出入境手续各类问题，用餐及住宿中出现的问题，境外观光中游客的各类问题，票证丢失问题的处理方法。

表2-48　课程结构与学时建议

模块	主题／课程	授课学期数	学分	建议学时
一	领队职业素养	1	0.5	8
二	领队工作流程	1	1.5	32
三	领队服务技能	1	1	12
四	领队特殊问题处理	1	1	12

2. 课程内容

（1）领队职业素养。

【内容要求】

①领队素养与知识储备。

②领队服务准则。

③领队具备的专业条件。

④领队行为禁忌。

【目标要求】

让学生了解获取领队资格的基本条件，掌握国家关于领队的法律法规，领队在上岗前需储备的知识与技能，领队的注意事项与行为禁忌。

【教学要求】

①学生通过分组合作、课堂讨论等方法开展探究式学习，在完成工作任务的过程中实现"做中学"。

②教学借助在线学习平台、微课、云盘、录制视频、在线视频、在线调查等多种现代信息技术，整合教学资源，优化教学过程。

教学方法	☑讲授　☑讨论或座谈　□问题导向学习　☑分组合作学习　☑案例教学 □任务驱动　□项目教学　□情景教学　□演示汇报　□实践教学　□参观访问 □引导文教学　□其他

【场地要求】

多媒体教室。

（2）领队工作流程。

【内容要求】

①接受带团任务。

②召开行前说明会。

③出入境业务。

④境外带团服务工作。

⑤送团及后续工作。

【目标要求】

①掌握行前说明会的流程和内容。

②模拟召开行前说明会。

③掌握出入境的服务流程，手续办理流程。

④掌握境外的带团工作流程。

【教学要求】

①学生通过分组合作、课堂讨论等方法开展探究式学习，在完成工作任务的过程中实现"做中学"。

②教学借助在线学习平台、微课、云盘、录制视频、在线视频、在线调查等多种现代信息技术，整合教学资源，优化教学过程。

教学方法	☑讲授 ☑讨论或座谈 □问题导向学习 ☑分组合作学习 ☑案例教学
	□任务驱动 □项目教学 □情景教学 □演示汇报 □实践教学 □参观访问
	□引导文教学 □其他

【场地要求】

多媒体教室。

（3）领队服务技能。

【内容要求】

①填报各种出入境相关表格。

②具备带团讲解能力。

③解决出入境突发状况。

【目标要求】

①掌握不同国家出入境相关表格填报方法。

②掌握境外不同景点的讲解技巧。

③掌握出入境突发状况的解决方法。

【教学要求】

①学生通过分组合作、课堂讨论等方法开展探究式学习，在完成工作任务的过程中实现"做中学"。

②教学借助在线学习平台、微课、云盘、录制视频、在线视频、在线调查等多种现代信息技术，整合教学资源，优化教学过程。

教学方法	☑讲授 ☑讨论或座谈 □问题导向学习 ☑分组合作学习 ☑案例教学 □任务驱动 □项目教学 □情景教学 □演示汇报 □实践教学 □参观访问 □引导文教学 □其他

【场地要求】

多媒体教室。

（4）领队特殊问题处理。

【内容要求】

①机场手续问题。

②出入境手续问题。

③用餐及住宿问题。

④观光活动中的问题。

⑤票证丢失问题。

【目标要求】

①解决机场及出入境手续各类问题。

②解决用餐及住宿中出现的问题。

③解决境外观光中游客的各类问题。

④掌握票证丢失问题的处理方法。

【教学要求】

①学生通过分组合作、课堂讨论等方法开展探究式学习，在完成工作任务的过程中实现"做中学"。

②教学借助在线学习平台、微课、云盘、录制视频、在线视频、在线调查等多种现代信息技术，整合教学资源，优化教学过程。

教学方法	☑讲授　☑讨论或座谈　□问题导向学习　☑分组合作学习　☑案例教学 □任务驱动　□项目教学　□情景教学　□演示汇报　□实践教学　□参观访问 □引导文教学　□其他

【场地要求】

多媒体教室。

（四）课程内容与课程目标支撑矩阵

表2-49　课程内容与课程目标支撑矩阵

序号	任务单元／知识点章节目录	C1	C2	C3	C4	C5	C6	C7	C8	C9
1	领队职业素养		M		H				L	L
1.1	领队素养与知识储备									
1.2	领队服务准则		M		H				L	
1.3	领队具备的专业条件									
1.4	领队行为禁忌									
2	领队服务流程	L						H	M	
2.1	接受带团任务									
2.2	召开行前说明会									
2.3	出入境业务			M		H				L
2.4	境外带团服务工作									
2.5	送团及后续工作									
3	领队服务技能			L					H	M
3.1	填报各种出入境相关表格									
3.2	带团讲解能力									
3.3	解决出入境突发状况			L					H	M
4	领队特殊问题处理									
4.1	机场手续问题									
4.2	出入境手续问题			L					H	M
4.3	用餐及住宿问题									
4.4	观光活动中的问题									
4.5	票证丢失问题			L					H	M

（五）学生考核与评价

1.课程考核设计

本课程采用全过程、多维度的过程性考核与终结性考核相结合的方式。过程性考核包括出勤、作业、小组活动、演示汇报等，终结性考核主要采用期末考试笔试的形式。课程建立多元评价方式，全面考核学生的综合素质和能力。对于教师来说，项目教学更加注重活动的过程，要把过程评价与终结评价相结合，注重过程评价，学生自评、互评与教师评价相结合，课内与课外评价相结合。

平时过程性考核分值占比 50%，期末终结性考核分值占比 50%。

表2-50　课程考核与评价设计

评价维度	过程性考核							终结性考核
分值占比	10%		30%			10%		50%
评价分项	单元测验	作业	项目实战	演示汇报	小组讨论	学习总结	专题调研	期末考试
次数	5	10	3	5	5	5	5	1

2.学业质量水平

从课程的角度概述学业质量水平的分级及其依据。

表2-51　学业质量水平说明

质量维度 （质量等级）	A（优）	B（良）	C（中）
出勤率	100%	90% 以上	80% 以上
作业质量	均分 90 分以上	均分 80 分以上	均分 70 分以上
单元及期中测试	均分 90 分以上	均分 80 分以上	均分 70 分以上
课程贡献	提出启发式问题 1 个及以上，或回答问题 4 次以上，或与教师讨论、小组讨论后形成思考报告 1 篇	课堂回答问题 2 次以上	课堂回答问题 1 次以上

（六）课程实施与保障

1.教学要求

（1）落实立德树人，培养学生专业服务技能。在课程内容设计上采用成果导向、项目开发理论，多应用角色扮演、疑难解答以及案例分析

的教学方式，根据专业对应工作岗位及岗位群实施典型工作任务分析；学生未来就业不需要的知识内容予以剔除，充分体现工学结合、深度融合的特点，达到立德树人，培养学生综合服务技能的要求。

（2）落实立德树人，培养学生职业的情感认同。通过课堂角色扮演，针对学生已经掌握的相关专业知识，在教师讲解后，学生分别扮演不同的角色，设身处地分析与解决所面临的问题，从所扮演的角色出发，运用所学的知识，自主分析与决策，提高学生实际决策的技能。身临其境的模拟活动能增强学生对职业的情感认同。

（3）落实立德树人，培养学生的创新精神与合作精神。在教学中教师设计体验情境，注重学生的体验学习，通过"项目为中心，任务为驱动"的教学模式来增强学生的综合职业能力，在教学组织上采用以工作任务或实际工作岗位项目为驱动的教学模式，以岗位项目任务的形式组织教学。课前根据不同的任务下发任务书和相关学习参考资料，让学生了解课程的基础知识。进入情境教学环节后，学生通过亲身实践活动进行学习，完成任务。每一个教学和实训的环节都强调注重学生的体验——设计相应的体验情境，让学生在体验中学习、感悟、升华，使学生牢牢掌握专业知识，提高专业技能和素养。理论知识由学生自主获得，教师根据情况进行补充。教师通过启发、提问等形式，引导学生自主学习、分析、思考。教师要针对不同工作难题，提出不同角度的解决方案，提升学生的创新能力。这样以小组合作学习的形式来完成工作任务，可以培养学生的合作精神、交流能力，提升学生的综合职业素养。

2.师资要求

【基本要求】

（1）旅游相关专业，硕士以上学历，了解旅游基础知识，熟悉世界及我国旅游业发展态势，熟悉客源国情况。

（2）拥有导游证等职业技能证书，双师型教师，具有较高的旅游职业素养，热爱旅游，热爱本职工作。

【团队能力提升】

目前旅游管理专业教师团队共16人，其中教授1人，副教授5人，全部持有职业技能证书，其中持有导游证教师6人，兼职教师8人，一线工作5年以上8人。"双师型"教师占比100%,行业企业专家占比50%。

担任本门课程的主讲教师均为中青年教师，拥有硕士学位、中级以上职称，有企业5年以上工作经历，对旅游行业有较深入的认识和理解。团队教师还需要多参加职业教育培训，多运用新方法、新思维，在教学中融入新业态、新标准，到企业中多进行岗位实践，不断提升职业实践技能与素养。

（七）教材要求与选择

教材选择：《出境旅游领队实务》。

（八）参考书籍与网络资源

参考书籍：《领队实务》《出境旅游领队工作案例解析》《出境旅游领队实务》。

网络资源：中国旅游局网站，广东省旅游局官网，珠海市文化广电旅游体育局。

（九）场地与设备要求

（1）场地面积：满足课程人数要求。

（2）场地规格：以正方形或宽敞形为佳，避免狭长形或不规则形状。

（3）场地通风：教室宽敞通风，夏季空调凉爽，冬季室内温暖。

（4）场地灯光：灯光明亮并可分组调节，投影布上方不能有灯光。

（5）分组布置：分成N组，每组安排6～8人为佳。

（6）场地布置：桌面、地面干洁卫生，校外实践教学基地有安全保障。

（7）场地设备：多媒体教学设备、校外实践教学基本教学材料（如显微镜、望远镜、手电筒等）。

（8）其他建议：课程需一定的经费支撑，用于学生外出调研、参观或者考察等。

（十）授课进程与安排

表2-52 课程资源需要和授课课安排

序号	任务单元/知识点章节目录	线下教学		课程资源建设						线上教学				
		理论学时	实践学时	视频（个）	虚拟仿真类（个）	非视频（个）	习题（道）	试题（题）	项目/案例（个）	线上学时	课程公告	交流互动	作业次数	单元测验
1	领队职业素养		1							2				
1.1	领队素养与知识储备										1			2
1.2	领队服务准则													
1.3	领队具备的专业条件													
1.4	领队行为禁忌	2	2											
2	领队服务流程													
2.1	接受带团任务			*	*	*	*	*	*					
2.2	召开行前说明会			*	*	*	*	*	*					
2.3	出入境业务													
2.4	境外带团服务工作			*	*	*	*	*	*					
2.5	送团及后续工作													
3	领队服务技能													
3.1	填报各种出入境相关表格			*	*	*	*	*	*					

续　表

序号	任务单元/知识点章节目录	线下教学		课程资源建设						线上教学				
		理论学时	实践学时	视频（个）	虚拟仿真类（个）	非视频（个）	习题（道）	试题（题）	项目/案例（个）	线上学时	课程公告	交流互动	作业次数	单元测验
3.2	带团讲解能力													
3.3	解决突发入境突发状况													
4	领队特殊问题处理			*	*	*	*	*	*					
4.1	机场出入境问题			*	*	*	*	*	*					
4.2	出入境手续问题													
4.3	用餐及住宿问题													
4.4	观光活动中的问题			*	*	*	*	*	*					
4.5	票证丢失问题													
…														

注：一般建设课程资源目的在于辅助学生理解重难点。

（十一）开发团队

表2-53

序号	姓名	部门/企业名称	承担的工作任务	签名
1	魏微	旅游管理专业	"金课"建设，制定课程标准、教案、教学日历	
2	李任欣	旅游管理专业	负责授课、案例汇总及更新，参与制定课程标准、教案、教学日历	
3	李顺光	广东省拱北口岸中国旅行社	校外实践教学	

二、G Polytechnic Practice of Outbound Tour Leaders

Table 2-46

Faculty	Tourism College
Major	Tourism Management
Course Code	17067320
Course	Practice of Outbound Tour Leaders
Written by	Wei Wei
Reviewed by	Zhou Liang

（一）Course Nature and Tasks

This course is a compulsory professional expansion course for the sophomores of tourism management. It belongs to the course of theory and practice.

This course is designed to meet the professional requirements of outbound tour leaders in travel agencies. By teaching the qualifications and qualities of outbound tour leaders, entry-exit laws and regulations, work processes, service methods and interpretation skills, accident handling and prevention and other contents, it aims to cultivate students to master the basic theoretical knowledge and practical operation of outbound tour leaders, and strengthen the cultivation of students' honesty, trustworthiness, good communication, love. The sense of responsibility and the quality of cooperation should improve the students' professional skills and service awareness to meet the needs of the growing outbound tourism industry for tourism talents.

The prerequisite courses of this course include Introduction to Tourism, Tour Guide Business, etc. The follow-up courses are Service Psychology, Banquet Design and Management.

(二) Course Objectives and Requirements

1. Knowledge objectives

(1) Understand relevant national policies and regulations on outbound tour leaders.

(2) Understand the role of tour leaders in the overall process of outbound tourism.

(3) Master rich knowledge of history and geography, policies and regulations, travel and life, customs, etc.

(4) Understand the knowledge of tourist source and destination. Have the basic knowledge of tourist source and destination, including the basic knowledge of residents' cultural traditions, customs and taboos, economic and cultural aspects of tourist source and destination.

(5) Identify the team leadership procedures for different types of teams.

(6) Be familiar with the common forms of the team leader.

2. Capability objectives

(1) Be able to complete the reception, sending off, coordination and connection of the tourist team according to the reception plan.

(2) Be able to master the basic theory of team leader and team leadership skills.

(3) Be able to master common methods of team leader explanation.

(4) Be able to master cross-cultural communication ability.

(5) Be able to handle the relationship between tour leaders and tourists.

(6) Be able to properly handle various emergencies.

3. Quality objectives

(1) Have good professional ethics and professional ethics.

(2) Have healthy physical and psychological quality.

(3) Have good etiquette.

（4）Have a strong team spirit.

Table 2-47： Matrix of Course Objectives for Major Training Specification
Decomposition Index

Dimension	Code	Course Objectives	Ea1	Ea2	Ea3	Ea4	Ea5	Ea6	Ea7	Ea8
Knowledge	C1	Understand relevant national policies and regulations on outbound tour leaders	M	H	H	M	L	H	L	L
	C2	Understand the role of tour leaders in the overall process of outbound tourism	H	H	M	H	L	M	M	M
	C3	Master rich knowledge of history and geography, policies and regulations, travel and life, customs, etc	H	M	L	M	L	H	M	M
	C4	Identify the team leadership procedures for different types of teams	H	M	L	M	L	H	M	M
	C5	Be familiar with the common forms of the team leader	H	M	L	M	L	H	M	M
Skills and abilities	C6	Be able to complete the reception, sending off, coordination and connection of the tourist team according to the reception plan	M	H	H	L	H	H	H	H
	C7	Be able to master the basic theory of team leader and team leadership skills	M	H	M	H	H	H	H	H
	C8	Be able to master common methods of team leader explanation	M	H	M	H	H	H	H	M
	C9	Be able to master cross-cultural communication ability	H	M	L	M	L	M	L	H
	C10	Be able to handle the relationship between tour leaders and tourists	H	H	M	H	H	H	H	L
	C11	Be able to properly handle various emergencies	M	H	L	H	M	H	H	L
Value	C12	Have good professional ethics and professional ethics	H	H	H	L	L	M	L	L
	C13	Have healthy physical and psychological quality	M	H	H	L	H	H	H	H
	C14	Have good etiquette	M	H	H	L	H	H	H	H
	C15	Have a strong team spirit	H	M	L	M	L	M	L	H

（三）Course Structure and Content

1. Course Structure

This course has 4 credits with 64 class hours, including 32 theoretical hours, 32 practical hours, and 16 online teaching hours.

In order to meet the requirements of teaching objectives, this course has four modules.

（1）Professional quality of team leaders : let students understand the basic conditions for obtaining the qualification of team leaders, master the national laws and regulations on team leaders, the knowledge and skills to be stored before taking up their posts, the precautions and behavior taboos of team leaders.

（2）Team Leader's workflow : it aims to simulate the briefing through the process and content, master the entry-exit service process and handle the formalities. Grasp several links of overseas group leading workflow and the whole business process.

（3）Team Leader service skills : learn to fill in various forms related to entry and exit. Grasp the ability to explain with the group. Solve exit entry emergencies.

（4）Handling of special problems of the team leader : master the handling methods of airport and entry and exit procedures, problems in meals and accommodation, problems of tourists in overseas sightseeing, and ticket loss.

Table 2-48：Course Structure and Class Hours

Module	Topic	Credit	Class Hours
1	Professional quality of team leaders	0.5	8
2	Team leader's workflow	1.5	32
3	Team leader service skills	1	12
4	Handling of special problems of the team leader	1	12

2. Course Content

（1）Professional quality of team leaders.

【Content】

① Team leader quality and knowledge reserve;

② Leader service criteria;

③ Professional qualifications of the leader;

④ Team leader behavior taboo.

【Objectives】

Let the students understand the basic conditions for obtaining the leader qualification, master the national laws and regulations on the leader, the knowledge and skills to be stored before taking up their posts, the precautions and behavior taboos of the leader.

【Teaching Requirements】

① Students carry out inquiry learning through group cooperation, classroom discussion and other methods to achieve "learning by doing" in the process of completing work tasks.

② Teaching integrates teaching resources and optimizes the teaching process by virtue of various modern information technologies such as online learning platform, micro class, cloud disk, video recording, video online, online survey, etc.

【Site Requirements】

Multi-Media Classroom.

（2）Team Leader's workflow

【Content】

Accept the mission. Hold a pre-trip briefing. Exit entry business. Overseas group service. Sending the delegation and follow-up work.

【Objectives】

① Master the process and content of the pre-trip briefing.

② Simulate the pre-trip briefing.

③ Master the entry-exit service process and go through the formalities.

④ Grasp the overseas group leading workflow.

【Teaching Requirements】

① Students carry out inquiry learning through group cooperation, classroom discussion and other methods to achieve "learning by doing" in the process of completing work tasks.

② Teaching integrates teaching resources and optimizes the teaching process by virtue of various modern information technologies such as online learning platform, micro class, cloud disk, video recording, video online, online survey, etc.

【Site Requirements】

Multi-Media Classroom.

（3）Team Leader service skills.

【Content】

Fill in and submit forms related to entry and exit. Ability to interpret with the group. Solve entry-exit emergencies.

【Objectives】

① Master the entry and exit related forms of different countries.

② Master the interpretation skills of different overseas scenic spots.

③ Master the solutions to exit entry emergencies.

【Teaching Requirement】

① Students carry out inquiry learning through group cooperation, classroom discussion and other methods to achieve "learning by doing" in the process of completing work tasks.

② Teaching integrates teaching resources and optimizes the teaching process by virtue of various modern information technologies such as online learning platform, micro class, cloud disk, video recording, video online, online survey, etc.

【Site Requirements】

Multi-Media Classroom.

（4）Handling of special problems of the team leader.

【Content】

Airport formalities. Exit and entry formalities. Meals and accommodation. Problems in sightseeing activities. Ticket loss.

【Objectives】

① Master all kinds of airport and entry and exit formalities.

② Grasp the problems in dining and accommodation.

③ Master various problems of tourists in overseas sightseeing.

④ Master the handling method of ticket loss.

【Teaching Requirements 】

① Students carry out inquiry learning through group cooperation, classroom discussion and other methods to achieve "learning by doing" in the process of completing work tasks.

② Teaching integrates teaching resources and optimizes the teaching process by virtue of various modern information technologies such as online learning platform, micro class, cloud disk, video recording, video online, online survey, etc.

【Site requirements 】

Multi-Media Classroom.

（四）Course Chapter and Course Objective Support

Table 2-49：Course Content and Course Objective Matrix

Chapter	Tasks/Contents	C1	C2	C3	C4	C5	C6	C7	C8	C9
1	Module 1：Professional quality of team leaders	H		M					M	
1.1	Quality and knowledge reserve of team leader	H	M		L				M	
1.2	Team Leader service guidelines	H		M					M	
1.3	Professional qualifications of the team leader	M	H	H	H	H	H	H	H	M
1.4	Team leader behavior taboo	M	H	H	H	H	H	H	H	M
2	Module 2：Team leader's workflow	M	H	H	L	H			H	
2.1	Leader service process	H	H	H	H				H	M
2.2	Accept tour group task		H	H		H			H	
2.3	Hold a pre-trip briefing		H	H	H	M	H	H	H	
2.4	Overseas tour group service		H	H		H	H		M	
2.5	Sending the tour group and follow-up work	M	M	H					H	H
3	Module 3：Team leader service skills		H	H	H	H			H	M

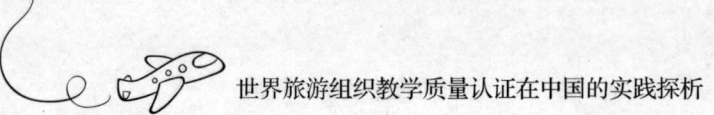

Continued Table

Chapter	Tasks/Contents	C1	C2	C3	C4	C5	C6	C7	C8	C9
3.1	Fill in various forms related to entry and exit		H	L					H	
3.2	Ability to interpret for tour groups			H						
3.3	Solve entry-exit emergencies	M	M		H		M	H	H	L
4	Module 4 : Handling of special problems of the team leader	M		M	H		H	H		
4.1	Airport formalities	M		M			M	H		
4.2	Entry and exit formalities	M	H	H	H	H	H	H	H	M
4.3	Meals and accommodation		H	H	H				H	H
4.4	Problems in sightseeing activities	M	H	H	H	H	H	H	H	M
4.5	Ticket loss	M	H	H	H	H	H	H	H	M

（五）Student Assessment and Evaluation

1. Course Assessment Design

This course is assessed by both formative assessment and summative assessment, with the usual and final scores accounting for 50% respectively.

The assessment of this course is a combination of the whole process, multi-dimensional process assessment and final assessment. The process assessment includes attendance, homework, group activities, presentation report, etc. The final assessment is in the form of final written examination. The course establishes multiple evaluation methods to comprehensively assess the comprehensive quality and ability of students. For teachers, project teaching pays more attention to the process of activities, combining process evaluation with final evaluation, focusing on process evaluation, combining student self-evaluation, mutual evaluation with teacher evaluation, and combining in class and extracurricular evaluation.

Table 2-50: Course Examination and Evaluation Design

Evaluation dimension	Formative Assessment								Summative Assessment
Percentage	10%				30%			10%	50%
Evaluation items	Unit test	Midterm test	Home-work	Demons-tration	Project	Group discussion	Sum-mary	Investi-gation	Atten-dance	Final test
Times	5	10	3	5	5	5	5	1	28	1

2. Academic Quality Level

Table 2-51: Academic Quality Level

Quality Dimension/ Grade	A	B	C
Attendance Percentage	100%	90%+	80%+
Homework Quality	90+	80+	70+
Unit test	90+	80+	70+
Course Contribution	Raise at least 1 question in class and inspire students to think	Answer questions at least 2 times	Answer questions at lease once

(六) Course Implementation

1. Teaching Requirements

(1) Implement Morality and Cultivate Students' Professional Service Skills.The course content design, the results oriented and project development theories are adopted, and the teaching methods of role playing, troubleshooting and case analysis are used more. The typical task analysis is carried out according to the corresponding posts and post groups of the specialty. The knowledge content that students do not need for future employment shall be resolutely eliminated, so as to fully reflect the characteristics of combination of work and learning and deep integration. Meet the requirements of establishing morality and cultivating students' comprehensive service skills.

(2) Cultivate Students' Professional Emotional Identity.Through

classroom role play, students have mastered relevant professional knowledge. After the teacher explains, students play different roles to analyze and solve the problems they face. Starting from the role they play, they use the knowledge they have learned to analyze and make decisions independently to improve students' practical decision-making skills. The immersive simulation activities can enhance students' professional emotional identity.

（3）Implement Moral Education and Cultivate Students' Spirit of Innovation and Cooperation. In teaching, teachers design experiential situations, pay attention to students' experiential learning, and strengthen students' comprehensive professional abilities with the teaching mode of "project centered and task driven". In teaching organization, teachers adopt the teaching mode of "work task or actual work post project driven", and organize teaching in the form of post project tasks. Before class, assignment books and relevant learning reference materials are distributed according to different tasks, so that students can understand the basic knowledge of the course. After entering the situational teaching link, the students learn and complete the task through their own practical activities. Each link of teaching and training emphasizes on students' experience-designing corresponding experience situations, so that students can learn, feel and sublimate through experience, firmly grasp professional knowledge, and improve professional skills and accomplishments. Theoretical knowledge is acquired by students on their own initiative and supplemented by teachers according to the situation. Teachers guide students to learn, analyze and think independently through inspiration, questioning and other forms. For different work problems, propose solutions from different perspectives to improve students' innovation ability. This kind of work task is completed in the form of group cooperative learning, which cultivates students' cooperation spirit and communication ability, and improves their comprehensive professional quality.

2. Teacher requirements

【Basic Requirement】

（1）Major in tourism, master degree or above, understand the basic

knowledge of tourism, be familiar with the development trend of world tourism and China, and be familiar with the situation of tourist source countries.

【Team Ability Improvement】

（2）At present, there are 16 teachers in tourism management, including 1 professor and 5 associate professors, all of whom hold professional skill certificates, including 6 teachers with tour guide certificates and 8 part-time teachers; 8 people have more than 5 years of working experience in the front line. "Double qualified" teachers accounted for 100%. Industry enterprise experts account for up to 50%.

The main teachers of this course are young and middle-aged teachers, with master's degree and intermediate professional title or above. They have more than 5 years of experience in enterprises, and have a deeper understanding and understanding of the tourism industry. Team teachers also need to participate in vocational education training, use new methods and new ideas, and integrate new formats and new standards into teaching. The enterprises under the Company shall carry out more post practice and constantly improve their professional practical skills and accomplishments.

（七）Textbook Selection

Zhai Li, Practice of Outbound Tour Leaders,2021,Huazhong University of Science and Technology Press, ISBN : 9787519122713.

（八）Reference Books and Network Resources

（1）Xie Yanjun, Practice of Outbound Tour Leaders, 2017, Tourism Education Press, ISBN : 9787563722440.

（2）Huang Huiyue，Team Leader Work Cases, 2018, Tourism Education Press, ISBN : 9787563715657.

（3）Zeng Zhaoxi，Practice of Outbound Tour Leaders，2019，Press of Renmin University of China，ISBN : 9787300271798.

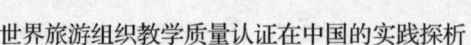
（4）Website of China Tourism Administration, http：// www.cnta.gov.cn.

（5）Website of Guangdong Provincial Tourism, http：//whly.gd.gov.cn/.

（6）Zhuhai Municipal Bureau of Culture, Television, Tourism and Sports, http：//wgltj.zhuhai.gov.cn/.

（九）Site And Equipment Requirements

The teaching site should meet the requirements for the number of students, and square or rectangle classroom is preferred. The classroom is spacious and ventilated, the air conditioning is cold enough in summer, and the room is warm in winter. The light is bright and can be adjusted in groups. The ground is dry and clean, and the off-campus practice teaching base is safe. Multimedia teaching equipment and basic teaching materials for off-campus practical teaching（such as microscope, telescope, flashlight, etc.）are complete.

Suggestion: it is suggested to add some basic courses of pedagogy as pilot courses to supplement students' basic pedagogical knowledge.

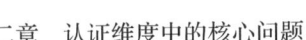

（十）Teaching Process and Arrangement

Table 2-52: Course Resource Requirements and Teaching Arrangements

Chapter	Tasks/Contents	Offline Teaching		Course Resource						Online Teaching			
		Theory Hour	Practice Hour	Video	Virtual	Non Video	Exercises	Test	Project hour	Course Announcement	Interaction	Homework	Test
1	Module 1: Professional quality of team leaders												
1.1	Quality and knowledge reserve of team leader	4	0	2		5			1	1	50	1	1
1.2	Team leader service guidelines	4	0	2		5			1	1	50	1	
1.3	Professional qualifications of the team leader												
1.4	Team leader behavior taboo	2	2	2		5			1	1	50	1	1
2	Module 2: Team leader's workflow	2	2	6		5	1	10	1	1	50	4	1
2.1	Leader service process	2	2	4		10	1	10	1	1	50	2	1

Continued Table

Chapter	Tasks/Contents	Offline Teaching		Course Resource							Online Teaching			
		Theory Hour	Practice Hour	Video	Virtual Video	Non Video	Exercises	Test	Project	hour	Course Announcement	Interaction	Home-work	Test
2.2	Accept tour group task	2	2	4		5	1	10		2	1	50	2	1
2.3	Hold a pre-trip briefing	2	2	2		5	1	10		1	1	50	1	1
2.4	Overseas tour group service	2	2	6		10	1	10		1	1	50	4	1
2.5	Sending the tour group and follow-up work	0	4	4		8			8	1	1	50	4	
3	Module 3：Team leader service skills	0	4	4		10	1	10	10	1	1	50	4	1
3.1	Fill in various forms related to entry and exit													
3.2	Ability to interpret for tour groups	4	0	2		5				1	1	50	2	1
3.3	Solve entry-exit emergencies	4	0	2		5				1	1	50	2	1

Continued Table

Chapter	Tasks/Contents	Offline Teaching		Course Resource							Online Teaching			
		Theory Hour	Practice Hour	Video	Virtual	Non Video	Exercises	Test	Project	hour	Course Announcement	Interaction	Home-work	Test
4	Module 4: Handling of special problems of the team leader													
4.1	Airport formalities	0	4			2	1		10					
4.2	Entry and exit formalities	0	4				1	10						
4.3	Meals and accommodation	1												
4.4	Problems in sightseeing activities	1												
4.5	Ticket loss	1												
	Total	32	32	20	0	80	8	80	28	12	12	600	28	8

Note: the purpose of general construction curriculum resources is to help students understand the key and difficult points.

（十一）Development Team

Table 2-53

No.	Name	Department/Company	Tasks	Signature
1	Wei Wei	Tourism Management	curriculum standards, teaching plans and teaching calendars	
2	Li Renxin	Tourism Management	Teaching cases updating; Participate in the formulation of curriculum standards, teaching plans and teaching calendars	
3	Li Shunguang	Guangdong Gongbei Port China Travel Agency	Off-campus practical teaching	

三、G 学院"中国旅游地理"课程标准

表2-54

学院（部门）	旅游学院
适用专业名称	旅游管理
课标编码	03AA082
课程名称	研学旅行实务
执笔人	
审核人	

（一）课程性质

"中国旅游地理"是旅游管理专业的一门专业拓展能力选修课程，是服务于旅行社导游、计调、外联等工作过程的综合基础课，对旅游资源、旅游景点的认知是导游、计调、外联等工作过程必备的知识准备。本课程开设在第三学期，它的前修课程是"旅游概论""导游业务"，它的后续课程是"计调业务""旅行社经营管理"等。

（二）基本理念

本课程教学遵循导游、计调、外联的职业性原则，从职业工作岗位

需求出发，以"典型工作任务"为载体，按照工作任务由简单到复杂，由单一到综合的原则选取，教学做相结合，利用现有师资、校内实训环境等条件组织教学。教师按照职业教育的特点和本课程的目标与要求，设计学习情境和工作任务，学生分组完成特定任务。以此培养学生的旅游资源认知能力、旅游客源地理分析能力、区域旅游产品（线路）开发能力。使学生在掌握专业知识的同时，提升方法能力和社会能力。

（三）设计思路

按照"以职业能力目标为导向，构建基于工作体系的高职课程体系"的总体设计要求，以工作任务模块为中心构建的工作项目课程体系，彻底打破学科课程的设计思路，紧紧围绕工作任务完成的需要来选择和组织课程内容，突出工作任务与知识的联系，让学生在职业实践活动的基础上掌握知识，增强课程内容与职业岗位能力要求的相关性，提高学生的就业能力。依据工作任务完成的需要、高等职业院校学生的学习特点和职业能力形成的规律确定课程的知识、技能等内容。依据各学习项目的内容总量以及在该门课程中的地位分配各学习项目的课时数。

1.确定开发主体

校企合作，成立中国旅游地理课程开发小组，可以由学校专人教师、旅行社线路设计与开发人员以及景区工作人员组成。

2.设计与开发流程

以学生是学习主体为中心，突出职业能力培养，行业企业合作开发，学生积极参与，依据以工作过程为导向的职业教育理论，根据技术领域和职业岗位的任职要求，参照导游、计调、外联工作标准，确定开发的流程。

"中国旅游地理"课程的设计基本思路是与旅游行业企业骨干一线员工共同分析导游、计调、外联职业岗位职责和职业能力，共同设计旅游管理专业（旅行社方向）课程体系。对真实的导游、计调、外联职业岗位的典型工作任务进行反复深入的分析，根据职业工作特点，设计学习情境，实施"课堂＋景区"教学模式，以真实项目和仿真项目为导向选取和整合、序化教学内容。根据导游、计调、外联职业工作分工的不同，设计项目课程结构，构建成各自相对完整、相对独立，类别性强，课时适量，易于在建构中学习，适于形象思维型智能特点，与相应职业资格标准吻合，整体由简单到复杂的中国旅游资源的认知、中国旅游客源地理认知、中国旅游产品的认知、中国旅游区划及主要旅游资源线路等学习情境。

本课程设置了32课时，2学分，考核方式主要是以考查为主，尽量采用灵活的考核方式来激发学生的潜能与学习的兴趣。

（四）课程目标

1. 总体目标

通过任务引领的项目活动，使学生掌握旅游地理的地域分异规律，能够进行旅游资源调查与分析，学会进行旅游线路设计、旅游目的地形象设计，同时培养学生多学科、多角度分析问题的思维能力，使其具有生态保护意识与创新设计意识，在提升专业技能的同时，提高团队协作技能、旅游市场开拓能力以及职业道德。

2. 具体目标

（1）知识目标。

①能识别各类旅游资源的旅游价值、空间分布规律。

②能描述我国重要旅游景点的空间分布。

③能区分中国不同地域的景观特色，能正确解释其地理成因及旅游人地关系等。

（2）能力目标。

①具备对中国各区域旅游资源调查与分析的能力。

②能设计各类专题旅游线路设计。

③学会区域旅游设计（旅游目的地系统设计、资源整合旅游产品组合、旅游形象设计）。

④会搜集、整理、提炼电子资料（互联网、视频）及纸质（书本、报刊）介质上的旅游地理知识。

（3）素质目标。

①具有严谨的学习态度和工作作风。

②具有团队协作的精神。

③具有一定的旅游审美能力。

④具有较高的职业道德和职业素养。

（五）内容标准（课程内容与要求）

表2-55

学习项目	学习模块／学习任务名称	知识内容和要求	技能内容和要求	教学方法	参考学时	
					理论	实践
项目一	走进"中国旅游地理"课程	列举与阐述基本的旅游地理学的理论	运用旅游地理的地域分异和人地关系分析问题	多媒体	2	
项目二	旅游资源的认知及调查评价	各类旅游资源的特征、分类；评价旅游资源的方法	能区分各类旅游资源；能对旅游资源进行评价、分级	案例教学	2	2
项目三	中国旅游产品	旅游产品的特点、种类、趋势	能准确列举、各个类别的产品	多媒体	4	
项目四	任务一：东北关东文化旅游区	区域内的主要资源与特色	设计一条区域内的旅游线路并简介	案例情境	2	
	任务二：华北黄土文化名山沃野海景风光旅游区	区域内的主要资源与特色	设计一条区域内的旅游线路并简介	案例情境	4	
	任务三：华东吴越淮河文化山水园林都市旅游区	区域内的主要资源与特色	设计一条区域内的旅游线路并简介	案例情境	4	
	任务四：华中荆楚巴蜀文化名山胜水旅游区	区域内的主要资源与特色	设计一条区域内的旅游线路并简介	案例情境	2	
	任务五：东南沿海民乐文化海岛风光旅游区	区域内的主要资源与特色	设计一条区域内的旅游线路并简介	案例情境	4	2
	任务六：西南民族风情岩溶山水风光旅游区	区域内的主要资源与特色	设计一条区域内的旅游线路并简介	案例情境	4	
	任务七：青藏藏传佛教文化高原雪域草原风光旅游区	区域内的主要资源与特色	设计一条区域内的旅游线路并简介	案例情境	2	
	任务八：西北思路文化绿洲草原大漠风光旅游区	区域内的主要资源与特色	设计一条区域内的旅游线路并简介	案例情境	2	

（六）实施建议

1.教学组织形式与实施建议

本课程在多媒体教室进行，根据教学内容的需要，为更好调动学生积极性，按照旅游地理区划将学生分成8组，每组同学负责一个区域，完成相应的任务：简介区域的主要资源种类及特点；推荐一条区域内的经典线路；设计一条线路并进行设计说明。

实施效果较为理想，学生易于接受并且具有一定的积极性。

2. 教材选用与编写建议

本课程选用的教材是机械工业出版社出版、杨载田老师主编的《中国旅游地理》，本教材最大的特点在于将每个旅游区划的特点都非常鲜明地呈现了出来并做了精准的概况，有助于学生理解和把握。

3. 考核评价建议

（1）考核方式：本课程以考查为主，按照各个小组完成任务的情况以及各个小组人员在分工的各个环节的表现来考查学生的专业技能、协作、执行等能力。

（2）成绩评定：本课程考核成绩采用百分制。每个学生的分数来自教师评价得分、小组互评得分、学生自评得分。

4. 课程资源的开发与利用建议

本课程有完整的课件和教案，尚未进行课程网站建设。但积极开发和利用网络课程资源，充分利用有关的电子书籍、电子期刊、多媒体课程资源数据库、学校和高教园区数字图书馆、相关网站等信息资源，使本课程教学媒体从单一媒体向多种媒体转变，使教学活动从信息的单向传递向双向交换转变，使学生从单独学习向合作学习转变。

5. 教学条件配置建议

教室选用多媒体教室。教师应具备一定的旅游行业从业经验，特别是旅行社计调、线路设计等方面的经验。

6. 其他说明

加强课程经费投入，增加学生实地考察的机会。

（七）附录

本课程的相关参考资料。

书籍：《旅游地理学》《中国旅游地理》《中国旅游市场概论》《人文地理学》《中国旅游统计年鉴》《中外旅游业管理》

网络资源：中国旅游网及其他门户网站旅游链接，各省、直辖市、自治区的旅游局网站。

三、G Polytechnic National Geography Course Criterion

Table 2-54

Course Title	National Geography
Course Code	3AA082
Credits	2
Total Credit Hours	32

（一）Nature of the Course

It is an optional course of professional development ability for Tourism Management majors, as well as a comprehensive elementary course serving tour guides, OPs, and external liaison personnel of travel agencies. It is also an recognition of tourism resources and scenic spots, as well as the knowledge preparation for tour guides, Ops and external liaison personnel, etc. This course will be opened in the 3rd semester following the courses of Tourism Outline and Tour Guiding, and followed by the courses of Operating Business and Operation Management of Travel Agencies, etc.

（二）Basic Philosophy

The teaching of this course follows professional principles of tour guides, OPs and external liaison personnel by starting from the demand of professional positions, with "typical work task" as the carrier and selecting the contents according to the principle of "from simple to complex, from single to comprehensive", in which teaching, learning and practicing are integrated, and current teachers and in-school practical training environment, etc. are utilized to organize teaching. Teachers design learning-situated context and work tasks according to the features of vocational education and the objective and requirements of this course; students are grouped to finish specific tasks so as to cultivate students' cognitive competence of tourism resources, geoanalysis competence of tourist sources and ability in development of regional tourism products (routes), and improve their learning method and social competence while grasping professional competence.

(三) Design Idea

A work project course system is based on the overall design requirement of "oriented by vocational ability goal, to build work system–based higher vocational education curriculum system", with work task module as the core. Thoroughly break the traditional design thought of subject curricula, select and organize course contents by closely centering on the demand of accomplishing work tasks; highlight the connection between work tasks and knowledge; help students grasp knowledge based on vocationally practical activities; enhance the correlation between course contents and professional position ability, and improve students' employability. Define the knowledge, skills and other contents of the course according to the requirement of accomplishing work tasks, learning features of higher vocational college students and the rules formed based on vocational ability. Distribute class hours of learning curricula according to their total contents and their position in the course.

(1) Define the main body of development. Establish a development team of China Tourism geography courses, composed of school professional teachers, route design and development personnel of travel agencies as well as staff in scenic areas, through cooperation between schools and enterprises.

(2) Design and Development Process. With "students are learning subjects" as core, highlight the cultivation of vocational ability, supported by the cooperation between the industrial enterprises for development; and active participation of students. According to working process–oriented vocational education theory as well as the job requirements of technical field and vocational position, define the development process with reference to working standard of tour guides, OPs and external liaison personnel.

The basic design thought of National Geography is to jointly analyze position responsibilities and vocational ability of tour guides, OPs and external liaison personnel with key front–line employees of enterprises in tourism

industry, and design course system of Tourism Management major (Travel Agency Orientation). Make profound analysis on typical work tasks of tour guides, OPs and external liaison personnel repeatedly, design learning context according to job features; and select, integrate and arrange in sequence the teaching contents guided by real projects and emulated projects. According to different division of labor of tour guides, Ops and external liaison personnel, design the project course structure and create the learning contexts as cognition of China tourism resources, China tourist source geography, cognition of China tourism products, China tourist area division and key tourism routes, etc., which are developed from simple to complicated in general and relatively complete and independent, quite classified, with proper class hours and easy to be learned in structuring, suitable for imaginative thinking-type intelligent features and identical to corresponding professional qualification standards.

This course includes 32 class hours, with 2 credits, and is mainly evaluated by examinations in a flexible manner to motivate students' potential and interest in learning.

(四) Course Objectives

1. Overall Objectives

Through task-oriented project activities, help students grasp regional differentiation rules of tourism geography, able to make research and analysis on tourism resources, learn to design tourism routes and images of tourism destinations; and cultivate students' thinking ability to analyze issues in a multidisciplinary and multi-perspective way, help them enhance consciousness of ecological protection and innovative design, as well as improve teamwork spirit, tourism market development capability and professional ethics while enhancing professional skills.

2. Specific Goals

(1) Knowledge objectives.

① Able to recognize tourism value and spatial distribution pattern of all kinds of tourism resources.

② Able to describe spatial distribution of key scenic spots in China.

Able to distinguish landscape features in different regions in China and correctly explain corresponding geographical reasons and tourism man-land relationship, etc.

(2) Capability objectives.

① Having the capability of research and analysis on different regional tourism resources in China.

② Able to design tourism routes with all kinds of themes.

③ Grasp regional tourism design (systematic design of tourism destinations, resources integration & tourism product combination, tourism image design).

④ Able to collect, clear up and extract tourism geographical knowledge in electronic materials (Internet and video) and paper media (books, newspapers and periodicals).

(3) Quality objectives.

① Having rigorous learning attitude and style of work.

② Having teamwork spirit.

③ Having some tourism aesthetics.

④ Having high professional ethics and professional quality.

（五）Content Standards（Course Content and Requirement）

Table 2-25

Study Project	Study Module/ Name of Study Tasks	Knowledge Content and Requirement	Skill Content and Requirement	Teaching Method	Study Hours for Reference	
					Theory	Practice
Project 1	Introduction to China Tourism Geography	List and expound basic theories of Tourism Geography	Analyze issues by using regional differentiation and man-land relationship of Tourism Geography	Multimedia	2	
Project 2	Cognition of tourism resources and research & appraisal	Features and classification of all kinds of tourism resources; appraisal method for tourism resources	Able to classify all kinds of tourism resources; able to evaluate and classify tourism resources	Case Teaching	2	2
Project 3	China tourism products	Features, types and trend of tourism products	Able to list all kinds of tourism products and make analysis	Multimedia	4	
Project 4	Task 1: Guandong Culture Tourist Area in Northeast China	Key resources and features within the region	Design a tourism route within the region and make an introduction	Case Context	2	
	Task 2: Loess Culture Tourist Area with Famous Mountains, Fertile Land and Seascape in North China	Key resources and features within the region	Design a tourism route within the region and make an introduction	Case Context	4	

Continued Table

Study Project	Study Module/ Name of Study Tasks	Knowledge Content and Requirement	Skill Content and Requirement	Teaching Method	Study Hours for Reference	
					Theory	Practice
	Task 3: Wu Yue Huaihe River Metropolis Tourist Area with Landscape and Gardens in East China	Key resources and features within the region	Design a tourism route within the region and make an introduction	Case Context	4	
	Task 4: Jing Chu Ba-Shu Culture Tourist Area with Famous Mountains and Rivers in Central China	Key resources and features within the region	Design a tourism route within the region and make an introduction	Case Context	2	
Project 4	Task 5: Folk Music Culture Tourist Area with Famous Mountains and Islands in China's South-East Coastal Areas	Key resources and features within the region	Design a tourism route within the region and make an introduction	Case Context	4	2
	Task 6: Karst Landscape Scenery Tourist Area with National Customs in Southwest China	Key resources and features within the region	Design a tourism route within the region and make an introduction	Case Context	4	
	Task 7: Tibetan Buddhism Culture Tourist Area with Plateau, Snow Land and Prairie in Tibetan Plateau	Key resources and features within the region	Design a tourism route within the region and make an introduction	Case Context	2	
	Task 8: Silk Road Culture Tourist Area with Oasis, Prairie and Desert in Northwest China	Key resources and features within the region	Design a tourism route within the region and make an introduction	Case Context	2	

（六）Implementation Suggestions

1. Teaching Organization form and Implementation Suggestion

This course will be opened in a multimedia classroom, which will better arouse students' enthusiasm according to the requirement of teaching content. Students will be divided into 8 groups according to tourism geographical regions, and each group of students will be required to finish corresponding tasks for one specific region: make a brief introduction to the types and features of major resources; recommend one typical route within the region; design a route and give design description.

The implementation efficacy is quite good, and students are easy to accept, with certain enthusiasm.

2. Selection and Compilation Suggestions of Teaching Materials

This course adopts the *China Tourism Geography*, chief editor Yang Zaitian, published by China Machine Press. It is featured by a vivid presentation and precise introduction to the characteristics of each tourism region division.

3. Evaluation Appraisal Suggestions

（1）Evaluation mode: this course will be evaluated based on examinations. Task completion by each group and the behaviors of students in each group in all links will be judged to examine students' professional skills, coordination and implementation abilities.

（2）Result evaluation: this course will be evaluated by adopting centesimal system. Each student's score will be calculated from teachers' evaluation, mutual evaluation among groups and self-evaluation by students.

4. Suggestions on Development and Use of Course Resources

This course has complete courseware and teaching plan, with relevant website yet to be built. However, online course resources have already been developed and utilized. Change the teaching media of this course from single media to multimedia, change teaching activities from unidirectional transmission of information to two-way exchange, and change students' study

from individual study to cooperative study, by fully utilizing relevant e-books, e-periodicals, multimedia course resources database, digital libraries in schools and higher education zones, related websites and other information resources.

5. Suggestions on Teaching Condition Configuration

Multimedia classrooms are preferred. Teachers shall have certain experiences in tourism industry, especially in OPs and route design in travel agencies.

6. Other Notes

Enhance investment in course expenditure and increase opportunities of field visit for students.

（七）Appendices

Reference books : *Tourism Geography China Tourism Geography China Tourism Market Outline Human Geography China Tourism Statistical Yearbook Management of China and Oversea Tourism* .

Network resources : China tourism website and other portal website tourism links. Tourism administration websites of all provinces, municipalities directly under the Central Government and autonomous regions.

第四节 教师

一、教师选拔标准

教师队伍建设是职业教育整体改革的关键，职教教师素质与能力的保障与提升是职业教育顺利发展的基础和关键。从国家各项政策文件以及职校调研中可以获知当前职教教师最缺乏的不是专业理论知识，而是职业技术能力（或称为专业实践能力）和专业教学能力。相对而言，职业技术能力是根本和基础，是专业能力的重要组成部分。

G 学院教师聘用条件如下。

The necessary requirements for Tourism Faculty of G Polytechnic are as follows.

（一）思想政治条件

Ideology and Politics

遵守国家法律和法规，遵守《广东省高等学校教师职业道德规范》，持有高等学校教师资格者。

We hope to hire a teacher who observes the national laws and regulations as well as the *Occupational Moral Standard for Guangdong college Teacher*, and acquires the qualification of university teacher.

（二）学历（学位）、资历条件

Educational Background（Degree）and Qualifications

具备下列条件之一。

Any applicant who has met one of the following requirements will be acknowledged as an outstanding teacher.

（1）获得博士学位。

Acquiring doctor's degree.

（2）获得硕士学位，工作 2 年以上。

Acquiring master's degree who has over two years working experience.

（3）大学本科毕业，在相关领域工作 5 年以上。

Acquiring bachelor's degree who has over five years working experience in a related field.

（4）主持开发新产品或推广新技术、新工艺、新产品，或直接解决生产建设中重大技术问题，或主持完成国家或省(部)级重大科研课题 2 项以上，并取得明显的社会和经济效益者，以杰出人才加以引进。

Taking charge of the development of new products and the promotion of new technology, new technique and new products, figuring out an important technological problem in production and construction independently, leading and completing more than 2 major scientific research projects at national or provincial（ministerial）level, and gaining significant social and economic benefits.

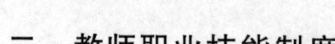

二、教师职业技能制度

（一）高职院校教师职业技能制度是高职院校实现内涵式发展的要求

20 世纪末我国高等教育扩招以来，高职教育迅速发展，经过 20 年的发展，高职院校的办学规模不断扩大，在校学生数量不断增加，高职教育发展取得了丰硕的成果，但其在发展过程中的一些问题也逐渐暴露。高职教育必须同时兼备职业性、教育性，但从实际情况来看职业性与教育性之间的"天平"始终失衡，导致部分高职毕业生存在理论知识不扎实、技能水平有待提升、缺乏创新精神、职业素养不高等问题，使得高职教育难以被企业与社会认可，高职院校发展面临瓶颈。从一定程度上讲，师资队伍建设是导致这些问题的重要原因。为了进一步平衡职业教育的职业性与教育性，促进高职院校的内涵式发展，必须建设一支高素质的"双师型"教师 队伍。

（二）高职院校教师职业技能制度是高职院校创新人才培养的关键环节

在传统教育教学理论的影响下，一些高职院校的人才培养存在重理论、轻实践的弊端，但大部分岗位的工作内容具有较强的操作性，对劳动者的实操能力提出了很高的要求，并非具备理论知识就可以胜任。针对这一问题，作为人才培养的关键环节—— 教师，具有不可推卸的责任。如果高职院校教师缺乏相关的实践经验，学生自然难以学以致用并提高其实践能力。对于高职院校而言，培养"双师型"教师队伍是创新人才培养模式的关键环节，是优化人才培养结构的突破点。

（三）高职院校教师职业技能制度是高职院校提高师资队伍水平的有效途径

有些高职院校教师大多负责理论教学，实践能力不足，无法为学生的实习实训提供有效指导。针对这种情况，企业可以为教师提供较好的

学习场所，在企业导师的指导下，教师可以学习操作技能，并结合自身的专业理论在生产活动中实现学以致用，切实提高自身的实践能力与应用能力，从而有效提高高职院校师资队伍整体水平。

（四）高职院校教师职业技能制度是高职院校提高毕业生就业能力的有效方式

当前，高职院校毕业生就业竞争力有待进一步提高。在产业结构转型背景下，社会对高素质、具有创新意识的技能型人才需求不断增加，而部分高职院校毕业生往往创新能力仍有待提高。同时，部分高职院校毕业生难以适应产业结构调整对岗位技能的新要求，出现结构性失业问题。教师是学生能力培养的主导者，必须具备一定的实践能力，了解企业、行业的用人需求。高职院校重视"双师型"教师队伍培养是提高毕业生就业能力的必然要求。

表2-56　G学院旅游管理专业教师的职业技能证书一览表

序号	姓名	职业资格证（中文）	职业资格证（英文）
1	段女士	餐厅服务员二级技师	Senior Restaurant Service Technician, Band 2
2	周先生	茶艺师二级技师	Senior Tea Art Specialist
3	陈先生	高级电子商务师	Senior Electronic Business Engineer
4	冯女士	旅游经济师	Travel Economist
5	马先生	会展策划师二级	Senior Exhibition Planner
6	万先生	经济师	Travel Economist
7	杨先生	高级旅游咨询师	Senior Travel Consultant
8	郭女士	高级茶艺师	Senior Tea Master
9	胡女士	旅行社经理	Travel Agency Manager
10	杨女士	商务英语培训师	Business English Trainer

第五节　管理

一、教学管理理念以人为本，关注师生发展诉求

教学管理是以人为主体和作用对象的实践活动，教学管理的核心是对人的管理。教师和学生作为教学管理工作的具体实施主体和直接作用

对象，其教学积极性和参与能动性深刻影响着教学管理的质量和效率，因此，"以人为本"的理念是提升管理有效性的基本前提。教学管理人本化理念的形成是认识人、对待人和培养人的动态过程。认识人体现在明确教师和学生的现实诉求与发展动力；对待人指通过各种激励手段和人文关怀来满足这些诉求、挖掘内在潜力；培养人则指依靠加强专业建设、优化课程结构、改进教学方法和创新管理制度等来增益教师的专业实践能力、促进学生的职业生涯发展。换言之，教学管理理念的人本化以充分调动师生的积极性和能动性并激发其创造性为逻辑起点。

二、教学管理模式协同有序，提升系统整体效率

教学管理作为职业院校实施人才培养、开展教学活动的基础和保障，其工作内容不仅繁杂，而且相对独立分散。以教育部印发的《高等学校教学管理要点》（教高司〔1998〕33号）为参照，教学管理的基本内容一般包括教学计划管理、教学运行管理、教学质量管理与评价以及教学基本建设管理。这一由主体、组织和环境三大要素组成的管理系统中，每个一级要素都嵌套了多个二级要素，各要素之间的相互作用和关系表现出较为丰富的层次性、因果性和非线性特征。根据协同学理论，当系统内部相互掣肘或离散时，就会造成整个管理系统内耗增加，系统内各子系统难以发挥其应有的功能；反之，若有相对独立性的子系统对管理主体和客体、组织目的及环境等进行协同，便能产生一个在结构和功能等方面远超原系统的、具有新的生命体的组织系统，进而更加有效地实现系统的整体功能效应。教学管理系统作为一个复杂的开放性系统，其内部一切活动都离不开主体、组织和环境的协同化。

三、教学管理机制灵活常态，保障队伍专业能力

教学管理工作兼有行政管理与学术管理的双重职能，不仅要进行一般的行政性管理，还要根据办学指导思想和人才培养目标等进行教育教学研究，承担学校教学工作的学术性管理职能，因此教学管理人员应是"懂得教育的有管理专长的专业人员"。美国教全国育协会（NEA）曾就"专业化"提出过8项标准：①应属高级心智活动；②应受长时间的专业教育；③应具有专门的知识领域；④应能不断地在职进修；⑤应有健全

的专业组织；⑥应以服务社会为目的；⑦应属永久性的职业；⑧应建立并能遵守专业规范或公约。

四、教学检查制度

G学院教学常规检查文件G学院院教字〔2007〕13号反映了该学院对教学质量的基本管理。

教学工作是学校的中心工作，建立教学检查制度是维护良好教学秩序，确保教学工作有序运行，保证教学质量的有效措施。为使教学运行规范有序，及时发现和解决教学工作中出现的问题，将教学工作的管理与监控落到实处，特制定本制度。

（1）教学检查包含日常教学检查、期初、期中、期末教学检查及专项教学检查。

（2）日常教学检查以随机抽查的方式进行。校领导、教务处、学工部、各院（系、部）教学管理人员、督导组成员、学生信息员均作为日常教学检查的成员。采取听课、抽查学生作业、与学生交谈、召开学生座谈会等方式了解教师日常教学和学生到课等情况，对日常教学秩序进行监督和检查。

（3）期初教学检查指每学期开学前一周，教务处检查开学的准备工作及教学设施情况。各院（系、部）检查教师的教学任务落实与准备工作，在正式上课的第一周内，教务处及各院（系、部）领导全面检查教师上课情况、学生学习情况、教学辅助设备运行状况及教材发放等情况，教学日历、课表、学生名单等教学管理资料的准备情况；同时检查上学期的成绩登录、成绩分析报告、试卷归档、考试工作总结等各项期末工作的落实情况和本学期各教研室和教学单位的教学教研工作计划和安排等情况。对检查中发现的问题要及时采取措施或通报有关部门及时解决。

（4）期中教学检查每学期安排一次，时间为第九周至第十三周。

①检查的主要内容。

a.教学秩序检查。教师执行授课计划（教学日历）情况；教师调（停）课、代课、准时上下课等情况；实验（训）教学安排及实验（训）设备完好等实验（训）室管理工作情况。

b.课堂教学检查。教师备课、授课、批改作业、辅导答疑情况；教材的选用情况；多媒体教学及课件使用情况等。通过听课检查课堂教学内容和教学方法。

c.实验（训）教学检查。实验（训）教学计划执行情况；实验（训）指导教师准备实验（训）情况，如备课及有关实验（训）条件的准备情况；指导实验（训）和批改实验（训）报告情况；实习计划执行及实习指导教师指导实习情况。

d.学风状况检查。学生到课率、上课听讲及完成作业、实验（训）、实习等情况，学生上课精神状态、遵守作息制度和课堂纪律情况，学生早读、晚自习情况等。

②检查的要求。期中教学检查采取各院（系、部）自查与学校抽查相结合，常规检查与专项检查相结合，一般检查与重点检查相结合的方式进行。具体要求如下：

a.各院（系、部）分别召开教师座谈会和学生座谈会，掌握课堂教学、实验（训）教学运行情况，听取教师和学生对教学工作的意见和建议。

b.各教研室对照教学日历检查本教研室所有任教课程的教学进度，检查教师备课情况，抽查学生作业批改情况，组织同行教师相互听课或进行教学观摩等。实验（训）室负责检查实验（训）开出情况、实验（训）教学计划执行情况、教研工作计划执行情况。各院（系、部）对教研室、实验（训）室的教学及管理工作进行检查并做出评价。

c.学校和院（系、部）教学督导员、院领导及相关处室负责人深入课堂、实验（训）室听课。

d.教务处会同学工部组织人员抽查教学秩序及学风情况。按照学校统一部署抽查部分院（系、部）的教学情况，同时召开学生及教师座谈会，了解整体教学运行情况。

e.教务处、院（系、部）通过调查表的形式在所任教的学生中进行课堂教学情况调查，做好记录和统计，并妥善保管好调查表。

（5）期末教学检查。每学期的最后两周进行期末教学检查。各院（系、部）要督促教研室、任课教师做好命题、考试、评阅、试卷分析、成绩登记等工作并加强考风考绩检查。做好听课笔记的收集、学生评教数据的处理和分析、教师教学质量评价、各教研室和教学单位的学期

教学教研工作和下学期的教学工作安排、各种文件和教学档案的归档的工作。

（6）不定期教学检查。不定期抽查主要是对教学秩序、课堂教学、学风状况等环节进行检查，以便能够及时发现问题解决问题，进一步确保教学工作有序进行，形成良好的教风学风。检查方法将采用不定期检查与学生信息员实时反馈教学信息相结合的方法。检查方法如下：

①不定期组织检查人员检查教师到岗情况、学生到课情况以及课堂纪律情况、教师精神面貌、学生精神面貌并及时通报检查情况。

②编辑学生教学信息员简报，及时反映教学动态。

③组建学生信息员群，鼓励学生主动收集和传递教学信息，实时反馈发现的问题，并跟踪整改情况。

（7）专项教学检查。根据每学期的教学目标和重点拟定专项教学检查内容，教学教研计划执行、课堂教学质量、教学秩序、教学文档、专业建设、课程建设、实验实习教学、毕业设计（论文）、考试与阅卷等各方面均可作为专项教学检查内容。专项检查可以单独进行，也可以结合定期教学检查进行。

（8）教学检查结束后，各院（系、部）均应认真总结，及时归纳、提炼教学改革的好思想、好方法、好手段，对教学中出现的问题要进行认真分析，并提出具体整改措施。教务处汇总各院（系部）材料后要予以通报，推广教学改革成果，对存在的共性问题，提出切实可行的措施予以改进和解决，以进一步规范教学管理，提高教学质量。

（9）各院（系、部）结合本部门的具体情况，制定出教学检查工作的实施细则。

五、课堂评价

（一）理论课程评价表

表2-57

教师姓名		所在部门		班级		授课地点					
授课名称						授课时间					
指标	权重	二级指标（指标内涵）	权重值	评价等级					得分
				A	B	C	D	E	
教学态度	0.15	以身作则，为人师表；严谨治学，从严执教；结合课程内容，重视学生思想教育；建立良好的师生关系，做学生的良师益友	0.7						
		精心准备教案、教具及课件制作	0.3						

续 表

教学内容	0.30	根据行业企业发展需要，遵循学生职业能力培养的基本规律，以真实工作任务／项目及其工作过程／流程等为依据整合、序化教学内容	0.2		
		教学内容符合教学日历和课程标准，学习情境（主题单元）设计突出职业性和应用性	0.2		
		有具体恰当的项目和任务，并能通过完成这些项目和任务，达到对学生专业能力、方法能力和社会能力的培养要求	0.2		
		教学环节设计合理，教学组织井然有序、有特色，内容过渡自然，教学环节紧凑，节奏适度	0.2		
		选用先进、适用的教材，与行业企业合作编写工学结合的特色教材、课件、案例、习题，实训实习项目、学习指南等教学相关资料。布置课后作业或训练项目，引导学生自主学习	0.2		

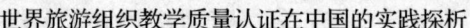

续 表

指标	项目权重	二级指标（指标内涵）	权重值	评价等级					得分
				A	B	C	D	E	
教学方法与手段	0.30	整体设计合理，教学突出重点，抓住关键，教学难点处理得当，时间分配安排合理，利用充分	0.2						
		体现任务驱动，项目导向、案例教学等行动导向的教学方法，实现教学做一体化	0.2						
		根据课程内容和学生特点，灵活运用案例分析、分组讨论、角色扮演、启发引导等教学方法，引导学生积极思考、乐于实践，提高教学效果	0.2						
		教学语言的组织清晰生动，节奏适度	0.2						
		教学过程突出以学生为主体，体现师生互动，引导学生积极思考、乐于实践，改变课堂上信息单向传递的现象	0.2						
教学效果	0.25	完全达到教学目标，对学生职业能力培养和职业素养养成有明显促进作用	0.5						
		学生响应程度积极，响应气氛活跃	0.5						
听课人			总分						
课堂情况		教师是否迟到	是否提前下课		应到学生数				
		实到学生数	迟到学生（约）		早退学生（约）				
评价与建议									

续　表

教师姓名				所在部门		班级						
实训名称							实训地点					
							实训时间					

指标	项目权重	二级指标（指标内涵）	权重值	评价等级					得分
				A	B	C	D	E	
教学态度	0.10	以身作则，为人师表；严谨治学，从严执教；结合课程内容，重视学生思想教育；建立良好的师生关系，做学生的良师益友	1.0						
实训目标	0.10	实训指导书规范，教学资料齐全，发放及时。实训场地清洁整齐。教师认真记载学生出勤情况和教学进程表	1.0						
实训内容	0.30	以真实工作任务／项目及其工作过程／流程等为依据整合、序化实训内容	0.4						
		实训内容与岗位实际能力要求紧密；实训内容与职业能力培养紧密联系，从应用的角度进行整合改造，知识学习实应用性（主题单元）设计	0.3						
		有具体恰当的项目和任务，并能通过这些项目和任务的完成，达到对学生的能力培养要求	0.3						
操作指导	0.30	教师讲解清楚，示范操作规范；指导实训认真负责，回答问题耐心细致，注重对学生严谨务实训练作风的培养	0.4						
		实训组织有序，有特色，内容过渡自然，实训环节紧凑，节奏适度；反馈及时，应变能力强，时间分配安排合理，利用充分	0.3						
		关注学生操作情况，指导及时，耐心、态度认真	0.3						
成绩考核	0.10	考核内容具体，评分标准明确。考核办法有创新，有利于提高学生职业能力	1.0						

续表

指标	项目 权重	二级指标（指标内涵）	权重值	评价等级					得分
				A	B	C	D	E	
教学效果	0.10	学生学习积极主动，达到了实训的目的。学生对实训教学效果反映好	0.10						
听课人			总分						
课堂情况	教师是否迟到	是否提前下课		应到学生数					
	实到学生数	迟到学生数（约）		早退学生数（约）					
评语与建议									

（二）实训课程质量评价表

表2-58

课程类型	指标	项目权重	二级指标（指标内涵）	权重值	评价等级				
					A 99	B 80	C 60	D 40	E 20
理论及实践课程指标	教师素养	0.2	备课充分，对学生既严格要求又关心爱护	0.5					
			教师按时上课，不迟到，不提前下课	0.5					
	教学内容	0.30	教学内容提炼较好，以技能培养为中心，学生比较容易接受	0.4					
			讲课条理清晰，深入浅出，重点突出，语言生动，富有感染力	0.3					
			讲课理论联系实际，善于运用案例，实例进行教学或示范	0.3					
	教学过程	0.20	态度和谐，善于启发学生参与教学活动，活跃课堂气氛，重视对学生独立分析和解决问题能力的培养	0.30					
			能够有效使用各种教学手段辅助教学（如教学网站、投影仪、课件、录像、实物、模型等）	0.30					
			布置作业，批改及时并讲解作业或实验的要点与难点	0.20					
			使学生明确课程学习目的，及时对教学内容进行小结和总结，讲练结合紧密	0.20					
	教学效果	0.30	通过学习这门课程，学生能力得到提高，感觉收获很大	0.50					
			认为这位教师教学水平高	0.50					

续　表

课程类型	指标	项目权重	二级指标（指标内涵）	权重值	评价等级 A 99	B 80	C 60	D 40	E 20
生产性实训指标	教师素养	0.20	对学生既严格要求又关心爱护	0.5					
			提前到岗，准备充分	0.5					
	教学过程	0.60	严格按照生产实训规范要求学生（安全规则、着装、操作规程）	0.30					
			讲解示范清楚	0.30					
			在学生操作过程中认真指导	0.20					
			对实训报告的撰写要求严格，批阅及时和认真	0.20					
	教学效果	0.20	使学生明确课程学习目的和考核标准	0.50					
			认为这位教师教学水平高	0.50					

第六节　全球旅游道德规范

一、旅游管理专业人才培养方案

加强旅游道德规范的课程描述。

Course Description of Strengthening Tourism Ethics in Tourism Management Professional Training Program.

（一）素质培养目标（Quality Training goal）

（1）道德素质：能够遵纪守法，具备良好的思想品德、社会公德和职业道德，树立正确的世界观、人生观和价值观，具有较强的敬业精神和社会责任感。

Moral ethics : able to abide by laws and regulations, have good ideology and morality, social morality and professional ethics, establish a correct world outlook, outlook on life and values, and have a strong sense of professionalism and social responsibility.

（2）文化素质：具有较高的文学艺术素养、人文科学素养和审美素养，具备适应职业变化的终身学习能力。

Cultural quality : have high literary and artistic literacy, humanities literacy and aesthetic literacy, and have the ability to adapt to lifelong learning.

（3）身心素质：拥有健康的体魄，养成良好的体育锻炼和卫生习惯，具备健全的心理和乐观的人生态度，具有良好的心理承受能力和社会适应能力。

Physical and mental quality : Have a healthy body, develop good physical exercise and health habits, have a sound psychological and optimistic attitude towards life, have a good psychological endurance and social adaptability.

（4）职业素质：具有严谨务实、深入细致的工作作风和爱岗敬业、团结协作、勇于开拓创新的精神风貌。

Professional quality : have a rigorous and pragmatic, in-depth and meticulous work style and dedication, unity and cooperation, and the courage

to explore and innovate.

二、相关课程设置（Related Course Settings）

（1）旅游学概论：要求学习者尊重旅游者的人身自由、行动自由、风俗习惯自由、宗教信仰自由等，让旅游者真正体验到旅游的乐趣和舒适。

Introduction to Tourism : require learners to respect the personal freedom, freedom of movement, freedom of customs, freedom of religious belief, etc., so that tourists can truly experience the fun and comfort of tourism.

（2）广东文化与风俗：让学生了解并遵守广东特有的勤俭持家、崇尚经营、兼收并蓄等文化习俗，尊重少数民族的传统与文化，同时理解和传播这种文化。

Guangdong Culture and Customs : Let students understand and abide by the unique cultural and customary practices of Guangdong, such as Diligent and thrifty household management, advocating management, inclusive and other cultural customs, respecting the traditions and culture of ethnic minorities, and understanding and spreading this culture.

（3）导游基础知识：秉承旅游致富、旅游改变生活的理念，了解中国部分落后地区的旅游资源并立志开发、建设、发展旅游经济，使当地居民普遍受益。

Basic Knowledge of Tour Guides : adhering to the idea of getting rich by tourism and changing life by tourism, understanding the tourism resources in some backward areas of China, especially in the minority areas, and aim to develop and construct the tourism economy so as to benefit the local residents generally.

（4）旅游法规：了解并熟悉旅游业的相关法规，尊重各民族的传统习俗；平等互助、合作共赢。

Tourism Laws and Regulations : understand and be familiar with the relevant laws and regulations of the tourism industry, respect the traditions and customs of all ethnic groups, and help each other equally and co-operate for a win-win situation.

（5）导游业务：通过旅游开发、旅游合作，既发展经济，又保护环

境，使旅游成为可持续发展的惠及子孙后代的绿色经济。

Tour Guide Business : through tourism development and tourism cooperation, not only develops the economy, but also protects the environment, making tourism a sustainable green economy for future generations.

（6）前厅与客房管理：通过游客在酒店的舒适体验，大力促进服务质量的提升，并改善当地的旅游环境。

Hotel Lobby and Guest Room Management : through the comfortable experience of tourists in the hotel, vigorously promote service quality, and improve the local tourism environment.

（7）餐饮运行与管理：通过对游客热情周到服务，使之感受中国饮食的美誉，从而提高餐饮行业的服务水平。

Operation and Management of Catering : through the warm and thoughtful service to customers, let them feel the reputation of Chinese food, thus improve the service level of the catering industry.

（8）旅行社经营与管理：旅行社合法经营，所有旅游产品做到定位准确、价格透明、服务上乘，形成旅游行业的规范有序状态，并促进经济的发展。

Operation and Management of travel Agency : Travel agencies operate legally, and all tourism products are accurate in positioning, transparent in price, and excellent in service, form a standardized and orderly state of the tourism industry, and promote economic development.

（三）专业核心课程简介

表2-59

课程名称	主要教学内容	技能考核项目与要求	参考学时／学分
导游业务	（1）如何成为导游人员； （2）认识导游服务； （3）完成团队带团； （4）完成散客带团； （5）处理与预防突发事件； （6）应对游客个别要求； （7）导游人员的带团技能； （8）导游综合知识讲座	（1）能灵活运用导游服务的原则和规范为游客提供规范化和个性化的地陪、全陪导游服务； （2）熟悉突发事件处理程序和方法，能有效防范突发事件产生； （3）熟悉处理个别要求的基本原则和方法，并能灵活运用	54学时／3学分
前厅与客房管理	（1）预订服务； （2）礼宾服务； （3）接待服务； （4）商务中心与总机服务； （5）客房对客服务； （6）客房的清洁保养； （7）宾客关系管理； （8）客房的安全、物资、人力资源管理； （9）前厅与客房服务技能实训	（1）能够正确使用前厅设备，进行预订服务，散客／团体行李寄存和提取服务，客人入住登记和结账服务，电话问讯和留言服务； （2）能够按服务标准为客人提供迎送、送餐、访客、擦鞋、小酒吧等服务，处理客人遗留物品； （3）具备中式／西式铺床技能，熟悉清扫客房的程序和方法； （4）掌握客人投诉的原因及处理方法，能够灵活处理宾客投诉； （5）能够进行客房消防、财务安全的预防和应急处理，了解客房工作存在的职业安全问题，了解客房设备、用品、布件管理的方法	68学时／4学分

续　表

课程名称	主要教学内容	技能考核项目与要求	参考学时／学分
餐饮运行与管理	（1）构建餐饮管理体系； （2）控制餐饮服务现场； （3）筹划与设计菜单； （4）策划餐饮促销活动； （5）控制餐饮成本； （6）采购与验收食品原料； （7）控制餐饮服务质量； （8）餐厅服务技能实训	（1）能根据餐饮企业的规模设计其组织机构和人员配置； （2）能够制定中西餐零点、宴会、管事等员工工作流程及标准； （3）能够应用食品营养知识设计菜谱，完成一份完整的菜单设计； （4）能够进行菜肴的销售分析和盈利分析，完成一份主题餐饮营销策划方案的撰写； （5）能制定餐厅收银员工作流程及标准，填写餐饮营业日报表，对关键环节提出成本控制思路； （6）能够准确评估供应商，了解食品原料质量标准，完成一次完整的食品采购与验收，提出食品采购成本控制的合理化建议； （7）能用科学的方法全面评估服务质量，处理宾客投诉； （8）能够开展中西餐的托盘、餐巾折花、摆台、点菜、上菜、分菜、斟酒、斟茶、撤换餐具、迎送客人等服务	68学时／4学分
旅行社经营与管理	（1）旅行社组织构造； 2旅行社的设立； 3旅行社产品设计与开发； 4旅行社产品销售； 5旅行社计调管理； 6旅行社人力资源管理	（1）熟练掌握国际国内旅行社的设立流程； （2）能够设计旅游线路，熟练掌握旅游产品的开发的各个环节，并结合该产品的特点，运用相关营销理论，确定适合的营销方案； （3）通过模拟操作，熟练掌握旅行社计调、外联等相关工作内容	68学时／4学分
旅游市场营销	（1）旅游景区营销与策划； （2）旅游酒店营销与策划； （3）旅游交通企业营销与策划； （4）旅行社营销与策划	（1）具有独立运用科学方法进行旅游市场调研的能力； （2）具有采集使用信息，分析归纳、总结交流经验，技能、技巧的能力； （3）具有将旅游市场营销理论与实践经验结合运用的能力	68学时／4学分

二、选修课心理健康教育的课程描述

表2-60

课程名称 Course Title	心理健康教育	课程编码 Course Code	XLBX01600
学期 Semester	2018—2019学年度第一学期	学分 Credits	2
面授学时 Credit Hours	32	周学时 Class Hours a Week	2
课程类型 Course Type	本课程为旅游管理专业基础（必修）课程		
课程目标 Course Aims	高校学生心理健康教育课程是知识集中讲授、心理体验与行为训练为一体的公共课程。该课程旨在使学生明确心理健康的标准及意义，增强自我心理保健意识和心理危机预防意识，掌握并应用心理健康知识，培养自我认知能力、人际沟通能力、自我调节能力，切实提高学生心理素质，促进学生全面发展		
课程内容 Course Content	第一讲：大学生心理健康概述 通过本部分的学习，学生能了解心理健康的标准意义、了解异常心理的表现，树立正确的心理健康观念。 （一）大学生心理健康导论 教学目标：通过教学使学生了解心理健康知识、大学生心理健康的特点，树立正确的心理健康观念，能够自主地调整心理状态、维护自身的心理健康。 教学内容： （1）认识心理活动的特点和实质； （2）了解大学生心理发展的特点； （3）掌握大学生心理健康的标准； （4）了解影响大学生心理健康的主要因素		

课程内容 Course Content	教学方法：课堂讲授、课堂活动、案例分析。 G学院大学生心理健康教育的特色： （1）理念：快乐教育。"四个快乐"，即心理中心是快乐中心、心理健康教育是快乐教育、心理咨询是快乐咨询、心理健康工作者是快乐天使。 （2）G学院的心理健康标准："三快"和"三满意"标准。 （二）大学生心理咨询 G学院大学生心理健康教育的特色： （1）理念：快乐教育。"四个快乐"，即心理中心是快乐中心、心理健康教育是快乐教育、心理咨询是快乐咨询、心理健康工作者是快乐天使。 （2）G学院的心理健康标准："三快"和"三满意"标准。 （二）大学生心理咨询 教学目标：通过教学使学生了解心理咨询的基本概念和功能、心理咨询的内容与类型，建立正确的心理咨询观念以及自助求助的意识。 教学内容： （1）心理咨询的概念和功能； （2）大学生心理咨询的意义和特点； （3）大学生心理咨询的内容与类型； 教学方法：课堂讲授、课堂活动、角色扮演 介绍G学院心理中心的地址、热线电话779620（2）7796109 介绍校大学生心理健康协会和二级学院大学生心理健康协会，欢迎大学生积极加入

续　表

课程内容 Course Content	(三)大学生心理困惑及异常心理 教学目标：通过教学使学生了解常见的大学生心理困惑及异常心理，了解心理疾病，懂得哪些状态可以通过自我或心理咨询进行调整，哪些心理疾病需要专业医疗机构诊治。 教学内容： (1)大学生常见的心理困惑及异常心理； (2)大学生常见的心理疾病及其应对。 教学方法：课堂讲授、小组讨论、案例分析。 重点： (1)让学生掌握本课程的基本要求、教学计划； (2)心理健康的标准； (3)大学生的常见心理问题。 难点：黑白灰理论。 第二讲：认识自我，健全人格 (一)大学生自我意识的培养 教学目标：通过教学使学生认识自我发展的重要性，了解并掌握自我意识发展的特点，能够识别在自我意识发展过程中出现的偏差及原因，并能够对其进行调适，建立自尊自信的自我意识。 教学内容： (1)自我意识概述； (2)大学生自我意识发展的特点； (3)大学生自我意识偏差及其调适； (4)自我意识的评估。 教学方法：课堂讲授、心理测试、案例分析、体验活动

续 表

| 课程内容
Course Content | （二）大学生人格发展与心理健康
教学目标：通过教学使学生了解人格的基本知识，当代大学生的人格特征和自我人格发展状况，掌握大学生常见人格缺陷的表现、形成原因及调适方法。
教学内容：
（1）人格概述；
（2）大学生的人格特征；
（3）人格发展异常的表现与评估；
（4）大学生人格完善的途径和调适方法。
教学方法：课堂讲授、心理测试、案例分析。
强调：健康人格是人格的完整性、同一性；不健康的人格有双重人格、多重人格、分裂人格。
难点：性格、气质类。
第三讲：大学生情绪管理
教学目标：通过教学使学生了解自身的情绪特点，掌握情绪调适的方法，自主调整情绪，保持良好的情绪状态。
教学内容：
（1）情绪概述；
（2）大学生情绪特点及其影响；
（3）培养良好的情绪；
（4）不良情绪的表现及调适。
教学方法：课堂讲授、情景表演、案例分析、团体训练。
重点：情绪调整方法。
难点：ABC理论（理性情绪疗法） |

续　表

| 课程内容
Course Content | 第四讲：大学生人际交往

教学目标：通过教学使学生了解人际交往的意义、特点及类型，理解影响大学生人际交往的因素，掌握基本的交往原则和技巧，了解人际关系障碍的类型及调适方法，增强人际交往能力。

教学内容：
（1）人际关系概述；
（2）大学生人际交往及影响因素；
（3）大学生人际交往原则及技巧；
（4）大学生人际关系障碍及调适。

教学方法：课堂讲授、情景表演、案例分析、团体训练。

强调：大学生宿舍人际关系。

讨论：如何协调舍含人际关系。

第五讲：大学生恋爱与性心理

教学目标：通过教学使学生了解自身性生理和心理的发展，认识大学生恋爱心理的特点，了解大学生在性心理和恋爱心理方面存在的问题，形成对性心理和恋爱心理的正确认识。

教学内容：
（1）性心理的发展和大学生性心理的特点；
（2）大学生性心理问题及调适；
（3）大学生恋爱心理发展的规律特点和常见问题；
（4）培养健康恋爱观和恋爱择偶观；
（5）艾滋病的预防。

教学方法：课堂讲授、案例分析、小组讨论。

讨论："同性恋"问题，婚前性行为问题 |

续　表

课程内容 Course Content	第六讲：大学生挫折心理与应对 教学目标：通过教学使学生正确理解压力和挫折，了解大学生压力及挫折的主要来源，了解挫折对人生的意义，学会正确应对挫折。 教学内容： （1）挫折概述； （2）大学生挫折的产生与特点； （3）挫折对大学生心理的影响； （4）挫折心理的应对，自我调适方法。 教学方法：课堂讲授、心理测试、案例分析、小组讨论
课程内容 Course Content	第七讲：大学生生命教育与心理危机干预 教学目标：通过教学使学生认识生命、尊重生命、珍爱生命，帮助大学生识别心理危机的信号，掌握初步的干预方法，预防心理危机，维护生命安全。 教学内容： （1）生命的意义； （2）大学生心理危机的表现与识别； （3）大学生心理危机的预防与干预。 教学方法：课堂讲授、心理测试、角色扮演、小组讨论
学习成果 Learning Outcomes	通过课程学习，学生要在知识、技能和自我认知三个层面达到以下目标。 （1）知识层面：通过本课程的学习，学生了解心理学的有关理论和基本概念，明确心理健康的标准及意义，了解大学阶段人的心理发展特征及异常表现，学生要掌握自我探索技能、心理调适技能及心理发展技能，如学习发展技能、 （2）技能层面：通过本课程的学习，学生要掌握自我探索技能、心理调适技能及心理发展技能，如学习发展技能、环境适应技能，压力管理技能，沟通技能，问题解决技能，自我管理技能、人际交往技能和生涯规划技能等

续 表

学习成果 Learning Outcomes	（3）自我认知层面：通过本课程的学习，学生树立心理健康发展的自主意识，了解自身的心理特点和性格特征，能够对自己的身体条件、心理状况、行为能力等进行客观评价，正确认识自己、接纳自己，在遇到心理问题时能够进行自我调适或寻求帮助，积极探索适合自己并适应社会的生活状态
教学方法 Teaching Methods	课程采用理论与实践相结合、讲授与训练相结合的教学方法，如课堂讲授、案例分析、小组讨论、心理测试、团体训练、情景表演、角色扮演、体验活动等。 在教学过程中，要充分利用"互联网+"，利用相关的图书资料、影视资料、心理测评工具等丰富的教学手段。
评价方法 Assessment Methods	（见下表）
参考书目 Recommended Textbooks and Reference Books	《大学生心理健康教育》 《大学生团体心理素质训练》

Assessment based on 测评依据	Percentage 百分比
平时成绩（考勤、课堂表现、作业完成情况等）	40%
期末考试成绩	60%
Total Marks 总分	100%

Marks will be given as percentages as follows，分数转换成百分比，如下所示。

0%~59%　　Fail　　不及格
60%~69%　　Pass　　及格
70%~79%　　Credit　　中等
80%~89%　　Good　　良好
90%~00%　　Distinction　　优秀

第三章　G 学院旅游管理专业参加世界旅游组织教学质量认证自评报告

第一节　自评报告中文版示例

UNWTO TEDQUAL CERTIFICATION PROCESS SELF EVALUATION

Summary Information on the Particulars of the Tourism Educational Programme in Process of Certification

（Maximum number of pages to be filled out : 50 pages.）

I. GENERAL INFORMATION

表3-1

Name of the Institution/Programme
G 学院旅游管理专业
Brief Description of the Programme

G 学院是广东省人民政府 1985 年批准设立、教育部备案的一所全日制公办普通高等学校。校园面积 1.34 平方千米，建筑面积超过 0.5 平方千米，其中教室 5.45 万平方米，图书馆 3.05 平方千米，体育场馆 0.01 平方千米，实习实训场所（含校内教学企业）0.18 平方千米。教学仪器设备 1.97 万台，馆藏图书 140 多万册，电子图书数字资源量7806 GB。G 学院现有全日制在校生约 22 000 人，专任教师近 1 000 人，是广东省规模最大的高职院校之一。是"国家示范性高职院校建设计划"骨干高职院校，也是广东省一流高职院校建设单位

G 学院旅游管理专业设置于 2004 年，2009 年成为学校重点专业，2015 年成为首批广东省高职教育品牌专业建设点。

该专业面向旅行社、酒店、景区景点等旅游企业第一线，培养掌握旅游管理基本理论、具有熟练的旅游操作技能，具备较强的外语交际能力、经营管理能力和开拓创新能力的高素质技术技能型人才。

该专业面向全国招生，现有在校生 666 人，已向社会输送 2 200 多名毕业生。该专业现有专任教师 23 人，其中教授 3 人，副教授 5 人；博士 4 人，硕士 18 人，学士 1 人。另外，该专业聘请了 20 位旅游企业经理、旅行社中高级导游、行业协会精英为兼职教师。

该专业建有英语语音室、模拟导游实训室、前厅与客房实训室、中餐实训室、西餐实训室、酒吧实训室、茶艺实训室、形体与礼仪实训室等校内实训基地，校内实训基地面积达 1 200 多平方米。校外实习基地有广东省拱北口岸中国旅行社、珠海长隆国际海洋度假区、深圳 JW 万豪酒店等

Brief Description on the Type of Educational System

G 学院为广东省教育厅主管的省属公办普通高等职业学校，该校旅游管理专业属于普通高等学校高等职业教育类型，专科层次，学制为三年、全日制。根据中华人民共和国教育部颁布的《普通高等学校高等职业教育（专科）专业目录（2015 年）》，该专业属于高等职业教育中的旅游大类、旅游类，专业代码为 640101。该专业与中等职业教育衔接的专业为"旅游服务与管理专业"，与本科教育衔接的专业为"旅游管理专业"

Brief Description on the Type of Accreditation Received by the Programme

本项目申请获得的认证类型为三年期有效的旅游教育质量认证

II. INFORMATION BY AREA OF ANALYSIS

Area of Analysis

Part I The Employers : Public and Private Sector

表3-2

1.1 INCLUSION OF THE EMPLOYERS NEEDS IN DEFINING THE MISSION, ACTION PLAN AND CURRICULUM CONTENT	
1.1 a) Mission 使命	G 学院是国家示范性骨干高职院校，学校发展的目标是成为国内一流、世界知名的高等职业学校。同时，G 学院是广东省唯一的"互联网＋"创新创业示范校，具有极强的科技特色。旅游管理专业作为首批广东省品牌专业建设点和十三个省级二类品牌专业之一，是 G 学院办学特色的具体体现。 　　我们将旅游管理专业的使命确定为，培养具有熟练的旅游实践能力和英语应用能力、适应广东省和粤港澳大湾区旅游业需要的高素质涉外旅游技能型人才
1.1 a) Mission 使命	G 学院专业就业岗位群：①旅行社岗位群，包括旅行社导游、计调、销售、会议等部门中高级服务员和经营管理人员；②酒店岗位群，包括前厅、客房、餐厅、销售、康体、娱乐、会议等部门的中高级服务员和经营管理人员；③其他旅游企业岗位群，包括国际邮轮公司、旅游运输公司、景区景点、餐饮企业、度假区、会展公司及其他旅游相关企业的从事服务、策划、销售、经营管理的中高级服务员和经营管理人员
1.1 b) Action Plan 行动计划	G 学院旅游管理专业建立在中国著名的旅游城市——珠海，珠海位于中国倾力打造的粤港澳大湾区范围内，粤港澳大湾区被称为世界四大湾区之一，是能够与东京湾区、旧金山湾区、纽约湾区并称的世界级湾区。随着中国经济发展水平的提升，人均可支配收入持续增长，社会公众对于旅游提出了更高的要求。本专业在设立之前，深入调研了国内不同收入水平人群的旅游需求，乘着粤港澳大湾区高端酒店业迅猛发展的东风，加上游客对国际邮轮项目的关注增多，结合地方经济发展特色，特别是珠海市发展"三高一特"（高端制造业、高新技术产业、高端服务业、特色海洋经济和生态农业）产业中提到的现代服务业要求，将开办旅游管理专业作为满足解决人民日益增长的美好生活需要和不平衡不充分发展之间的矛盾的重要手段，将办好、办强旅游管理专业作为服务地方经济增长的支撑力量。 　　企业需求调研（包括问卷调研）是在充分调研的基础上，征求企业（潜在的雇主）等各方的意见和建议，编制、修改和完善人才培养方案，并制定课程标准；成立校企合作理事会，发挥企业在人才培养和专业建设中的作用；人才培养的企业满意度调查（毕业生跟踪调查和用人单位满意度调查）等

1.1 INCLUSION OF THE EMPLOYERS NEEDS IN DEFINING THE MISSION, ACTION PLAN AND CURRICULUM CONTENT	
1.1 b) Action Plan 行动计划	旅游管理专业将办学立足点确定为，依托粤港澳大湾区培养具有熟练的旅游实践能力和英语交际能力高素质涉外旅游技能型人才。为将办学理念真正落到实处，旅游管理专业不断通过内引外联凸显办学特色，不仅吸引相关旅游企业参与人才培养方案、课程标准、实训室的建设，同时与企业合作建立现代学徒制试点班和企业订单制培养班。旅游企业作为人才培养的重要主体，参与旅游管理专业人才的培养，可以使旅游管理专业培养的人才更加适应企业岗位需求，人才培养多少、如何培养、培养到什么程度可根据企业的需求来决定。以上做法可以最大限度地满足旅游企业用人需求，缩短旅游企业人力资源培育周期，节约企业人力资源成本，增加企业效益，深受企业欢迎
1.1 c) Curriculum content 课程内容	旅游管理专业力争实现优良的人才培养效果，为国家经济发展输送更多人才，特制定了人才培养方案修订的基本原则，即"三年一大改，每年一小改"，紧密结合社会经济发展形势来设计人才培养方案。目前旅游管理专业所使用的人才培养方案为 2016 年版（适用于 2016、2017 级学生）。旅游管理专业注重与本地区大型旅游集团长隆集团合作，与本地区外国品牌酒店珠海万豪、珠海喜来登、深圳 JW 万豪等酒店，与本地区龙头旅行社广之旅、南湖国旅、珠海拱北口岸中旅、深圳宝安中旅等企业，以及香港云顶邮轮集团合作，为之培养合格人才。在人才培养过程中，本专业注重收集各个用人单位对于学生的满意度调查数据，根据企业反馈结果及时进行每年度的人才培养方案修订工作，为每三年一次的人才培养方案较大调整积累基础数据，使人才培养方案的修订能够紧跟社会经济发展趋势，紧跟企业用工需求，最大限度地为企业考虑、为学生考虑、为旅游业可持续发展考虑。在 2020 年人才培养方案的执行过程中，旅游管理专业通过举办"旅游企业运营与旅游行业发展"研讨会、开拓新的实训就业市场等活动，与用人企业进行了深入研讨，为人才培养方案的修订打下了坚实的基础，能够保障人才培养工作高质量完成。下表为部分专业核心课程简介，具体的人才培养方案及开课进度表见佐证材料

续　表

1.1 INCLUSION OF THE EMPLOYERS NEEDS IN DEFINING THE MISSION, ACTION PLAN AND CURRICULUM CONTENT				
	专业核心课程简介			
	课程名称	主要教学内容	技能考核项目与要求	参考学时/学分
1.1c) Curriculum content 课程内容	导游业务	（1）如何成为导游人员；（2）认识导游服务；（3）完成团队带团；（4）完成散客带团；（5）处理与预防突发事件；（6）应对游客个别要求；（7）导游人员的带团技能；（8）导游综合知识讲座	（1）能灵活运用导游服务的原则和规范为游客提供规范化和个性化的地陪、全陪导游服务。（2）熟悉突发事件处理程序和方法，能有效防范突发事件产生。（3）熟悉处理个别要求的基本原则和方法，并能灵活运用	54学时/3学分
	前厅与客房管理	（1）预订服务；（2）礼宾服务；（3）接待服务；（4）商务中心与总机服务；（5）客房对客服务；（6）客房的清洁保养；（7）宾客关系管理	（1）能够正确使用前厅设备，进行预订服务、散客/团体行李寄存和提取服务、客人入住登记和结账服务、电话问讯和留言服务	68学时/4学分
	前厅与客房管理	（8）客房的安全、物资、人力资源管理；（9）前厅与客房服务技能实训	（2）能够按服务标准为客人提供迎送、送餐、访客、擦鞋、小酒吧等服务，处理客人遗留物品；（3）具备中式/西式铺床技能，熟悉清扫客房的程序和方法；（4）掌握客人投诉的原因及处理方法，能够灵活处理客人投诉；（5）能够进行客房消防、财务安全的预防和应急处理，了解客房员工存在的职业安全问题，了解客房设备、用品、布件管理的方法	68学时/4学分

续 表

1.1 INCLUSION OF THE EMPLOYERS NEEDS IN DEFINING THE MISSION, ACTION PLAN AND CURRICULUM CONTENT				
1.1c) Curriculum content 课程内容	餐饮运行与管理	（1）构建餐饮管理体系； （2）控制餐饮服务现场； （3）筹划与设计菜单； （4）策划餐饮促销活动； （5）控制餐饮成本； （6）采购与验收食品原料； （7）控制餐饮服务质量； （8）餐厅服务技能实训	（1）能根据餐饮企业的规模设计其组织机构和人员配置； （2）能够制定中西餐零点、宴会、管事服务员工作流程及标准； （3）能够应用食品营养知识设计菜谱，完成一份完整菜单设计； （4）能够进行菜肴的销售分析和盈利分析，完成一份主题餐饮营销策划方案的撰写； （5）能制定餐厅收银员工作流程及标准，填写餐饮营业日报表，对关键环节提出成本控制思路； （6）能够准确评估供应商，了解食品原料质量标准，完成一次完整的原料采购与验收，提出食品采购成本控制的合理化建议（7）能用科学的方法全面评估餐饮服务质量，处理客人投诉； （8）能够开展中西餐的托盘、餐巾折花、摆台、点菜、上菜、分菜、斟茶、斟酒、撤换餐具、结账、迎送客人等服务	8学时／4学分
	导游英语	（1）广东概览； （2）中山纪念堂和陈家祠； （3）深圳中国民俗文化村； （4）珠海渔女； （5）佛山祖庙； （6）梅州客家围屋； （7）丹霞山； （8）潮州菜； （9）鼎湖山和七星岩； （10）开平碉楼	（1）能够用英语解说和评价旅游景点； （2）能够撰写广东省主要景点英语导游词	68学时／4学分

续　表

1.1 INCLUSION OF THE EMPLOYERS NEEDS IN DEFINING THE MISSION, ACTION PLAN AND CURRICULUM CONTENT			
1.1c) Curriculum content 课程内容	旅行社经营与管理	（1）旅行社组织构造；（2）旅行社的设立；（3）旅行社产品设计与开发；（4）旅行社产品销售；（5）旅行社计调管理；（6）旅行社人力资源管理	（1）熟练掌握国际国内旅行社的设立流程；（2）能够设计旅游线路，熟练掌握旅游产品的开发的各个环节，并结合该产品的特点，运用相关营销理论，制定适合的营销方案；（3）通过模拟操作，熟练掌握旅行社计调、外联等工作相关内容	68学时/4学分
	旅游市场营销	（1）旅游景区营销与策划；（2）旅游酒店营销与策划；（3）旅游交通企业营销与策划；（4）旅行社营销与策划	（1）具有独立运用科学方法进行旅游市场调研的能力；（2）具有采集使用信息、分析归纳、总结交流经验、技能、技巧的能力；（3）具有将旅游市场营销理论与实践经验结合运用的能力	68学时/4学分

1.2 ADAPTATION OF THE PROGRAMME TO NEW TRENDS AND REQUIREMENTS OF THE EMPLOYERS	
1.2 a)Existence of Monitoring Mechanisms to Assess Needs 已有的管理机制	旅游管理专业经过精心筹备，成立了专业指导委员会，由国内旅游领域权威专家组成，具体组成名单包括柯先生（珠海市旅游总会秘书长）、刘先生（珠海市文体旅游局主任）、李女士（珠海海湾大酒店人事主管）、李先生（广东省拱北口岸中国旅行社培训部经理）、王女士（珠海度假村酒店培训部经理）、杨先生（广东省拱北口岸中国旅行社高级经理）。专业建设指导委员会的成立，一方面有利于人才培养目标符合广东省及珠海市的地方经济发展需求，另一方面用工企业代表的参与可以使学校教学过程更加符合企业实际需要，使人才培养工作真正落到实处。

续　表

1.2 ADAPTATION OF THE PROGRAMME TO NEW TRENDS AND REQUIREMENTS OF THE EMPLOYERS	
1.2 a)Existence of Monitoring Mechanisms to Assess Needs 已有的管理机制	旅游管理专业建设指导委员会的建立，真正实现了旅游管理专业人才培养的政校行企协同育人，摆脱了传统的专业封闭办学模式，通过专业建设指导委员会的有力协调，可以更加便捷地实现政校行企资源的有效整合，有利于为旅游管理专业人才培养设置较高的起点，有利于利用多种资源开展旅游管理专业人才培养工作，有利于从根本上保障人才培养质量，有利于利用政校行企资源不断拓展学生就业出口，实现旅游管理专业毕业生好就业、就好业。专业建设指导委员会指导下的现代学徒制试点班的开设，有利于从根本上改变大学院独自办学的困境，使企业真正融入人才培养的全过程，学生入学、学生毕业完全是按照企业选人、用人标准来进行衡量，学生学业过程由学校与企业共同负责，企业可以完全按照真实工作需求来合理安排人才培养方案及课程设置等。以上多种做法的共同使用，从根本上确保了旅游管理专业人才培养的高质量、高规格。 （1）针对旅游企业不断变化的用人需求，旅游管理专业立足专业人才培养现状，认真总结、提炼现代学徒制试点班及企业订单班的经验教训，注重认真捕捉旅游企业不同需求，有针对性地开发一些特色课程。比如，针对旅游企业新的运营电商平台及微信公众号运营工作需求，在课程设置上开发特色旅游电商平台运营课程，设置微信公众号运营课程，培养学生软文的撰写、文案的策划能力，这些都是与传统的旅游人才培养不一致的地方，但恰恰是当前旅游企业所急需的
1.2 b）Adjustment Actions 改进措施	（2）旅游管理专业将培养高端涉外导游作为专业实现跨越式发展的基本落脚点，包括高端涉外旅游实训室的打造，能够教授双语涉外旅游课程的师资准备，与境外高水平旅游管理学院联合培养应用型人才等工作都已经提上了日程，这一切的努力都是为了满足涉外旅游企业不断增长的高端旅游人才需求以及存量旅游人才的继续教育需求。旅游管理专业秉承一切服务于企业的办学宗旨，将企业迫切需要解决的问题当成专业发展突破的首要目标，与企业同呼吸、共命运，真正将服务地方经济发展与支撑企业转型升级落到实处。旅游管理专业努力与高端涉外旅游企业构建命运共同体，通过人员互聘、资源互通等手段，树立中国高端涉外旅游人才培养的独特办学品牌，整合各方面资源，逐步建立中国顶尖、世界闻名的旅游人才培养基地

1.2 ADAPTATION OF THE PROGRAMME TO NEW TRENDS AND REQUIREMENTS OF THE EMPLOYERS	
1.2 b）Adjustment Actions 改进措施	（3）本专业根据"互联网+"的发展趋势，建设旅游信息化实训室，加强旅游电子商务实训教学；鼓励学生参加"互联网+"创新创业大赛。本专业根据中国邮轮市场的变化，开设了邮轮服务与管理、邮轮英语等课程；加强创新创业教育，培养创新创业人才

Area of Analysis

Part II The Student

表3-3

2.1 COMMUNICATION AND PROMOTION OF THE PROGRAMME （BEFORE AND DURING THE ADMISSION PROCESS） 学生入学前的交流与推广

2.1.1 旅游管理专业学生入学选拔方式

旅游管理专业学生当前的入学选拔主要通过两种方式：一种是每年的全国统一的普通高考，通过全省统一的高考分数线进行录取选拔；另一种是学校自主招生进行选拔，通过学校出题进行笔试和面试，有针对性选拔，选拔出更多更适合本专业发展的学生。

2.1.2 旅游管理专业学生构成

旅游管理专业的学生除了普高学生外，每年会录取一定比例的中职学生。为了录取到更加优秀的中职学生，在每年招生录取前学院都会派出教师前往合作的或优秀的中职院校进行洽谈，寻求更多的合作，并且在相关学校进行宣传，通过制度和宣讲吸引更多的优秀学生。目前从中职招收具有3+证书和通过自主招生的学生，每年的中职招生计划在不断扩大，从2004年起即开始招收中职学生，近几年中职学生占全部学生的40%~50%。从2015年开始，旅游管理专业开始招收学徒制学生。

2.1.3 旅游管理专业学生入学录取条件和流程

招生录取执行教育部规定的"学校负责，招办监督"的录取要求，招生录取严格遵守教育部、省招生办公室的有关政策和规定，以考生高考成绩为基本依据，本着公平、公正、公开的原则，综合衡量德智体美各方面，择优录取。在省招生委员会划定的录取最低控制分数线上，在保证完成招生计划的前提下，制定具体录取标准，按照理科类、文科类、美术类、体育类、高职"3+证书"（含退役士兵）类、以普通高中学业水平考试成绩为录取依据的高职分类考试招生，进行分类录取。广东省普通高中毕业生，高中学业水平考试等级成绩须符合《关于印发<广东省普通高校招生考试改革调整方案>的通知》（粤教考〔2008〕28号）的要求。

在广东省，报考普通高考、以普通高中学业水平考试成绩为录取依据的高职分类考试招生文科类、理科类的高中毕业生，物理、化学、生物或政治、地理、历史三门学业水平考试均须获得等级成绩，且至少有一门达到C级及以上等级。报考普通高考美术类、体育类的高中毕业生，物理、化学、生物或政治、地理、历史三门学业水平考试成绩至少有两门达到D级及以上等级

续　表

2.1 COMMUNICATION AND PROMOTION OF THE PROGRAMME (BEFORE AND DURING THE ADMISSION PROCESS) 学生入学前的交流与推广

文科类、理科类专业采取"分数优先"的原则，按照分数由高到低的顺序，优先录取分数排在前面的考生，再录取分数排在后面的考生。高考文化课成绩相同时，依据各省的排名方法按顺序录取。在安排专业时，要参考考生填报的专业志愿顺序进行安排。当考生填报的专业志愿都未被录取时，若考生服从专业调剂，调剂到未满额专业，若拒不服从专业调剂，做退档处理。

"3+ 证书"类（含退役士兵）专业采取"志愿优先"的原则，先录取第一志愿填报 G 学院校旅游管理专业的进档考生，如未完成招生计划，再录取第二志愿填报的进档考生，依此类推。专业录取按"专业志愿优先"原则

2.1.4 与学生及其家长的交流活动

在每年招生前，旅游管理专业会派出教师参加高校与家长的专场交流会，让更多家长了解学校和专业。在招生简章中会详细介绍各专业的培养目标、课程设置、师资力量、教学规划以及收取费用，让学生清晰了解所学专业的基本情况，以便做出正确的专业选择。

在学生报到当天，各学院会安排专门的教师和场地给有疑问的家长，介绍专业基本情况和学生在校学习和生活的基本情况，从多角度增加与家长的交流机会。

过去三年期间，旅游管理专业的交流活动在不断完善和进步，得到了学校、家长、学生的认可，保证了学生在入校前和入校后充分了解自己的专业。

2.1.5 学生录取前的课程、师资准备以及费用计划

在学生入校前，各专业均已完善专业教学计划和课程教学进度表，每三年调整一次，保证教学计划根据学生和社会发展的需求变化而进行变化，现在最新版的教学计划是2016 版旅游管理专业教学计划。旅游管理专业师资充足，结构合理，能较好完成教学任务。旅游管理专业的学费按照学校统一规定进行收取

续　表

| 2.2 INTRODUCTION OF THE STUDENTS IN THE PROGRAMME (POST ADMISSION) |

旅游管理专业近五年每年录取人数为 200 人左右，并从 2015 年开始招收学徒制学生。具体数据见下表。

2004—2017 级旅游管理专业招生录取学生情况

年级	专业	录取总人数	职高人数	普高人数
04 级	旅游管理	200	100	100
05 级	旅游管理	180	90	90
06 级	旅游管理	180	90	90
07 级	旅游管理	210	105	105
08 级	旅游管理	300	150	150
09 级	旅游管理	200	100	100
10 级	旅游管理	180	90	90
11 级	旅游管理	220	110	110
12 级	旅游管理	219	100	119
13 级	旅游管理	210	90	120
14 级	旅游管理	217	90	127
15 级	旅游管理	236（含学徒制）	100	136
16 级	旅游管理	240（含学徒制）	100	140
17 级	旅游管理	240（含学徒制）	100	140
18 级	旅游管理	200（含学徒制）	100	100
19 级	旅游管理	230（含学徒制）	100	130
20 级	旅游管理	230（含学徒制）	100	130

近五年对职高和普高学生对比，可以发现这两类学生有一些不同的特点。职高学生因为在高中阶段就开始接触专业，对专业和职业的认知度更高，入学前职高生普遍已考取职业资格证书，进入 G 学院后，在专业课程的学习上更容易接受，特别是实操课和技能大赛，优势更明显，不过在英语学习上有一定的劣势，基础比较薄弱。普高学生理论基础扎实，英语水平相对更高，有一定优势，不过对职业的认识还处于空白阶段，实操能力较弱。

学生在入学之初，会由专业主任对其进行入学教育，包括专业概况、课程介绍、就业岗位、职业精神和素养、专业教师团队等，为学生打下基础，同时邀请往届优秀师兄师姐回校与新生交流，邀请业界专业人士对新生进行专业认知教育

2.3 ATTENTION GIVEN TO STUDENTS' NEEDS ——ADMINISTRATIVE, ACADEMIC, SOCIAL WELFARE AND CURRICULUM SUPPORT 学院在管理、学术、福利和课程支持等方面对学生的关注

2.3.1 管理方面的关注

学院关注学生的成长，在行政方面充分考虑学生的现状，为学生提供个性化的服务和帮助。学院行政办公室和辅导员办公室在工作日一直为学生开放，可以为学生办理各种相关事宜。办公室配置勤工俭学同学，随时帮忙处理学生提出的各种问题。学生的学业成绩包括平时成绩和期末考核成绩，由专业教师出题并进行评定，录入成绩系统，学生通过个人账号查询，如果对成绩有异议可以书面提出成绩核对请求。

2.3.2 学术方面的关注

学生在校期间，学院会安排不定期的专家讲座、企业宣讲、校内专题活动等，学生根据自己专业所需进行选择。学院协助学生拓展知识面，提供更多企业实习岗位。专业教师会加入各班级微信群和 QQ 群，对学生在校期间的各种问题进行解答和帮助。

2.3.3 学生福利方面的关注

在校期间，学习成绩优异、德智体美劳全面发展的学生可以申请国家奖学金、国家励志奖学金，学校还设立了"优秀学生""优秀学生干部"等综合奖学金，"学习优秀奖""创作成果奖""文体活动奖""考级考证优秀奖""精神文明奖""学习进步奖""优秀学生活动组织奖"七项单项奖励。特困生可以申请国家助学贷款和国家助学金。学校也设立了贫困学生助学金，根据学生不同经济状况，分甲、乙、丙三个等级，助学金额为 1000～2000 元/学年。学校设立了勤工助学管理中心，为在校大学生提供勤工助学岗位。学校配备专门的管理部门和老师负责。每年学校学生处发出通知，学院辅导员办公室组织和材料收集，各班班主任实施，收集学生资料，审核并进行申报。近五年，每年均有15%到20%的学生受到奖励或者补助，保证优秀的学生得到奖励，家庭困难的学生得到资助或者助学贷款，助学贷款覆盖所有有困难且提出申请的学生，确保学生顺利完成学业。

2.3.4 课程方面的关注

旅游管理专业在设置课程时充分考虑到学生的自身特点和学科发展的系统性，融入学生的职业核心能力，为学生综合素质的提高、专业技能的提升以及可持续发展打下基础。专业课程的设置充分考虑到市场的需求以及学科发展的需求，旅游管理专业的课程计划分为五大模块，包括综合素质课、专业基础课、专业核心课、专业综合实践、专业拓展等，具体设计关注学生的个体需求和专业发展的需求

续 表

2.4 ASSESSMENT OF THE STUDENT'S PERFORMANCE
对学生表现的评估

教师对于学生学业的综合评价，不同的课程评价方法也不尽相同。实训课程主要通过考查学生的技能掌握情况来给予学生学业的评价，通常体现在期末的技能测试及平时的技能学习及实践情况中；理论课程主要通过期末考试和平时表现来对学生进行综合评价。理论课教师对于期末考试题的题型包括主观题和客观题，给学生的答题时间一般是90分钟到120分钟，考查学生对于基本专业理论知识的掌握情况。理论课平时成绩主要通过学生在日常学习中的课堂出勤、课堂表现（包括课堂纪律、课堂回答问题、课堂讨论等）、学生作业等综合给出。学生通过理论课和实训课等各专业课的学习，基本理解了本专业需要的理论知识，基本掌握了本专业需要的专业技能，为学生今后从事旅游行业储备了丰富的专业知识及岗位技能。这具体表现为，学生的理论课程的学业成绩绝大部分及格，极少部分学生有不及格现象，不及格的学生通过学期补考后基本上都通过了考试，学期的最终学业成绩达到合格；学生绝大部分通过了实训课程的技能测试，学业成绩为合格。同时，学生通过校企合作企业顶岗实习，对于实际工作岗位中要求的技能也进一步熟练和掌握，能够直接为企业创造经济效益。学校要求每位学生在毕业前都至少要有一个技能证书，所以每一位旅游管理专业的学生在校期间都通过了包括导游证等在内的一项技能证书，为学生的就业提供了帮助。相当一部分学生在校期间通过了大学英语四级考试，还有一部分学生通过自己的努力通过了大学英语六级考试，为自己职业国际化发展创造了条件。针对目前社会职业岗位要求从业人员熟练操作计算机办公软件的现状，旅游管理专业的学生在校期间积极参加大学生计算机等级考试，取得计算机等级证书。课余期间，学生积极投身于各种学生社团工作，比如酒店协会、导游协会等。各社团除了组织各项校级技能大赛，比如酒店技能大赛、导游技能大赛等以外，还加强与酒店和旅行社的联系，增强对实际工作岗位的了解。学生的社团活动丰富了学生的业余生活，也提供给学生一个锻炼自己各方面能力的平台。学院每年举办校级酒店技能大赛、中英文导游技能大赛及茶艺比赛，选拔出优秀者参加省级和全国级的比赛，取得了一系列优异的成绩，有学生还因在省级导游比赛中的优异表现获得省劳动奖章。近年来，在全国级和省级大赛中旅游管理专业的学生获得了全国一等奖及省级一等奖等一系列优异的成绩

2.5　EVALUATION OF STUDENTS' SATISFACTION LEVEL REGARDING THE PROGRAMME AND ADDITIONAL SERVICES 学生对本专业以及其他服务的满意度评价
学校针对学生的课程学习制定了一系列的政策，针对学生课堂出勤设置了 APP 考勤助手，监督学生的上课出勤情况。学生请事假和病假都有严格的请假程序。这一管理程序和方法监督了学生的课堂出勤，督促了学生的上课和学习。同时，学校设置了学生最满意课程奖，体现学生对于课程教学的督促和评价。教师的教学水平也越来越高。学期进行过程中设有学生座谈会，教师了解学生对于相关课程的意见和建议，然后针对这些意见和建议提出整改方案。每一学期期末都有学生评教环节，评价指标共有 12 项，并设置有学生评语汇总，体现学生的满意度详情，学生对于绝大部分教师的教学方法都是满意的。学校针对优秀的教师还设置有教学优秀奖，鼓励教师积极探索教学方法。部分学生在校期间也会利用课余时对于学校的学习和生活环境，学生是满意的。比如，教室里都安装了空调，改善了学生上课的环境，有利于学生在天气炎热的夏天能够安心学习；学校食堂重新进行了装修，学生的就餐环境得到了很大的改善；整个校园都有免费的无线网络，便于师生随时随地上网，加快了信息交流的速度。间兼职，比如带团等，可以学以致用，也体现了学生对学院和对专业的认同感。 　　对于学校的学习和生活环境，学生是满意的。比如，教室里都安装了空调，改善了学生上课的环境，有利于学生在天气炎热的夏天能够安心学习；学校食堂重新进行了装修，学生的就餐环境得到了很大的改善；整个校园都有免费的无线网络，便于师生随时随地上网，加快了信息交流的速度。
2.6 FOLLOW-UP OF GRADUATED STUDENTS 对毕业生的跟踪调查
学校设置校友会，专门负责与校友进行联络等各项工作。学校每年针对毕业生都有一系列的跟踪调查材料，其中涉及毕业生的工资情况、毕业生的岗位与专业对口率及用人单位满意度等相关信息。除此之外，学校和学院还会定期邀请毕业生回校座谈，其中优秀毕业生还会被邀请为在校师生做出报告，从而跟踪和了解毕业生毕业后的一些情况。 　　针对在校生，学校还有辅助在校生就业的一系列政策和举措，设置了专门的招生就业处，负责学生的就业指导工作，在学生课程中也专门设置了就业指导课程，针对学生的就业进行全方位的指导。同时为了鼓励大学生创业，学校也有一系列的政策和举措，包括创新创业课程的设置、学校创新创业学院的成立，还积极组织学生参加国家和省级的各项创新创业大赛，积极传达国家和广东省对于大学生创业的一系列优惠政策。 　　目前本专业毕业生中有 40 多人在中国知名旅行社、广东省拱北口岸中国旅行社就业，有 90 多人在知名景点珠海长隆旅游度假区工作，还有数百人在广东省多家旅行社、国际品牌酒店、会展公司、外贸公司以及其他旅游公司工作

Area of Analysis

Part III The Curriculum and Pedagogical System

表3-4

3.1 METHODOLOGY USED TO FORMULATE THE CURRICULUM 课程体系整体设计的方法

3.1.1 人才培养目标

本专业以服务珠江三角洲和广东省经济社会发展为宗旨，培养德智体美劳全面发展，掌握旅游文化、旅游服务与管理的基础知识，具有熟练的旅游服务操作技能，具备较强的外语交际能力、经营管理能力和开拓创新能力，拥有良好的职业道德和诚信品质，面向酒店、旅行社、景点景区等旅游企业，适应旅游行业前厅、餐厅、客房、销售、计调、导游、督导管理等岗位需要的高素质技术技能型人才。

3.1.2 课程体系设计

（1）课程设计思路。以"宽口径、厚基础、强技能、高素质"为人才培养目标，以学生为本，以素质教育为主线，以建立符合学生认知规律和知识结构的体系、内容为重点，以加强实践实训教学、改革教学模式为手段，以建立科学规范的教学评价为尺度，以产学研一体化合作为切入点，加强专业课程建设，全面推进各课程的持续均衡发展。

（2）课程总体结构。旅游管理专业三年课程共计2 637学时，131学分。从纵向结构上来看，其分为综合素质课程（必修）、综合素质课程（选修）、专业课程必修模块（含专业基础、专业核心和专业综合性实践）、专业拓展课程模块四大模块。在本专业课程结构设置中，大学一年级设置通识教育课程和专业基础课程，二、三年级开设专业核心课程、专业实践课及专业拓展课。四大模块学分别占总学分的14.5%、3.8%、64.9%、16.8%。从横向结构上来看，专业必修课程共计85学分，其中，专业基础课、专业核心课和专业综合性实践课分别占37.6%、27.1%和35.3%。从课时分配上来看，实践课时达到总课时的一半以上，为56.9%，理论课时为43.1%。

（3）核心课程架构。重视专业核心能力的培养，专业核心课程共6门，合计394学时，覆盖旅行社及酒店两大主要目标就业行业领域。除导游业务考证课程外，其余均设置在大二学年，为提升学生的涉外旅游、跨文化交际能力，第四学期开设导游英语课程。

课程名称	学时	学分	开设学期
导游业务	54	3	二
前厅与客房管理	68	4	三
餐饮运行与管理	68	4	三
导游英语	68	4	四
旅行社经营与管理	68	4	四
旅游市场营销	68	4	四

3.1 METHODOLOGY USED TO FORMULATE THE CURRICULUM 课程体系整体设计的方法
3.1.3 课程方法制定 　　专业课程方法的制定上，首先，紧紧围绕"培养学生的什么能力，用什么样的课程培养学生的能力"这条主线开展广泛调研。调研对象包括：行业企业、校内教师、同类院校教师、在校生等。其次，通过调研找准本专业的目标就业岗位，对岗位展开深入剖析，提炼典型工作任务。最后，分析完成典型工作任务的知识、技能和素质，组合为课程。 　　同时，本专业还在每年12月份召开旅游类专业政校行企专家座谈会，就人才培养方案中的培养方向与培养目标、核心能力和课程设置等各个方面征求专家意见和建议。在经过前期调研、中期座谈研讨后，拟出人才培养方案和课程体系初稿，召集校企专家委员会探讨和论证，进行修订和完善，以求科学合理。 **3.1.4 课程计划实施** 　　学生6个学期中在校时间为4.5个学期，顶岗实习（含毕业设计）1.5个学期。 　　具体实施计划：制定专业课程课程标准—制订开课计划—选订教材—制订与填写教学日历—准备教案与课件—教师授课与作业批改—导听课与意见反馈—教师个人教学反思—课程小组教研讨论
3.2 CURRICULUM COHERENCE 课程的连贯性
3.2.1 本专业课程设置的连贯性 　　第一学年即第一、第二学期，主要为通识课程和基础课程，如综合英语课程、旅游概论课、导游考证课；第二学年即第三、第四学期，重点开设几门专业核心课程，如第三学期开设酒店方向专业能力课和专业英语课，为参加酒店类职业技能比赛做准备，第四学期开设旅行社方向专业能力课、导游专业英语课、旅游市场营销课、拓展课；第三学年即第五、第六学期，主要开设拓展课和顶岗实习。 　　三年的课程设置中，英语课贯穿始终，以满足涉外旅游及跨文化交际的需求。在课程的设置上，基于学生职业能力的培养，基础课程、专业核心课程、专业实践课及拓展课的开设循序渐进，前导和后续课程、同期课程的设置要合理，课程的连贯性强。 **3.2.2 中高职课程衔接的有序性及连贯性** 　　2015年，旅游管理专业成为面向往届中职或普通高职毕业生的现代学徒制试点专业。同年9月，G学院与深圳华强职业技术学校签订旅游类专业三二分段对接协议，并就中高职人才培养方案的对接进行了深入探讨，分析并厘清中职、高职旅游类专业各自面向的岗位（群）所需的知识、能力和素质要求，并确定中职、高职各自的人才培养目标定位。 　　基于中职、高职的知识、能力和素质分析，归纳课程，编写和完善课程标准，构建中高职旅游类专业相互衔接的一体化课程体系，编写中职、高职旅游类专业人才培养方案。在这个方面，旅游管理专业负责人万方秋老师带领专业团队教师成功申报2016年广东省教改课题——"基于职业标准的中高职旅游类专业一体化课程体系的构建"并进行研究。研究指出，高职课程的知识、能力、素质等在中职的基础上有较大的增量，呈现纵向延伸和横向扩展，即中职是基础，高职是提升，避免中职、高职部分专业课和实践课重复的情况，构建有效衔接的课程体系，提高中职、高职院校人才培养的质量和效益，并增强高职院校对中职学生的吸引力

3.3 EFFECTIVENESS OF THE PEDAGOGICAL METHOD 教学方法的有效性

3.3.1 合适的教学理念

（1）工作过程导向教学理念在本专业中的运用。高职教育应重视学生校内学习与实际工作的一致性，探索课堂与实习地点的一体化，积极推行订单培养，探索工学交替、任务驱动、项目导向等有利于增强学生能力的教学模式。这就要求高职院校教师在课程设计时必须从本课程培养学生所达到的相关技能目标出发，结合实际工作岗位，将工作过程分解成一个个工作任务，每项任务完成一个目标，最终使学生在完成工作流程的同时，掌握此工作岗位所要求具备的能力和素质。

旅游管理专业多位教师在课程改革中运用了工作过程教学理念。例如：郭卫娜、段金梅、冯淑玲、吴迪等老师多年来运用工作过程理论开展教学，结合酒店、旅行社实际工作岗位及岗位群对能力的要求，对岗位分解、课程的整合有了新的认识和思考。其中，郭卫娜老师发表了《基于工作过程的＜旅行社经营与管理＞课程改革与实践》等相关课程论文。

（2）成果导向教学理念在本专业中的运用。为了更好地应对现代科学技术对高等教育带来的挑战，本专业部分教师尝试采用成果导向教学理念去解决"培养什么样的人"以及"如何培养人"的现实问题。成果导向的教育理念以目标为导向，从专业需求出发，制定培养目标、考核要求以及课程体系，在最大程度上保证教育目标和结果的一致性。

在旅游管理专业课堂教学中，部分教师尝试结合成果导向教学理念进行教学改革，以学生的专业需求和实际情况为出发点，制定合理的教学方案，创新教学方式，丰富教学内容，使学生在学习过程中能充分理解和运用专业知识理论，提高自己的专业技能和学习能力。

在本教学理念的运用方面，旅游专业朱瀚老师在旅游管理专业基础英语课程实践中进行教学改革，并在 2015 年申报立项广东省教改项目"以成果为导向的课程机制在高职高专教学中的应用——以大学英语课程教学改革为例"，杨易老师申报校级教改项目为"基于 WPO 与 OBE 课程改革比较研究的酒店英语课程设计"。

3.3.2 教学方法的多样化和有效性

旅游管理专业的课程建设强调师生互动，充分调动学生的积极性、主动性和创造性。根据不同的教学目标、教学内容、教学对象，因材施教，传统教学方式，采用任务驱动、项目教学、小组作业、案例分析、角色扮演、实地调研等多种生动活泼的教学方法，努力培养学生获取知识的能力以及分析问题、解决问题和创造性思维的能力。

（1）信息化教学的推广和运用。本专业各课程小组应以有利于提高教学效果为原则，不断加强教学手段现代化的建设，积极推动信息技术在教学活动中的普遍运用。在信息化教学手段上，除了进行多媒体授课、多信息手段与学生进行课程交流外，旅游管理专业专任教师还就自己的专业领域和授课课程，积极申报和开发在线课程和微课课程，共立项校级在线开放课程 9 门，校级微课 1 门。专业教师积极提升自身信息化教学水平，各门在线开放课程均在积极建设中。逐步实现使用网络进行教学与管理，将相关的教学大纲、教案、习题、实验指导、参考资料等上传到课程网站，实现优质教学资源共享，带动课程建设，使其不断进步。此外，专业教师积极参加全省、全国信息化教学大赛。如：苏丹老师获得"第一中国外语微课大赛"广东省赛区二等奖，全国职业院校信息化教学大赛高职组信息化教学设计三等奖

3.3 EFFECTIVENESS OF THE PEDAGOGICAL METHOD 教学方法的有效性

（2）任务驱动、项目导向教学法。旅游管理专业多位教师在课程改革中运用了工作过程教学理念，采用任务驱动、项目导向的教学方法。强调以真实的案例、真实的任务来设计综合实训，努力做到理论教学与实践教学对接，实训环节与工作环境对接，素质培养与岗位素质要求对接。如理实一体化课程"旅行社经营管理""导游业务""旅行社计调实务""旅游市场营销"等，综合性实训课程"模拟导游""餐厅服务技能实训"等。如冯淑玲老师在"模拟导游"课程教学中，针对旅游职业岗位职能与素质，结合珠三角地区旅游业发展的实际情况与特点来设计课程内容，注重学生职业道德、讲解能力、应变技巧、带团规范、心理素质等方面的培养，以项目为导向、以任务来驱动，依托导游带团实际流程来设计课程，以研学旅行的方式实现教学目的，发表了《<模拟导游>课程研学旅行的探索与实践》一文。

（3）案例分析、角色扮演、实地调研等教学方法的运用。旅游管理专业课程的讲授应紧密联系行业发展动态，将调研收集的鲜活的行业案例运用到课堂中，让学生贴近行业企业一线。在"模拟导游""宴会设计""餐饮运行与管理"等课程中，教师或多方收集导游带团案例、宴会策划案例、餐饮业服务案例，或分小组扮演进行模拟导游、模拟餐厅服务员、迎宾员等角色，充分调动学生的动脑动手能力，活跃课堂气氛，提高学生的实践能力

3.4 EXISTENCE, ACCESS and USEFULNESS of the CURRICULUM SUPPORT FACILITIES 教学设施的建设、利用和效率

3.4 a) Infrastructure and pedagogical equipment 基础设施和教学设备	旅游管理专业已建成多间校内实训室，包括多媒体语言实验室 3 间，配置了相应的实训设备和配套软件；模拟导游实训室 1 间，面积 500 多平方米的综合性酒店实训中心（包括中餐厅、西餐厅、酒吧实训室、茶艺实训室、形体礼仪训练室等各 1 间），为学生的校内实习提供了保障。实训场地建设使用情况如下

续　表

3.4 EXISTENCE, ACCESS and USEFULNESS of the CURRICULUM SUPPORT FACILITIES 教学设施的建设、利用和效率								
3.4 a) Infrastructure and pedagogical equipment 基础设施和教学设备	序号	基本数据 实训室名称	地点	建筑面积（平方米）	工位数（个）	设备价值（万元）	设备情况	主要面向课程
	1	国际化双语职业人才培养基地	S4304	300	72	70	在用	旅游电子商务 办公自动化
	2	语音室	S1304	160	60	50.605	在用	酒店英语 情景英语
	3	语音室	S1303	240	75	44.518	在用	旅游英语
	4	语音室	S2503	173	70	60.824	在用	酒店英语
	5	形体礼仪实训室	S5304	150	50	14.097	在用	形体训练
	6	欧美文化体验室	S5306	170	80	6.8259	在用	旅游礼仪 演讲 情景英语
	7	模拟导游实训室	S2104	248	90	78.297	在用	旅游礼仪 模拟导游
	8	西餐厅实训室	S5301	110	50	4.790	在用	西餐实训
	9	酒店实训中心	S5302	240	50	27.044	在用	前厅实训 餐厅实训 调酒实训 茶艺实训
	10	化妆与形象设计实训室	C栋中厅	65	50	15.80	在用	化妆与形象设计
3.4 b) Infrastructure and equipment for pedagogical support and additional services 其他的教学设施设备及资源	近年来，学校加大了图书信息资建设的投入。馆藏文献现在以年增加10万册的速度稳步发展，每年订购中外文现刊及报纸1 350余种，引进了知网数据库、读秀数据库、超星电子图书数据库、方正Apabi电子图书数据库。目前，全馆入藏文献总量近16万册，其中纸质图书为105.43万册（包含过刊合订本18 239册，光盘28 313张），电子图书28万册，电子期刊折合图书14万册。在校生人均馆藏量近90册，基本形成了以中文纸质图书和外文原版纸质图书为主体，兼有电子期刊、电子图书、多媒体视听资源、自建特色数据库等数字资源，以及中外文期刊、中外文报纸共同组成的实体资源和虚拟资源相结合的馆藏文献资源，能较好地满足学生的学习需求							

3.4 EXISTENCE, ACCESS and USEFULNESS of the CURRICULUM SUPPORT FACILITIES 教学设施的建设、利用和效率	
3.4 c) Support measures for the safety and maintenance of pedagogical resources 教学设备及资源的管理及维护	实训室及实训设备实行学校工业中心、学院实训中心及专业三级管理制度。学校实训中心进行招标、采购等统一管理，学院进行日常运作及设备管理和维护，专门安排相关教师及勤工俭学学生负责专业器具的保养、耗材的登记管理及采购统计等，以保障日常教学的正常开展

Area of Analysis

Part IV The Faculty

表3-5

4.1 FACULTY SELECTION 师资选拔
学院旅游管理专业现有教师23人，其中女性15人，男性8人，均为中华人民共和国公民。其中，顾忆华、胡晓晶、郭卫娜等3位女教师任专业重要管理岗位。 师资选拔符合国家及专业要求，在2016年的最新一次教工招聘中，旅游管理专业对外招聘条件为硕士研究生及以上学历学位，职称讲师及以上，年龄40周岁以下，具有高等院校相应专业2年以上教学经验或在企业从事相应专业技术工作2年以上经验。所有招聘条件中均无性别、种族、宗教、政治倾向等歧视。 招考岗位按岗位要求，以面试形式执行，采取专业考核、思政测评及心理健康测评相结合的形式，具体细则如下： （1）专业考核：教师岗采取试讲及答辩的方式进行。其中试讲主要考核授课章节的组织与实施及授课效果。授课课程按专业自行准备，采用PPT授课模式讲授。本模块总分30分，设合格分数线21分，15分钟内完成；答辩主要考核教师的岗位任职能力及专业素养。由专业专家出具答辩题，现场答辩。本模块总分30分，设合格分数线21分，10分钟内完成。 （2）思政测评：考核政治思想水平及意识形态。由专业专家出具答辩题，现场答辩。本模块总分20分，设合格分数线16分，10分钟内完成。

续　表

4.1 FACULTY SELECTION 师资选拔

（3）心理健康测评：考核心理健康水平及状态。由专业专家出具答辩题，现场答辩。本模块总分20分，设合格分数线16分，10分钟内完成。

最终考核结果评分方式为各分项分值取平均分（小数点后2位且四舍五入），总分取各分项分的合计分。排名按总分从高到低依次排名。单项分未达合格线的取消考核成绩。

通过上述方式，外国语学院旅游管理专业在师资准入资格上把控严格，积极引进行业先进人才，注重学术水平与职业技能共同发展

4.2 ACADEMIC COORDINATION 学术协作

旅游管理专业以专业小组为核心，积极组织教师召开备课会议，集体研读课程标准和教材、分析学情、制订学科教学计划、分解备课任务、审定备课提纲、反馈教学实践信息。各任课教师根据集体备课的备课提纲和各班的学情，撰写教案，并发挥各人特长。

在课题的组织和研究上，专业教师段金梅主持并于2015年立项的珠海市哲学社会科学"十二五"规划2015—2016年度课题《珠海建设华南"会议之都"的策略研究》于2017年4月顺利结题，本专业的三名专任教师作为课题参与人提供了专业上的相关帮助。同样由段金梅老师主持的广东科学技术职业学院教学改革项目"高职旅游专业职业核心能力培养途径与课程建设研究"，也在专业教师的协助下正在紧锣密鼓地进行。周程明老师主持的珠海市社会科学"十二五"规划课题《珠海高校大学生对珠海旅游认知情况的调查与分析》于2016年在同专业的师资力量支持下顺利结题。

校企合作作为学校与企业建立的一种合作模式，能更有效地抓好教育质量，有针对性地为企业培养人才，注重人才的实用性与实效性。学校成立了"校企联合培养专业教师与校企互聘专业技术人员（教师）"工作领导小组，校长任组长，各教学部门负责人和相关职能部门负责人为成员。领导小组全面负责校企联合培养专业教师与校企互聘专业技术人员（教师）的组织管理与监督工作。根据校企协同育人改革要求，学院制定了一系列建设企业兼职教师队伍的文件，如《"校企互聘共培"教师队伍管理办法》等，实施专任教师和企业专家在校企工作岗位承担实质工作的"双岗双薪"、专任教师在行业企业兼职及参与企业技术研发等方案，打造了一支专业优秀教学团队，解决了企业专家任教难及专业教师社会服务能力弱的关键问题。

学院在与企业的合作中共同建立了一套专业教师培养流程，包括以下几种方式：

（1）校企双方选派专业教师（专任）和企业一线专业兼职教师参加国家相关部门组织的职业培训班进修学习。

（2）选派专业教师（专任）到行业企业实践锻炼或参加行业企业举办的职工职业技能培训班学习。

（3）与学校合作办学的行业企业开设专业教师（专任）培训班，对专业教师（专任）进行实操技能及企业文化方面的培训，提高专业教师（专任）的实操能力和实践教学能力，使专任教师在3年内达到兼职教师的实践教学水平。

（4）学校开设专业教师（兼职）培训班，结合学校发展实际，对来自企业一线的专业兼职教师进行培训，提高他们的教学水平和综合素质，使兼职教师在3年内达到专任教师的理论教学水平

4.2 ACADEMIC COORDINATION 学术协作

（5）学校每学期至少举办1次"专业专任教师—企业专业技术员"经验交流会，使学校专业教师和企业专业技术人员在交流中各取所长、各补所短。

（6）依托学校科研项目和课题，吸引企业高层次人才加入项目组参与课题研究，为学校专业教师（专任）提供项目研究实践方面的指导。

在旅游管理专业中，专业教师、学生和其他教辅行政人员之间是相互协作共同发展的关系。一般先设定专业目标，以此为前提设计学生培养方案，再以培养方案为核心进行教学计划安排与协调沟通

旅游管理专业教工每学期按照教学任务规定，平均举行教工例会2～3次（每月举行例会一次）。如在2017—2018学年外出培训学习心得分享会上，外国语学院在进行专业资源整合后针对品牌专业建设、课程建设薄弱环节选派了一批专任教师赴外地参加暑期培训。先后有9位教师登台汇报了他们的学习内容、收获和体会，并就如何将学习内容融入今后的教研教改中，分享了自己的想法。

参照学校相关规定，所有教师可自行选择正规的、高质量的培训机构或单位，培训内容与所学专业、所授课程、所进行的科研教改方向和正在开展的课程、专业建设内容相符即可进行申请。

本专业在强化教工和其他员工职业道德的问题上，首先要求从事教育行业的教师们都必须具备相应的教师资格证，其次配合学校继续教育部门安排，积极参与继续教育活动，鼓励教工参加相关学校培训工作。如2017年9月由学校组织的全校范围内骨干教师培训课，专业参加人数达50%以上。

在培养学生的过程中，旅游管理专业积极引入行业专家、兼职教师、学生未来就业企业管理者参与学生培养过程，举办各种旅游企业相关讲座，且由企业人员担任特定专业课的教学安排

4.3 PROFESSIONAL PERFORMANCE 专业业绩

旅游管理专业教师按照国家相关政策和规定，职称从助教、讲师、副教授至教授均可按相关规定进行晋升。

现有23人教师中，中英文导游考评员4位；持有导游资格证者4位；茶艺师二级资格3位，评茶师中级以上资格3人位，航空乘务教员资格2位，礼仪训练指导师2位，国际商务会展员资格1人。

教师科研、指导竞赛等业绩突出。自2004年专业设立以来，专业教师共获得全国教指委课题3项，省级教改课题2项，广东省教指委课题2项，市厅级课题6项，校级课题15项，并承担了大量的服务国内旅游行业的横向课题。出版教材专著16部，在国内外重要专业期刊和重要学术会议发表论文71篇。一大批高水平的科研成果为专业建设奠定了良好的基础。

教师课程建设、教学大赛取得重大进展，教学质量不断提高。2004年以来，本专业共立项并建设完成校级精品课程3门。近3年来，9门立项课程为校级在线开放课程，基本涵盖了本专业的所有核心课程。其中，朱瀚、苏丹老师分别获得全国教育教学信息化大赛二、三等奖，苏丹老师获得中国外语微课大赛省赛二等奖。冯淑玲、苏丹老师获得学生最满意课程奖。2017年，杨易、冯淑玲老师分别获得校长教学质量二、三等奖。另外，万方秋等老师申报的旅游管理专业教学成果获得学校第六届教学成果奖一等奖。

续　表

4.3 PROFESSIONAL PERFORMANCE 专业业绩
教师指导学生参加各级各类技能竞赛硕果累累。自 2013 年以来参加全国职业院校技能大赛，本专业教师指导学生获得全国职业院校技能大赛一等奖 1 项，二等奖 2 项，全国职业院校广东省选拔赛一等奖（中英文导游、中西餐赛项）8 项，二等奖（中英文导游、中西餐赛项）17 项。自 2012 年以来参加全国旅游院校技能大赛获得一二三等奖十多项。指导学生参加珠海市、斗门区、万山区旅游局组织的导游技能大赛，学生均获得优异成绩，如珠海市十佳优秀导游、斗门区导游大赛一等奖、万山区导游大赛一等奖等。本专业学生国赛二等奖获得者丁雅新，在 2016 年广东省导游职业技能大赛中，以第一名的成绩获得一等奖，并因此成为广东省五一劳动奖章获得者。各级各类竞赛的参与和获奖，真正做到了"赛、学、训、教、改、建"相融合，提高了教师的教学质量，扩大和彰显了我校旅游专业在全省乃至全国的影响力

4.4 CONTINUOUS KNOWLEDGE UPDATE 继续教育更新	
4.4 a）Training	旅游管理专业在正常的教学过程中为教师发展持续不断地组织内部培训，如 2017 年初为专业教师组织的茶艺师培训。外部培训与学院其他专业相通，符合规定的培训项目均可申请学院资助。据统计，2015—2017 年，旅游管理专业教师共计参加 58 次继续教育培训，培训内容以专业技能提升为主。外国语学院旅游管理专业 2011—2015 年共发表 18 篇论文，科研项目立项并结题 8 项，培训及社会服务项目 24 项。 根据近三年的培训记录，可以看出教工培训多集中在提升专业水平，拓展专业知识面及了解行业最新动态方面。教师培训项目的选择以是否符合专业目标为标准，由学院领导决定是否符合。培训项目内容的选择主要基于旅游市场发展的新动向。专业教师积极申报各类校级、市级、省级、国家级相关科研项目，并主动参加各种信息化教学大赛，不少参赛教师获得优异名次
4.4 b)Research Activities	旅游管理专业对教工科研活动予以高度支持，积极提供各种申报信息，并给予各类资源支持，如语音室等实训室也对有需要的教职工开放使用。 旅游管理专业科研活动主要以教师所执教的课程为中心，以公众的广泛需求为主，也有与企业合作而进行的具体项目研究。科研信息来源多种多样，如调研方式搜集及与旅游行业相互交流等途径。 旅游管理专业现有品牌建设经费 50 万元，专门用于科研等教学活动建设，该项目经费以按需使用为主

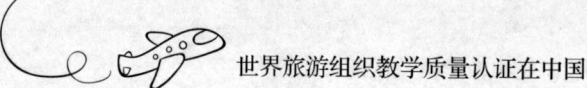

Area of Analysis

Part V The Management

表3-6

5.1 ORGANIZATION 管理架构		
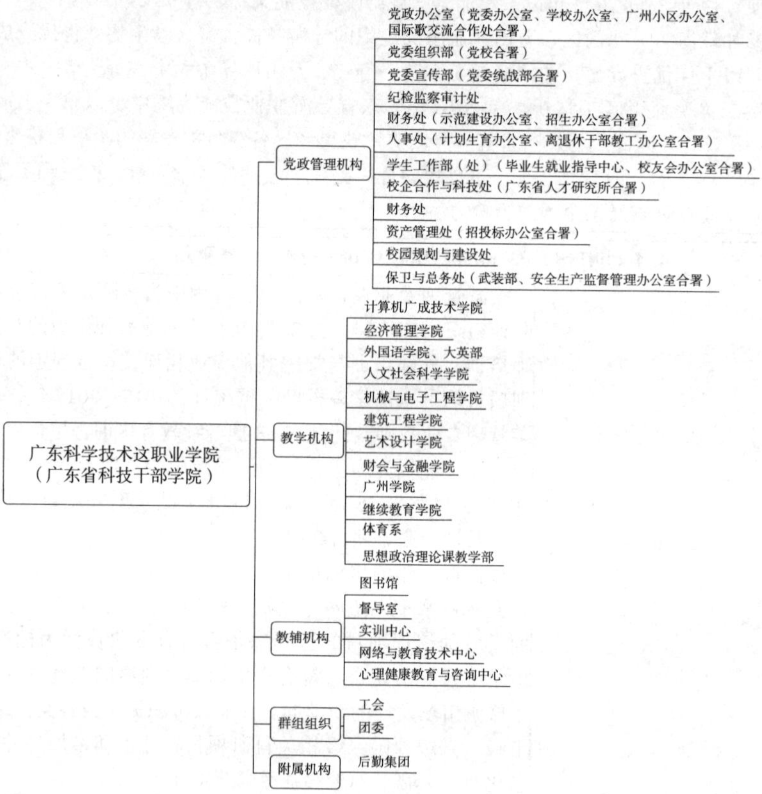 广东科学技术这职业学院 （广东省科技干部学院）	党政管理机构	党政办公室（党委办公室、学校办公室、广州小区办公室、国际歌交流合作处合署） 党委组织部（党校合署） 党委宣传部（党委统战部合署） 纪检监察审计处 财务处（示范建设办公室、招生办公室合署） 人事处（计划生育办公室、离退休干部教工办公室合署） 学生工作部（处）（毕业生就业指导中心、校友会办公室合署） 校企合作与科技处（广东省人才研究所合署） 财务处 资产管理处（招投标办公室合署） 校园规划与建设处 保卫与总务处（武装部、安全生产监督管理办公室合署）
	教学机构	计算机广成技术学院 经济管理学院 外国语学院、大英部 人文社会科学学院 机械与电子工程学院 建筑工程学院 艺术设计学院 财会与金融学院 广州学院 继续教育学院 体育系 思想政治理论课教学部
	教辅机构	图书馆 督导室 实训中心 网络与教育技术中心 心理健康教育与咨询中心
	群组组织	工会 团委
	附属机构	后勤集团

5.2 QUALITY ASSURANCE 质量保证	
5.2 a）Quality Plan 质量监管文件	（1）全面质量计划及其配套手册:《广东科学技术职业学院旅游管理专业人才培养计划》 （2）体现内外部利益相关者了解该计划的调查问卷（或评价系统）:《2016年专业设置调研问卷及报告》 （3）证明该计划实施的文件:《关于加强高职高专教育人才培养工作的意见》（教高〔2000〕2号）;《关于全面提高高等职业教育教学质量的若干意见》（教高〔2006〕16号）

5.2 QUALITY ASSURANCE 质量保证	
5.2 b）Monitoring 质量监管实施	一、质量监控指标体系 　教学质量监控体系由教务处、校企合作管理处（实训中心，合署）、督导室、学工处、招就处等相关部门共同建立健全各教学环节的质量标准，主要包括以下内容： 　①院（系、部）教学状态评估指标体系；②课堂教学质量评价体系；③实践教学环节评价指标体系；④毕业论文（毕业实习）评价体系；⑤校内"教学企业"分级评价标准及校外"教学企业"分级评价标准（试行）；⑥毕业生就业质量报告。 　二、质量监控团队 　（一）监控机构 　教学质量监控机构分校和院（系、部）两级。校级质量监控机构由校教学工作委员会、教务处、校督导室、学工处、招就处、校企合作管理处（实训中心，合署）等部门组成，负责对全校的教学状态和教学质量进行监控和评估，同时对院（系、部）的监控、评估结果进行确认。院（系、部）级质量监控机构由院（系、部）教学工作委员会、教研室等组成，负责对本院（系、部）的教学状态和教学质量进行监控和评估，并将监控、评估结果上报校级相关的质量监控机构。 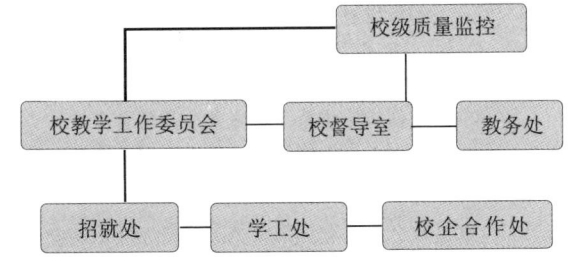
5.2 b）Monitoring 质量监管实施	（二）监控职责 　1.校教学工作委员会职责 　校教学工作委员会是在校长的领导下，对全校教学工作中的重大问题进行研究、决策、指导、规划、审定和监督等工作的重要组织。其在教学质量监控方面的主要职责如下： 　（1）对学校的教学质量监控和评价工作进行宏观管理与指导。 　（2）督促加强校、院（系、部）两级教学质量监控，以保障教学质量的全面提高。

5.2 QUALITY ASSURANCE 质量保证	
5.2 b）Monitoring 质量监管实施	2．教务处职责 （1）组织制定学校相关的教学工作质量标准或规范。 （2）制定学校专业建设、课程建设、教材建设等教学基本建设规划，并负责提出专项评估计划。 （3）组织制定监控体系所需的相关评估方案及评估指标体系、实施办法及配套文件。 （4）对教学过程的运行情况及效果进行检查、评估、监督。 （5）针对教学质量监控和评估中发现的问题，制定整改措施和建设方案。 （6）负责面向学生的教学质量调查，并向有关部门和教学单位提供反馈意见。 3．校企合作管理处（实训中心，合署）职责 （1）制定学校实训室、实训基地和"教学企业"基本建设规划，并负责提出专项评估计划。 （2）负责制定实训室与实训基地实践教学、顶岗实习环节评价方案，负责制定"教学企业"实践教学环节评价框架的方案。 （3）对顶岗实习进行跟踪巡视、检查监督。 （4）针对顶岗实习环节监控和评估中发现的问题，制定整改措施和建设方案。 4．校督导室职责 （1）制定与教学督导有关的质量监控体系所需的相关评估方案及评估指标体系、实施办法及配套文件。 （2）对学校教学过程进行跟踪巡视、检查及监督。 （3）对教学质量及教与学中存在的问题做出客观评价，提出建议和改进意见，并以教学督导信息的形式及时向有关部门反馈 5．学工处职责 （1）制定学生学习状态与效果的评估方案。 （2）针对教学质量监控和评估中发现的有关学生学习思想、学习态度、学习纪律等方面的问题，提出加强教育管理及学风建设的具体措施。 （3）组织开展学生学习状态与效果的评估。 （4）组织开展新生素质调研。 （5）组织开展人才需求状况分析。 （6）组织开展就业状况数据分析。 （7）组织开展毕业生跟踪调查。

续　表

5.2 QUALITY ASSURANCE 质量保证	
5.2 b）Monitoring 质量监管实施	6．招就处 （1）组织开展就业状况数据分析。 （2）组织开展毕业生跟踪调查。 （3）组织开展行业企业专家、用人单位满意度调查。 （4）组织开展就业对口率调查。 7．院（系、部）教学工作委员会职责 （1）依据学校的教学质量监控和评估指标体系及评估标准，开展评教、评学工作。 （2）负责对本院（系、部）教师教学质量的监控。 （3）负责对本院（系、部）学生学习状态与效果的评估。 （4）对本院（系、部）评估中发现的问题进行分析研究，提出整改与建设措施。 （5）配合校级教学质量监控机构开展其他工作。 8．学生信息员职责 （1）对学校或院（系、部）的教学计划、教学内容、教学方法及手段、教学管理及教学条件、教学评价、教师队伍等教学管理工作及时提出意见和建议，定期向教务处和所在院（系、部）反映。 （2）及时了解有关学生学习状况，反映学生在听课、实验、实习、作业、考试及社会实践等方面的情况。 （三）质量指标的应用及其结果。 麦可思学生质量评定报告

INFORMATION REGARDING THE INCLUSION OF THE PURPOSES AND PRINCIPLES OF THE GLOBAL CODE OF ETHICS FOR TOURISM INTO THE PROGRAMME

表3-7

1. The Employers
1.Did your institution/programme consider the principles of the Global Code of Ethics for Tourism in formulating the mission and the action plan? 2.Does the institution/programme collaborate with the public/private sector in the implementation of the principles of the Global Code of Ethics for Tourism? If yes, please give examples. （1）本专业建立地是中国著名的旅游城市——珠海，珠海位于中国倾力打造的粤港澳大湾区。随着中国经济发展水平的提升，人均可支配收入持续增长，社会公众对于旅游提出了更高的要求。本专业在设立之前，深入地调研了国内不同收入水平人群的旅游需求，结合地方经济发展特色，特别是珠海市发展"三高一特"产业中提到的现代服务业要求，将开办旅游管理专业作为化解人民日益增长的美好生活需要和不平衡不充分的发展之间的矛盾的重要手段，将办好、办强旅游管理专业作为服务地方经济增长的支撑力量。旅游管理专业为力争实现良好的人才培养效果，紧密结合社会经济发展形势，根据全球伦理规准则来设计人才培养方案。 （2）本专业为了适应旅游行业发展的新趋势以及实施全球伦理规范准则组建了专业教学理事会，建立了由国内旅游领域权威专家组成旅游管理专业建设指导委员会。专业教学指导委员会的成立，一方面有利于人才培养目标符合广东省及珠海市的地方经济发展需求，另一方面用工企业代表的参与可以使学校教学过程更加符合企业需要，使人才培养工作真正落到实处。同时与本地区大型旅游集团广州长隆集团有限公司合作，与本地区外国品牌酒店珠海万豪、珠海喜来登、深圳 JW 万豪等酒店以及本地区龙头旅行社广之旅、南湖国旅、拱北口岸中国旅行社、深圳宝安中国旅行社等企业合作，同时与云顶香港有限公司合作，校企双方围绕人才培养目标、课程设计和实施、实习实训、就业指向、学生管理、师资配备、考核评价等进行全方位的合作，并进行了一系列实践探索与全程跟踪调研。目前，首届现代学徒制班的同学已顺利毕业，预计未来这些同学会在自己的岗位上运用课堂所学，更好地为企业服务
2. The Student
1.In the admission of students, does your institution/programme respect the equality of people（sex, race, religion, political view, etc.)? Does your institution/programme promote the admission of the most vulnerable groups（persons with disabilities, ethnic minorities, indigenous people, etc.)? 2.Does your institution/programme promote understanding and respect among students? Please give some examples. 3.Does your institution/programme promote the mobility of students?

2. The Student

4.Does your institution/programme evaluate students on knowledge, skills and values? Please give examples.

5.According to Article 5 of the Global Code of Ethics for Tourism "Tourism professionals （…） should carry out studies of the impact of their development projects on the environment and natural surroundings". Do you ask the students of your institution/programme to carry out studies about tourism in your country/region or to be part of any cooperation for development activity?

6.Does your institution/programme have programmes that strengthen ethic values on the students' behaviour? Please give examples.

（1）旅游管理专业除了招收广东省的学生外还招收其他外省学生，包括新疆维吾尔自治区、四川省、安徽省、河南省、湖南省、贵州省、甘肃省、山西省以及陕西省等地的学生，有汉族、维吾尔族以及土家族等民族的学生。旅游管理专业除了普高学生外，每年会录取一定比例的中职学生。为了录取到更加优秀的中职学生，每年招生录取前学院都会派出老师前往合作的或优秀的中职院校进行洽谈，寻求更多的合作，并且在所在学校进行宣传，通过宣讲吸引更多的优秀学生。目前已经与多家中职学校达成3加2培养计划。

（2）学生在入学之初，会由专业主任对其进行入学教育，包括专业概况、课程介绍、就业岗位、职业精神和素养、专业教师团队等，为学生开始大学生活打下基础，同时邀请往届优秀师兄师姐回校与新生交流，邀请业界专业人士对新生进行专业认知教育。学生在校期间，学院会安排不定期的专家讲座、企业宣讲、校内专题活动等，学生可以根据自己专业所需进行选择，以协助学生拓展知识面，为学生提供更多企业实习岗位。学校组织学生参加各种茶话会、联谊会以增进同学之间的理解，加强学生之间的感情。

（3）旅游管理专业与本地区大型旅游集团广州长隆集团有限公司合作，与本地区外国品牌酒店珠海万豪、珠海喜来登、深圳JW万豪等酒店以及本地区龙头旅行社广之旅、南湖国旅、拱北口岸中国旅行社、深圳宝安中国旅行社等企业合作，同时与云顶香港有限公司合作，让学生到这些企业交流实习，也为这些企业培养合格人才。在2016年，日本酒店集团负责人莅临我校选拔赴日社会实践学生、2016级现代学徒制班学生参加认识实习、举办"旅游企业运营与旅游行业发展"研讨会，旅游管理专业开拓了新的实训就业市场。

（4）旅游管理专业的教师对于学生学业的综合评价包括学生的学业成绩，考级考证的情况，参加社团组织的情况、参加技能大赛的情况、参加课外实践的情况等，不同的课程评价方法也不尽相同。实训类课程主要通过考查学生的技能掌握情况来给予学生学业评价，通常体现在期末的技能测试及平时的技能学习及实践情况；理论课程主要通过期末考试和平时表现来对学生进行综合评价，理论课教师对于期末考试题的题型设计包括主观题和客观题，给学生的答题时间一般是90分钟到两个小时，主要考查学生对于基本专业理论知识的掌握情况，理论课平时成绩主要通过学生在日常学习中的课堂出勤、课堂表现（包括课堂纪律、课堂回答问题、课堂讨论等）、学生作业等平时表现来综合给出。学生通过理论课和实训课等各专业课的学习，可以形成良好的职业道德和敬业精神，熟练掌握旅游服务与管理技能

2. The Student

（5）旅游管理专业的专业课程都会要求学生们开展关于旅游对于自然环境的影响以及绿色旅游的相关研究。例如在旅游概论、中国旅游地理等课程中均讲授了旅游影响及可持续发展旅游的有关内容，并且要求学生完成可持续发展旅游的调查研究和宣传推广活动。

（6）旅游管理专业的课程设置中加入了思法基础与廉洁修身、心理健康教育、军训和入学教育（含军事理论）、就业指导、旅游法规、跨文化交际和旅游服务礼仪等加强学生道德价值观的课程。

3. The Curriculum and Pedagogical System

1. How does the curriculum contain the principles of the Global Code of Ethics for Tourism: (a) as a transversal issue in all subjects, (b) as a specific subject about ethics or (c) both?

2. How does your institution/programme inform the students and professors about the principles of the Global Code of Ethics for Tourism (seminars, specific classes, brochure, etc.)?

3. What is the pedagogical method used to teach the principles of the Global Code of Ethics for Tourism to the students? Do you think the students might remember the principles and are they able to apply them once they leave the institution? How do you ensure that this knowledge is acquired?

（1）旅游管理专业三年课程共计2 637学时，131学分。从纵向结构来看，分为综合素质课程（必修）、综合素质课程（选修）、专业课程必修模块（含专业基础、专业核心和专业综合性实践）、专业拓展课程模块四大模块。在本专业课程结构设置中，大学一年级设置通识教育课程和专业基础课程，二三年级开设专业核心课程、专业实践课及专业拓展课。并且将全球伦理规范准则贯穿到所有的专业课程中。其中"旅游概论"中有专门章节较多涉及全球伦理规范的相关内容，导游业务中包含对游客人格尊严的维护和宗教信仰、生活习俗的尊重和对法律的服从，酒店前厅与客房管理中强调以人为本、对旅客进行人文关怀等。

（2）旅游管理专业经常组织有关专家和行业精英来学院举办讲座，向旅游管理专业的学生宣讲全球伦理规范准则，并通过班级qq群、微信群等媒介宣讲旅游道德规范。

（3）旅游管理专业多位教师在课程改革中运用了工作过程教学理念，采用任务驱动、项目导向的教学方法来将全球伦理规范准则传递给学生。教师针对旅游职业岗位职能与素质，结合珠三角地区旅游业发展的实际情况与特点来设计课程内容，将全球伦理规范准则贯穿教学全过程，注重学生职业道德、讲解能力、应变技巧、带团规范、心理素质等方面的培养。在教学过程中，老师们使用雨课堂来进行教学，使用这种在线课堂的教师可以及时了解学生们是否掌握了课堂知识

4. The Faculty

1.What is the admission process of your institution/programme regarding Faculty? Does your institution/programme respect the equality of people（sex, race, religion, political view, etc.)?

2.Does your institution/programme promote equity of gender among the Faculty members? Please give examples.

3.Does your institution/programme promote understanding and respect among the Faculty members as well as between them and the students and other staff members?

4.Does your institution/programme promote the mobility of Faculty abroad（to study or to be trained)?

5.Does your institution/programme have programmes that strengthen ethic values on the Faculty and other staff members? Please give examples.

6.Does the Faculty of your institution/programme carry out studies about tourism in your country/region?

（1）广东科学技术职业学院旅游管理专业现有教师 23 人，其中女性 14 人，男性 9 人，均为中华人民共和国公民。在专业管理过程中，顾忆华、胡晓晶、郭卫娜等三人任专业重要管理岗位，均为女性。

在 2016 年的最新一次教工招聘中，旅游管理专业对外招聘条件有以下内容：

①硕士研究生及以上学历学位。

②职称为讲师及以上。

③年龄在 40 周岁以下。

④具有高等院校相应专业 2 年以上教学经验或在企业从事相应专业技术工作 2 年以上经验。

所有招聘条件中均无性别、种族、宗教、政治倾向等歧视。

（2）在旅游管理专业中，专业教师、学生和其他教辅行政人员之间是相互协作共同发展的关系。学校先设定专业目标，以此为前提设计学生培养方案，再以培养方案为核心进行教学计划安排与协调沟通。旅游管理专业也会组织教师集体备课，要求教师进行课题互助，并且开展校企合作开发课程、教材。

（3）参照学校相关规定，所有教师可自行选择正规的、高质量的培训机构或单位，培训内容与所学专业、所授课程、所进行的科研教改方向和正在开展的课程、专业建设内容相符即可进行申请。其中，万方秋老师和冯淑玲老师于 2016 年 7—8 月赴德国参加"德国'职业能力开发导向'双元制职教专业教学法研修班"（国培项目代码：38153013）。

（4）本专业在强化教工和其他员工职业道德的问题上，首先要求从事教育行业的教师都必须具备相应的教师资格证，其次配合学校继续教育部门安排，积极参与继续教育活动，鼓励教工参加相关学校培训工作。如 2017 年 9 月由学校组织的全校范围内骨干教师培训课，专业参加人数达 50% 以上。

（5）旅游管理专业的教师通过申报课题、发表论文、校企合作开发教材等形式开展本地区旅游方面的研究

5. The Management
1.Does your institution/programme respect economic, social and cultural environment and transmit the same to the students, professors and local community? Please, give examples.
2.Does your institution/programme observe and respect the social and cultural traditions of all peoples, including minorities and indigenous people? Does your programme promote their integration and teach students respect towards everyone?
3.Does your institution/programme help other institution/programme of least developed destinations to create/update their tourism programmes using as reference the principles of the Global Code of Ethics for Tourism while developing their mission, action plan, curriculum, etc.?
（1）旅游管理专业教师和学生尊重经济、社会和文化环境。学院要求学生和教师收看习近平总书记的重要讲话、党的十八大和党的十九大工作报告。党的十八大报告明确提出建设中国特色社会主义"五位一体"总体布局，建设中国特色社会主义的总体布局从"三位一体""四位一体"扩展为经济建设、政治建设、文化建设、社会建设、生态文明建设的"五位一体"，建设中国特色社会主义总体布局更加完善。 （2）旅游管理专业遵守和尊重包括少数民族和土著人民在内的所有民族的社会和文化传统，在旅游管理专业的专业课程——"导游基础知识"这一课程中，有一个单元介绍中国的少数民族，教师在介绍这个部分时，不仅要将相关的知识介绍给学生，还要求学生要尊重每一个人。 （3）旅游管理专业与2015年对口支援西双版纳职业技术学院，帮助西双版纳职业技术学院制定旅游专业的使命、行动计划、课程等，并且派遣专业老师去西双版纳职业技术学院给学院老师进行培训

第二节 自评报告英文版范例

INFORMATION BY AREA OF ANALYSIS

Area Part I The Employers: Public and Private Sector

Mission

G Polytechnic is a National Key College of Higher Vocational Education and National Demonstrative Vocational College for Innovation and Entrepreneurship. Adhering to the idea of "pursuit of excellency, distinction and innovation", we are fully dedicated to developing into a national first-rate and internationally celebrated leading vocational college that prepares

qualified talents, undertakes satisfactory social services, plays an exemplary role, and enjoys fine social reputation. The college is the unique demonstrative institution for innovation and entrepreneurship of "Internet plus" in Guangdong Province with its strong technical characteristics. Tourism management, one of the first batch of brand building specialties in Guangdong Province and one of the thirteen provincial brand specialties in the college, has fully demonstrated the characteristics.

The mission of tourism management specialty is to train high-quality and skilled graduates who are proficient in tourism practice and English communication and who are able to be adapted to the needs of tourism industry in Guangdong province and Guangdong-Hong Kong-Macao Greater Bay Area.

Tourism management is designed to train qualified staff for the following positions : ① Travel agency posts : middle and senior attendants and management staff in Tour Guide Department, Tour Operator Department, Sales Department, Conference Department, and so on; ② Hotel posts : middle and senior attendants and management personnel in Front Office Department, Housekeeping Department, Food & Beverage Division, Sales Department, Recreation and Entertainment Department, Conference Department, and so on; ③ Posts in other travel enterprises : middle and senior attendants and management personnel engaged in service, planning, sales and operation management of tourism travel companies, international cruise companies, scenic spots, catering enterprises, holiday resorts, exhibition companies, and other tourism-related enterprises.

Action Plan

G Polytechnic is based in Zhuhai, a well-known tourist city in China. Zhuhai is located in the Guangdong-Hong Kong-Macao Greater Bay Area which is known as the fourth world-class Grand Bay Area together with the Tokyo Bay Area, the San Francisco Bay Area and the New York Bay Area. With the development of China's economy, the per capita disposable income continues to grow, and the public place higher demands on tourism. Prior to its establishment, staff of the specialty have conducted an in-depth study on the tourism needs of people of different income levels in Mainland China. By taking advantage of the rapid development of the high-end hotel industry in the Guangdong-Hong Kong-Macao Greater Bay Area and the increasing attention given to international cruise lines by tourists, and acting in line with the requirements of local economic development, especially the requirements of modern service industry concerned in Zhuhai's development of the "three highs and one special" industries, we set up the tourism management specialty as an important means to solve the contradiction between the growing needs of the people and the unbalanced and insufficient development of the modern service industry, and to become a supporting force for local economic growth.

We have seriously studied the needs of enterprises (via a questionnaire survey) at the beginning of the establishment. We have formulated, modified, and improved the personnel training programs and set up curriculum standards after soliciting opinions and suggestions from the enterprises and potential employers on the basis of adequate investigation and research. We have established the college-enterprise cooperation council to make enterprises play a role in personnel training and specialty construction and carried out enterprise satisfaction surveys of personnel training through graduates' follow-up survey, employers' satisfaction survey, and so forth.

The education concept of Tourism Management is to train high-quality and skilled graduates who are proficient in tourism practice and English communication and who are able to be adapted to the needs of tourism industry in Guangdong province and Guangdong-Hong Kong-Macao Greater Bay Area. In order to truly implement this concept, the tourism management professionals not only attract relevant tourism enterprises to participate in the formulation of talent training programs, curriculum standards and the training room construction, but also cooperate with the enterprises to establish modern apprenticeship pilot classes and cooperation classes consisting of students booked in advance by large companies. Tourism enterprises participating in the training of tourism management specialty, makes it possible for the graduates

to better adapt to the needs of enterprises' positions. The scale and number of students to be trained, the training methods and the training level are decided according to the requirements of enterprises. Through the above practices, we can meet the employment needs of tourism enterprises to the maximum, shorten their incubation period of human resources, save their cost of human resources, and increase their efficiency and benefit, so these measures are warmly welcomed by tourism enterprises.

Curriculum content

In order to realize the effect of excellent talent cultivation and provide more talents for the national economic development, we have formulated the basic principle for the revision of the talent training program, namely, "a major change in three years and a minor change every year", closely integrating with the social and economic development. At present, the talent training program used is the 2016 version (for 2016 and 2017 students). We focus on the cooperation with the region's leading tourism group the Chimelong Group, main foreign brand hotels such as Zhuhai Marriott Hotel, Sheraton Zhuhai, Shenzhen JW Marriott and so on, leading travel agencies such as GZL Travel Service, South Lake International Travel Service, China Travel Service Gongbei Port, Guangdong, China Travel Service in Baoan Shenzhen and other agencies, as well as Hong Kong Genting Cruise Group, to train qualified personnel for them.

In the process of personnel training, we collect survey data on employers satisfaction to our students and make timely revisions of talent training programs according to the results of the enterprise feedback so as to accumulate basic data for major adjustment of talent training programs every three years, which enables the talent training programs to keep pace with the trend of social-economic development, meet the demands of enterprises and take the needs of enterprises, students and sustainable development of the tourism industry into consideration to the greatest extent. During the implementation of the talent training program made in 2016, we invited Japan Hotel Group leaders to select students to intern in Japan, organized the students of the modern apprenticeship classes to do cognition practice, held seminars on "the tourism enterprise operation and the development of tourism industry", and opened up new training and employment market and conducted in-depth discussions with employing enterprises. This has laid a solid foundation for the revision of the talent-training programs in 2018 and ensured the completion of high-quality personnel training. This Table is part of the professional core curriculum. For the specific talent-training programs and the class schedule, please refer to the supporting materials.

Introduction to Professional Core Curriculum

Course	Main Teaching Content	Items and Requirements of Skill Assessment	Class Hours/ Credits
Tour Guide Business	(1) How to become a tour guide. (2) Cognition of tour guide service. (3) Providing tour guide services to package tours. (4) Providing tour guide services to individual tours. (5) Preventing and dealing with problems and emergencies. (6) Dealing with visitors' individual requirements. (7) Tour guide's skills. (8) Lectures on tour guide's comprehensive knowledge	(1) Be able to provide standardized and personalized tour guide services to visitors by flexibly applying the principles and norms of tour guide services. (2) Be familiar with the emergency handling procedures and methods, and prevent emergencies effectively. (3) Be familiar with the basic principles and methods of dealing with individual requirements, and use them flexibly	54 class hours/ 3 credits

Continued Table

Course	Main Teaching Content	Items and Requirements of Skill Assessment	Class Hours/ Credits
Hotel Lobby and Room Management	(1) Reservation service. (2) Concierge service. (3) Reception service. (4) Business center and switchboard service. (5) guest room service. (6) Room cleaning and maintenance. (7) Guest relationship management. (8) Room security, materials, and human resources management. (9) Lobby and room service skills training	(1) Be capable of using the lobby equipment, and offering booking service, FIT / group luggage storage and retrieval service, guest check-in and check-out service, telephone inquiry and message service. (2) Be able to greet guests, handle guests' left-over items, provide room service, reception service, and bar service etc. according to the service standards. (3) To master the Chinese / Western-style bed-making skills, and know about the checking out procedures and methods. (4) To know about the reasons and the handling methods of guests' complaints and to handle guests' complaints flexibly. (5) Be able to conduct guest room fire protection, prevent financial insecurity and deal with emergencies, figure out the existing occupational safety problems of guest room staff, and learn about management methods of equipment, supplies, cloth pieces in guest rooms	68 class hours / 4 credits

Continued Table

Course	Main Teaching Content	Items and Requirements of Skill Assessment	Class Hours/ Credits
Catering Operation and Management	(1) The construction of the catering management system. (2) Control of food service site. (3) Planning and designing the menu. (4) Planning catering promotions. (5) Control of the cost of catering. (6) Procurement and acceptance check of the food raw materials. (7) Control of the quality of food service. (8) Restaurant service skills training	(1) Be capable of designing the organizational structure and arranging the staffing according to the scale of catering enterprises. (2) Be capable of formulating the work processes and standards of Chinese and Western snacks, banquet and management attendants. (3) Be capable of designing recipes and make a complete menu according to the food nutrition. (4) Be able to conduct analysis of food sales and profitability, and write a themed catering marketing scheme. (5) Be able to work out the workflow and standards of restaurant cashiers, fill in the restaurant business day statements, and put forward ideas for the cost control of the key links. (6) Be able to assess suppliers accurately, know about the quality standards of food raw materials, do a complete procurement and acceptance check of the raw materials, put forward suggestions on the cost control of food procurement. (7) Be able to assess the catering service quality scientifically and comprehensively, and handle guest complaints. (8) Be able to carry out the tray service of Chinese and Western dishes, fold napkin flowers, set the table, place an order, serve dishes, distribute cuisine, pour tea, pour wine, replace tableware, checkout, welcome and farewell guests, and other services	68 class hours / 4 credits

Continued Table

Course	Main Teaching Content	Items and Requirements of Skill Assessment	Class Hours/ Credits
English For Tour Guide	(1) Overview of Guangdong. (2) Dr Sun Yat-sen Memorial Hall and Ancestral Temple of the Chen Family. (3) Shenzhen China Folk Culture Village. (4) Statue of Zhuhai Fisher Girl (5) Foshan Ancestral Temple. (6) Meizhou Hakka Round House. (7) Danxia Mountain. (8) Chaozhou Cuisine. (9) Dinghu Mountain and Qixingyan. (10) Kaiping Diaolou	(1) Be able to explain and appraise the tourist attractions in English. (2) Be able to write the English tour guide words of the main attractions in Guangdong Province	68 class hours / 4 credits
Travel Agency Opera-tion and Management	(1) Organizational structure of travel agencies. (2) The establishment of travel agencies. (3) Product design and development for travel agencies. (4) Product sales of travel agencies. (5) Operator management of travel agencies. (6) Human resource management of travel agencies	(1) Be proficient in the constitution process of international and domestic travel agencies. (2) Be capable of designing tourist routes, mastering the development of tourism products, and working out suitable marketing schemes by combining the relevant marketing theories and the characteristics of the products. (3) Be proficient operation, outreach, and other related work in travel agencies through simulate operation	68 class hours / 4 credits
Tourism Marketing	(1) Tourist attractions marketing and planning. (2) Tourism hotel marketing and planning. (3) Tourism transport company marketing and planning. (4) Travel agency marketing and planning	(1) Be capable of doing tourism market research independently with scientific methods. (2) Be capable of collecting marketing information, analyzing and summarizing information, summing up and exchanging marketing experience, skills and tactics. (3) Be capable of applying tourism marketing theories into practice	68 class hours / 4 credits

Adaptation of the programme to new trends and requirements of the employers.

Existence of monitoring mechanisms to assess needs.

After elaborate preparations, the Tourism Management Program set up the steering committee of tourism management specialty of Guangdong Polytechnic of Science and Technology which is composed of domestic authoritative experts in the field of tourism. The experts are Ke Ming (Secretary General of Zhuhai Tourism Federation) , Liu Tie (Dean of Zhuhai Culture, Sports and Tourism Bureau) , Li Xiufang (Human Resources Supervisor of Zhuhai Grand Hotels Group) , Li Shunguang (Manager of Zhuhai Seasky Travel Agency) , Wang Shiqin (Training Manager of Zhuhai Holiday Resort Hotel) , and Yang Song (Senior Manager of China Travel Service Gongbei Port Guangdong) . The establishment of the steering committee is conducive to the talent training objectives in line with the needs of local economic development in Zhuhai City and Guangdong Province, and on the other hand, participation of representatives from tourism enterprises will enable teaching activities as well as our talent training in the college to better meet the actual requirements of enterprises.

The establishment of the steering committee of tourism management specialty has truly realized the cooperation among the government, the institute, the industry and enterprises in education, and got rid of the traditional closed−off education mode. The steering committee would help to integrate the social and school resources, set a higher starting point for the specialty, ensure the quality of personnel training fundamentally, and offer the students better employment resources. Under the guidance of the Steering Committee, the pilot program of modern apprenticeship will help radically change the traditional closed−off education mode, and the enterprises can truly integrate themselves into the entire process of personnel training. The enrollment and evaluation of students are carried out in line with the standards of enterprises, and the college and the enterprise are jointly responsible for the students' education. Enterprises could make the talent training programs

and curriculum according to the requirements of real work situations. All these measures would ensure high-quality and high-standard professional education.

Adjustment Actions

In view of the changing employment needs of tourism enterprises, we seriously sum up and refine the experiences and lessons of the modern apprenticeship pilot classes and the ordered classes consisting of students booked in advance by large companies and have developed some characteristic courses based on the different needs of tourism enterprises. For example, we have constructed a training room for tourism informatization to strengthen the teaching of tourism e-commerce based on the development of "Internet +". Courses like Cruise Service and Management and Cruise English are opened according to the changes in China's cruise market. The education of innovation and entrepreneurship are emphasized in order to cultivate innovative entrepreneurial talents.

Since many travel agencies begin to make use of the e-commerce platform and the WeChat official account, we have also developed the special e-commerce service platform operation course for the curriculum, set up the WeChat official account operation course, and cultivated students' copywriting ability, which are not included in traditional talent training programs but are precisely urgently needed by the tourism agencies. In order to meet travel agencies' growing demands for high-end tourist talents and the continuing education of the travel professionals, we are dedicated to cultivating high-quality foreign-related tourism skilled personnel, constructing high-end foreign-related tourism training rooms, training teachers capable of bilingual teaching and cooperating with overseas high-level Tourism Management Colleges in talent training. Adhering to the purpose of serving the tourism business, we actively engage in solving the agencies' urgent problems through adjusting talent training programs, truly serving the local economic development, and supporting the transformation and upgrading of enterprises. Tourism Management Program strives to construct a community of common destiny with the high-end foreign related tourism enterprises. By means of personnel exchange and resource sharing, we will establish a unique brand for the training of high-end foreign-related tourism talents in China, and gradually establish China's top and world-renowned tourist talents training base by integrating various resources and keeping pace with the tourism industry's development.

Area Part II The Students

Communication and Promotion of the Programme (before and during the admission process)

Admission Selection Method

The admission selection method of Program of Tourism Management students includes two types. One is via yearly National College Entrance Examination, which conduct the admission selection based on the provincial unified entrance examination score line. The other one is via independent enrolment, which is a targeted test organized by the college, including written test and interview, as a way of selecting more students who are more appropriate for the specialty.

Sources of Tourism Management Students

The college also recruits students from the secondary vocational schools in a certain ratio, besides high school students. To attract outstanding students t each year the college sends some staffs to secondary vocational schools to do a propaganda tour. The proportion of secondary vocational school students' enrolment ascends year by year. The year of 2004 is the first time for secondary vocational school students to be enrolled while in recent years the proportion of the secondary vocational school students reaches 40%~50%. In addition, Tourism Management Program began enrolling apprenticeship students since 2015.

Admission Conditions and Procedures

The admission strictly abides by the relevant policies, regulations of the Ministry of Education and Guangdong Provincial Admission Office, and follow

the rule that the school is responsible for admission and admission office provides supervision. Taking the National College Entrance Examination scores as the fundamental basis, in accordance with the principle of fairness, justice, openness, we give a comprehensive assessment in moral, intellectual, physical, aesthetics and labor education, and enroll only those who are outstanding. Based on the lowest admission score delimited by the admission office and on the condition of completion of admission plan, we specify the admission standards. The admission is conducted differently for different types of students including students of science, students of liberal arts, art students, sports students, 3+ certificate students (including veterans) and high school students.

In Guangdong Province, high school students are divided into students of liberal arts and students of sciences. The subjects involve physics, chemistry, biology, or politics, geography, history. The students have to pass all the three subjects and at least one of them must reach level C or above. For art and sports students, at least two subjects have to reach level D or above. When recruiting students, it is always to take the principle of "Score is the priority", which is to order the students' scores from high to low, and matriculate the students with higher scores first, then matriculate those with lower scores. If several candidates obtain the same scores, they will be ordered according to the unified ranking method of the province. When arranging the majors, the college refers to the choices ordered by the candidates. For the candidates whose first choices are not admitted, if obeying adjustment of majors, they may be adjusted to other majors; if candidates do not obey the adjustment, the candidates' files will be returned to them.

For 3+ certificate students (including veterans), it always takes the principle of "first choice is the preferred". Our college is giving priority to qualified students whose first choice is tourism management. If the enrollment plan has not been completed, we will enroll the candidates whose secondary choice is our college. So, the basic principle of admission is "first choice is preferred".

Communication with Students and Parents

Before the annual enrolment, the college will send teachers to attend the special meeting with parents, so that more parents can understand our college and the program. In order to let students clearly understand the basic situation of our major and make a better choice, the recruitment brochure will detail the training objectives, curriculum setting, faculty, teaching plans and fees.

On registration day, the college will arrange teachers on spot to introduce our major's basic situation and campus life to students and parents, thus increase communication chances with them. Over the past three years, the communication activity is continuing to be improved and progressed. The activity has been highly appreciated by the college, parents, and students. It is ensured that the students fully understand their own major before they are enrolled.

Curriculum, Faculty Preparation and Cost Planning

Before entering the school, each major has perfected the professional teaching plan and the curriculum teaching schedule. Every three years, the teaching plan changes according to the needs of students and social development.

Now the latest version of the teaching plan is the 2022 edition of tourism management professional teaching plan. Faculty is abundant in tourism management major and the structure is reasonable, which will ensure the teaching task being well completed.

The tuition of tourism management major is charged according to the unified regulations of the college. Since 2016, the tuition fees has been reduced to 5, 250 *yuan* from 6, 500 *yuan* yearly.

Introduction of the Student in the Programme (Post Admission)

Enrolment Number and Composition of Tourism Management Students

Tourism Management (including Tourism English) enrolled about 200 students annually in recent 5 years. In 2012, totally 209 students were enrolled and all of them are from high schools. In 2013, 152 high school students and 28 students from secondary vocational schools were enrolled. In 2014, 139 high school students and 81 students from secondary vocational schools were

enrolled. In 2015, 155 high school students and 81 from secondary vocational schools were enrolled. In 2016, 147 high school students and 103 students from secondary vocational schools were enrolled. The program started to enrol apprentices in 2015. Detailed data is shown in the following table :

Students Enrolled in the Tourism Management Program 2004–2017

Grade	Major	Total Number of Students	Students from Secondary Vocational Schools	Students from High Schools	Proportion of Students from Secondary Vocational Schools
2004	Tourism Management	200	100	100	50%
2005	Tourism Management	180	90	90	50%
2006	Tourism Management	180	90	90	50%
2007	Tourism Management	210	105	105	50%
2008	Tourism Management	300	150	150	50%
2009	Tourism Management	200	100	100	50%
2010	Tourism Management	180	90	90	50%
2011	Tourism Management	220	110	110	50%
2012	Tourism Management	219	100	119	54%
2013	Tourism Management	210	90	120	57%
2014	Tourism Management	217	90	127	58%
2015	Tourism Management	236(including apprentices)	100	136	58%
2016	Tourism Management	240(including apprentices)	100	140	58%
2017	Tourism Management	250(including apprentices)	80	170	68%

Feature of Students from Secondary Vocational Schools

In the past five years, the two type of students have shown different features. The students from secondary vocational schools show better cognition on the major and profession because they have learned about the major in previous study.

Students of this kind have generally obtained the vocational qualifications. After entering the college, it is easier to absorb the professional courses, especially show more advantages in the practical courses and skills competitions. However, they have a weaker foundation in English study, which is a disadvantage compared with the students from high schools.

Freshmen Orientation

After the students arrive in the school, the director of the program will carry out the orientation to the freshmen, including major profiles, curriculum, employment, professional spirit and literacy, faculty, etc. which helps the students to start brand new college life. At the same time, we invite the alumni to go back to the college and communicate with the freshmen, and also invite experts from the industry to give lectures about the major to them in addition to professional education, we usually ask the dean or secretary of the school to give the first class to the students.

Attention Given to Students' Needs – Administrative, Academic, Social Welfare and Curriculum Support

Administrative Support

The college pays close attention to the growth of students, and cares about the present situation of the students from the administrative aspect and provide personalized service and help to them. The administrative office and instructor office are open to students during the working day, the administrative staff help deal with handle various matters for the students. The offices also recruit some students as part-time staff to help solve problems proposed by the students. Students' academic performance includes results of routine assessment and final examination scores, which is determined and evaluated by professional teachers, and input into the online score system. Students can query the results through personal accounts. If students have objections to the results, they can submit request for score check in written form.

Academic Support

During the period of study, the college will arrange experts' lectures, job fairs, and special activities on campus for the students to participate according to their own needs, helping them broaden their knowledge and obtain more

internship positions.Professional teachers will join the class WeChat groups and QQ groups to answer online students' various questions and provide suggestion or guidance.

Student Welfare Support

The excellent students who are well developed in all-round aspects are eligible to apply for National Scholarships and National Encouragement Scholarships. The college also set up some comprehensive scholarships such as "Outstanding 1 student" "Excellent Student Cadre" and seven individual awards named "Excellent Study Award" "Creative Achievement Award" "Art and Sports Activities Award" "Award for Certificates and Grading" "High Morality Award" "Academic Progress Award" "Award for Outstanding Organization in Student Activities".

Poverty-stricken students can apply for national student loans and state grants. College also set up grants for them. The grants are divided into three levels of A, B, C according to the different economic conditions of the students. The amount is 1 000~2 000 *yuan* yearly. The College has set up a Part-time Work Management Centre to provide part-time jobs for college students. It is equipped with specialized management departments and staffs. In recent five years, there are 15% to 20% of the students have received subsidies or incentives each year. We ensure that the excellent student are rewarded and the students from poor families obtain the subsidies or loans. The student loans cover all the students who encounter difficulties and submit applications, to ensure the successful completion of their studies.

Curriculum Support

When elaborating the curriculum for Tourism Management Program, we take full account of the students' own characteristics and the systematic development of the discipline, and integrate the students' professional core competence, so as to lay a foundation for the improvement of students' comprehensive quality, enhancement of their professional skills and ability of sustainable development when setting the professional courses, we give full consideration to the market demand and the needs of the discipline development. Curriculum of tourism management specialty is divided into five modules, including comprehensive quality courses, professional basic courses, professional core courses, comprehensive professional practice, and professional development. The specific design concerns students' individual needs and the needs of professional development.

Assessment of the Students Performance

Comprehensive Evaluation of Students' Academic Achievements

Evaluation methods are different for different courses. For practical training courses, the students are evaluated mainly by skills they mastered, which are usually reflected in the final skill test and in daily skill study and practice. For theoretical courses, the students are comprehensively evaluated mainly by final examination and routine performance. Final exams of theoretical courses include subjective and objective questions, the students have 90 minutes to 2 hours to finish the test. The test papers cover the basic theoretical knowledge and professional knowledge. Students' routine performance includes attendance, the assignments, the performance in classes (respect of classroom discipline, interaction with teachers, discussion in classes, etc.) and so on.

Academic Achievement

The students mastered the theoretical knowledge and professional skills of the major after they had learned all kinds of courses, which prepare them to work in career of tourism. Students show good academic performance. Most of the students could pass the theoretical tests, and very few of them fail. The students who failed would take part in make-up exams, and the final result is up to standard. Most of the students could pass the skill tests of the training course.

Meanwhile, the students have opportunities to do internships in positions of enterprises cooperating with the college, they make progress in mastering the skills required by the real work and could make economic benefit directly to the enterprises. The college requires that every student should have at least one certificate of skill when they graduate, so every student majoring in tourism

has obtained a certificate of skill including certificate of tour guide, which is beneficial for them to be employed in the future. Most students have actively passed CET-4 (College English Test Band 4) , and some students have passed CET-6 (College English Test Band 6) , which creates conditions for international development of their career in the future.

In view of the requirement of computer skills by the social positions, most of the students majoring in tourism took part in the exams for National Computer Rank Examination and have obtained the certificate. Students are also actively engaged in all kinds of student activities during spare time. For example, they join Hotel Association, Tour Guide Association, English salon and so on. The associations not only organize all kinds of skills contest in college level, but also strengthen the contact with hotels and travel agencies to enhance students' understanding of the real work. The activities enrich the students' campus life and also provide them with a platform to practice themselves. Each year, our college organizes the hotel skill competition, tour guide skills contests in Chinese and in English and tea art competition, of which the winners will further take part in the contests in provincial and national level. In recent years, our students achieve a series of excellent prizes, including : the first prize of National Chinese Tour Guide Skills Contest, first prize of National English Tour Guide Skills Contest, first prize of Guangdong Province Tea Art Competition and so on.

Evaluation of Students' Satisfaction Level Regarding the Programme and Additional Services

Students' Sense towards College and Major

The college has formulated a series of policies for students' Curriculum Learning. The college sets APP of to supervise students' attendance. The procedure of asking for leave for reason of personal affairs and for illness is strict, which is a method of supervision of class attendance of the students. At the same time, the college has set the award for most satisfying course, which can reflect the students' supervision and evaluation to the course teaching, thus promotes the teaching level of the faculty. During the semester, student seminars are organized to better understand the students' opinions and suggestions regarding the related courses, based on which the teachers put forward the rectification plan. At the end of each semester, students will evaluate the teaching. The evaluation consists of 12 indexes and a collection of students' comments reflecting the satisfaction level of the students. The results shows that generally the students are satisfied with the teaching methods of most teachers. In order to encourage teachers to actively explore teaching methods, the college also sets excellent teaching awards for teachers.

Students' Satisfaction with School Environment

Students are generally satisfied with the environment of campus study and life. Each classroom is equipped with air conditioner, which enable students to study peacefully in the hot summer. All the canteens have been renovated, and the dining environment of the students has been greatly improved. The whole campus is covered by free Wi-Fi, which is convenient for teachers and students to access to the Internet anytime and anywhere, speeding up the information exchange.

The college particularly sets up Alumni Association to get in contact with alumni. Every year the Alumni Association will track the graduates, involving the employment situation, salary, the counterpart rate between the position and the major, employer's satisfaction, etc. In addition, Alumni Association invited graduates to go back to college to participate in activities including symposium, speech, report, and opening ceremony of new semester. These activities provide valuable experience for the students.

In order to improve student's employment situation, the college introduced a series of policies and measures. The college has set up Section of Recruitment and Employment to be responsible for the employment guidance of students. The college carried out a series of employment guidance courses to provide overall guidance in this aspect. It helps graduates get conscious of the employment situation, build up confidence and establish positive attitude. Meanwhile the college encourages students to start up business by themselves

by making a series of policies and measures including setting courses of innovation and entrepreneurship, establishing department of innovation and entrepreneurship, organizing students to participate in competitions of innovation and entrepreneurship in national and provincial level, and conveying the preferential policies to students' entrepreneurship encouraged by the nation and Guangdong Province.

Many students are employed in well-known enterprises. So far, there are more than 40 graduates employed by company of Gongbei Port travel agency, which is the famous travel agency in China and most powerful travel agency in Zhuhai. There are more than 90 graduates employed by company of Chimelong Group Limited, which is AAAAA Scenic Area in China and a popular holiday resort worldwide. In addition, hundreds of graduated students are working in other travel agencies, international brand hotels, event companies, foreign trade companies and other tourism enterprises, etc.

Area Part III Curriculum and Teaching System

Methodology Used to Formulate the Curriculum

Educational Objectives

To Serve the economic and social development in the Pearl River Delta and Guangdong province, the Tourism Management Program aims to cultivate occupation-oriented , high-level specialized talents with full development of morality, wisdom, physique, and aesthetics. It prepares students for mastering a basic knowledge of tourism culture, tourism service and tourism management both in theory and in practice, with a solid professional base of tourism management and operation, an excellent communicative ability of foreign languages, and a strong sense of renovation. After their graduation, students will be qualified to enter a variety of hospitality and tourism sectors including hotel management, human resources, PR companies, restaurants, hotels, and many other related companies.

Curriculum Design

The Principles of Curriculum Design : With the educational objectives of "solid foundation, broad caliber, excellent quality, highly developed ability", the program focuses on student- oriented quality education. In order to establish the students' cognition and knowledge structure systematically, it is crucial to make reform of the teaching method and to establish a scientific teaching evaluation standard. The integration of production, learning and research should be regarded as a breakthrough point to strengthen the professional curriculum construction, completely promote sustained and balanced curriculum development.

Curriculum Structure

The courses of this program are comprised of 2,637 class hours or 131 credits. From the perspective of the vertical structure, it can be divided into four modules : comprehensive quality courses 1 (compulsory) comprehensive quality courses 2 (elective) , professional required modules (including professional foundation, professional core, and professional comprehensive practice) , professional development. The curriculum provides students with general education courses and professional basic courses in the first year, and professional core courses, professional practice courses and professional development courses in the second and third year. The four modules account for 14.5%, 3.8%, 64.9%, and 16.8% of the total credits respectively. From the perspective of the horizontal structure, professional courses take up 85 credits, including professional courses 37.6%, professional core courses 27.1% and comprehensive practical courses 35.3%. From the distribution of class hours, the practical courses occupy more than half of the total class hours (56.9%) , and the theoretical class hours occupy 43.1%.

Framework of Professional Core Courses. In the curriculum, a lot of emphasis has been laid on the cultivation of professional core competencies, providing students with 394 class hours of 6 core courses, covering travel agencies and hotels——two major targeted areas of the tourist industries. Except the course about tour guide certificates, all the others are set up in the

second academic year. To improve the students' international tourism skills and intercultural communication ability, the course of "our Guide English" is offered in the fourth semester.

A List of Professional Core Courses

COURSES	Class Hours	Credits	Semester
Tour Guide Business	54	3	2nd semester
Hotel Lobby and Guest Room Management	68	4	3rd semester
Operation and Management of Catering	68	4	3rd semester
Tour Guide English	68	4	4th semester
Operation and Management of Travel Agency	68	4	4th semester
Tourism Marketing	68	4	4th semester

Curriculum Development

First, for the formulation of professional courses, an extensive investigation has been conducted centering the idea of "talent-conscious" and "curriculum-oriented". The interviewees include industry enterprises, professional teachers, graduates, on-school students and so on. Secondly, every December, some tourism professionals from tourism colleges, tourism industry and tourism enterprises would be invited to attend a seminar to discuss the educational orientation and objectives, core ability cultivation, curriculum settings and other aspects related to curriculum building. After the preliminary investigation, the mid-term discussion, the talent training program, and the curriculum system draft would be made. In order to make it more scientific and reasonable, the experts committee made up of staffs from schools and enterprises was convened to discuss and demonstrate, revise and perfect the curriculum before it is implemented. (The whole procedures of developing curriculum go like this : investigating the positions of the enterprises—refining typical tasks—analyzing what knowledge, skills and quality should be combined into courses—working out the curriculum) .

Curriculum Implementation

The total course duration is 6 semesters, among which 4.5 semesters at school and 1.5 semesters for the internship (including graduation design). For the course details, please see the Appendix: ① The Program of Cultivating Talents; ② The Allocation of Schooling Weeks in Each Semester; ③ The Calendar for Professional Teaching; ④ Teaching Plan of Tourism Management Program(version 2016).

Curriculum Coherence

Curriculum Coherence in this Program. In the first and second semester (the first academic year), general courses and basic courses are offered for students such as Basic English and Introduction to Tourism and Certification. During the third and fourth semester (the second academic year), students can take some specialized core courses, such as some professional competency courses for hotel orientation and Hotel English in the third semester, especially for students who are going to participate in the Hotel Occupation Skills Competition. Furthermore, to train student's professional ability, the fourth semester prepares some courses about travel agencies, such as Professional Tour Guide English, Tourism Marketing, and Course for Development. The fifth and the sixth semester (the third academic year) mainly focus on courses for development and internship.

In the courses of the three years, English courses have been carried out throughout the whole curriculum to meet the needs of foreign tourism and intercultural communication under the current globalization background. With a strong curriculum coherence, this program helps students cultivate occupation abilities through basic courses, professional core courses, professional practice courses and development courses subsequently and orderly. For the details, please see in the Appendix: Teaching Plan of Tourism Management Program (version 2016).

Curriculum Coherence between Secondary and Higher Vocational education period.

Since 2015, Modern Apprenticeship Pilot Project has been conducted in some secondary or higher vocational schools. In September of the same year, this program signed agreement on 3 plus 2 articulation education program

（first 3 years of education in secondary vocational schools and last 2 years of education in higher vocational schools ） with Shenzhen Huaqiang Vocational Technical School for the purpose of cultivating qualified talents integrally. A lot of details about the program of talent cultivation were discussed including the position analysis, requirements for vocational tourism professionals as a special group, and requirements for students' all-round ability and quality. The two parties are crystal clear about their own responsibilities in different education periods.

Based on the analysis of the required knowledge, ability and quality obtained in the secondary and higher vocational education, the programs for cultivation of talents in secondary and higher vocational education are eventually completed after integrating their own curriculum systems, with the clarified curriculum, and the perfected standards. In this regard, Professor Wan Fangqiu, the director of the program of Tourism Management with some other teaching staffs successfully applied one of the Teaching Reform Project of Guangdong Province in 2016. Their study pointed out that compared with secondary vocational schools, the required knowledge, ability and quality in higher vocational curriculum have a larger increment presenting vertical extension and horizontal expansion, i.e., secondary vocational education is the foundation, while higher vocational education is a promotion. To avoid the repetition of some courses such as practice courses and professional courses in the curriculum of the two periods, focuses should be put on constructing effective convergence of the curriculum system, improving the quality and efficiency of talent cultivation in higher vocational education, and enhancing the attractiveness of higher vocational education to students in secondary vocational schools.

Effectiveness of the Pedagogical Method

Appropriate Teaching Concept : Application of Working Process Oriented Teaching Concept. For higher vocational education, more attention should be paid to the consistency of students' course learning and field practice, explore the integration of courses and practice, implement the program according to positions requirements, explore the various teaching modes such as learning, task-driven teaching, project-oriented teaching and so on. This requires the teaching staff in higher vocational colleges to focus on how to achieve the educational objectives when they are making curriculum. It is necessary to combine the actual work with knowledge learning, divide the working process into small tasks. Each of them would be accomplished with a goal, which ultimately enables students to complete all the small tasks, and eventually obtain the required abilities of future positions.

Some teaching staffs such as Guo Weina, Duan Jinmei, Feng Shuling, Wu Di, and so on have been applying the two teaching modes mentioned above for many years. They have combined the requirements of the actual work of travel agencies and hotels with the curriculum. By doing this, they could have a new understanding and thinking about teaching methodology. Among them, lecturer Guo Weina（2016）did some research and published an article titled "Course Reform and Practice of Travel Agency Management Based on the Working Process-oriented Mode".

Application of Objective-based Teaching Method

In order to cope with the challenges brought by modern science and technology to higher education, a part of teaching staff have been experiencing the objective-based teaching methodology and hoping that they could solve the problems of "What kind of talents should we cultivate" and "How we should do". The concept of objective-based teaching is goal-oriented, which requires teachers to develop training objectives, assessment requirements and curriculum system from the perspective of the professional needs, eventually ensure the consistency of educational objectives and results to the greatest extent.

In the teaching of tourism management, some teachers have made teaching reforms by employing the concept of objective-based teaching. By taking the students professional requirements and the actual situation as the starting

points, they work out a rational teaching plan, innovate teaching methods, enrich the teaching contents, to help students have a full understanding of theoretical professional knowledge, thus ultimately improve their professional skills and learning ability. In this aspect, Mr. Zhu Han, one of the teachers who has been trying to figure out the problem about how to improve students' English ability in basic English courses. He did a lot of research and applied for a project about Guangdong provincial teaching reform : "Application of Curriculum Mechanism Based on Achievement-oriented in Higher Vocational education—Teaching Reform of College English Teaching in Guangdong Polytechnic of Science and Technology." Another Teacher, Yang Yi, declared the school-level teaching reform project "Hotel English Curriculum Design and Reform Based on the Comparative Study of WPO and OBE" .

Diversity and Effectiveness of Teaching Methodology

The program emphasizes the interaction between teachers and students, and fully mobilizes the enthusiasm, initiative, and creativity of the students. Teaching reform has been implemented continuously. According to the different teaching objectives, teaching contents, teaching objects, teachers adapt different teaching methods including Task-driven, Project-based, Group Work, Case Study, Role Playing, Field Research and so on against the traditional cramming teaching system, to cultivate students' ability of acquiring knowledge, solving problem and creative thinking.

Application and Promotion of Informatization Teaching

For the teaching staff, creatively understanding and developing modern teaching means is a task which brooks no delay. To improve the teaching effect, all the teaching staff have been using information technology widely in teaching activities. In addition to the multimedia courses, they also devote themselves to applying and developing online courses and MOOC courses (massive open online courses) for focusing on their own research fields and courses. There are 9 online open courses and 1 MOOC course open for students. All the teaching staff are actively improving their level of informatization teaching and many online courses are under construction. Network teaching and management have been realized gradually. The excellent teaching resources are shared by uploading the teaching syllabus, lesson plans, exercises, experiment guidance and reference on the course website.

In addition, the teaching staff actively take part in the informatization teaching contests both in provincial and national levels. Su Dan, one of the teaching staff won the second prize in "First National Foreign Language MOOC Competition, Guangdong Division", and the third prize in the "Vocational Education: National Informatization Teaching Design Competition for Higher Vocational Education".

Application of teaching methods: Task-driven and Project-oriented

Some teaching staff have adopted task-driven and project-oriented teaching methods on the base of "Working process" concept, which is one of the most popular teaching concepts in the curriculum reform, emphasizing on the real case and the real task in design training, and striving to achieve the integration of theoretical and practical training, practice training and working environment, and requirements for quality cultivation and position training. The following courses are good demonstrations: "Travel Agency Management", "Tour Guide Business" "Travel Planning Practice" "Tourism Marketing" "Simulation of Tour Guide" "Restaurant Service Skills Training" etc. For example, Feng Shuling has paid a lot of attention to cultivate students' professional morality, presentation ability, adaptability, sense of rules in tour guidance, psychological quality in her course design. According to the characteristics of tourism development in the Pearl River Delta region, she designed her course basing on the actual process of being a tour guide, and tried to achieve the purpose of combination of teaching, practice and research, with the publication of an article titled "Combination of Classroom learning and Field Practice in the Simulated Courses".

Application of Other Teaching Methods: Case Analysis, Role Playing,

Field Research and so on.

Due to the particularity of this program, most of the courses should be closely linked with the development of the industry, the study and collection of fresh industry cases should be used in the classes, which could let students be closer to the industry and enterprises frontier. The teaching staff who conduct the courses like "A Stimulated Course for Tour Guide" "Banquet Design" and "Catering Operation and Management", are required to collect a lot of real cases of being tour guides, party planners and catering servers. Role-playing is wildly used in class teaching. Students could have the chances to play the roles of tour guides, waiters, ushers and so on, which can involve them into the lively atmosphere and activate their thinking and operating potential, finally improve students' practical ability.

Existence, Access And USefulness Of The Curriculum Support Facilities

Infrastructure and teaching equipment

To fully develop students' practical abilities, 5 training rooms have been built particularly, including 3 language multimedia labs equipped with the appropriate training equipment and related software; 1 room for simulation of tour guide and 1 for practicing as tour guides. All the simulation equipment of exhibition facilities was sponsored by Zhuhai Import and Export Chamber of Commerce. Besides, there is an apprehensive hotel training center of over 500 square meters in Training Building No. 5, with various functional areas such as Chinese Restaurant, Western Restaurant, Bar, Tea Art, Body Etiquette and so on. The following are the details of the present condition and usage of the training rooms:

No.	Projects Names	Spots	Floor Area (Square Meters)	Seats	Equipment Value (Unit: Ten Thousands *yuan*)	Accessibility	Courses
1	International Bilingual Professional Talents Training Base	S4304	300	72	70	Accessible	Tourism e-commerce Office Automation
2	Language Lab	S1304	160	60	50.605	Accessible	Hotel English
3	Language Lab	S1303	240	75	44.518	Accessible	Tourism English
4	Language Lab	S2503	173	70	60.824	Accessible	Hotel English
5	Physique Etiquette Training Room	S5304	150	50	14.097	Accessible	Physique Training
6	European and American Cultural Experience Room	S5306	170	80	6 (8) 259	Accessible	Tourism Etiquette; Speech Situational English
7	Simulated Tour Guide Training Room	S2104	248	90	7 (8) 297	Accessible	Tourism Etiquette; Simulated Tour Guide
8	Western Restaurant Training Room	S5301	110	50	4.790	Accessible	Western Restaurant
9	Hotel Training Center	S5302	240	50	27.044	Accessible	Front office; Restaurant; Bartender; Tea art
10	Makeup and Image Design	The Middle Hall	65	50	15.80	Accessible	Makeup and Image Design

Other Teaching Facilities, Equipment and Resources

In recent years, there has been an increasing investment in the construction of library information resources in our school with an annual collection of 100 thousand volumes reaching a steady development. Every year saw a subscription of more than 1,350 kinds of Chinese and foreign language journals and periodicals. The CNKI database has been introduced, as well as Duxiu Database, Superstar E-Book database, and Founder Apabi e-book Database. At present, the library holds a total of nearly 1,600,000 volumes, including 1,054,300 paper ones (including 18,239 bound volumes paper books published and 28,313 pieces of CD-ROM) , 280,000 electronic books, and 140,000 electronic journals or books. Students' collection quantity reaches nearly 90 per capita. Chinese paper books and foreign original paper books comprise of the main body of the library, decorated with electronic journals, electronic books, multimedia resources and self-built database of digital resources. In a nutshell, the library is a wonderful place for students to explore knowledge.

Management and maintenance of teaching equipment and resources

To ensure the normal operation of the training rooms, training rooms and equipment are under management by three different administration levels : Industrial Center (GDPST) , Training Center (School of Foreign Language) and this program (Tourism Management) . Training center is in charge of bidding and purchase of equipment and facilities. Training Center for daily operation and management, and the teaching staff and students of this program responsible for maintaining and purchasing, accounting and so on.

Part IV: Faculty

Faculty Selection

The Department of Tourism Management consists of 24 faculty members (15 female and 9 male) , all of whom are citizens of The People's Republic of China. The standards of selecting faculty members are in line with the requirements of the state and the major. In the latest faculty recruitment in 2016, the major of tourism management posted the following conditions:

· A master's degree or above/lecturer or above.

· Under the age of 40.

· With more than 2 years' teaching experience in higher education organization, or with more than 2 years' position-related working experience as a full-time professional in an enterprise.

No discrimination in terms of gender, race, religion, political bias in all recruitment conditions.

According to the requirements of the positions, paper test and face-to-face interview are set to assess candidates' professional knowledge and qualifications. The detailed process are as follows:

Assessment of professional knowledge and skills

· The assessment for this step includes two parts: teaching demonstration and Q & A. Teaching demonstration requires the candidates to display their ways of preparing and presenting teaching content and the teaching effect. The full score for this part is 30 points, the passing line is 21 points, the time for this part is limited within 15 minutes.

· The Q & A mainly evaluate candidates' professional capacity and suitability for the position. Interviewers announce the questions and the candidates are required to give answers on site. The full score for this part is 30 points, the passing line is 21 points, and the time is 10 minutes.

Ideological evaluation:

· The evaluation in this step is to get a general ideal of the candidates' attitude towards the world, the country and life. Interviewers announce the questions and the candidates are required to give answers on site. The full score of this part is 20 points, the passing line is 16 points and it must be finished in 10 minutes.

Mental health assessment:

· The assessment in this step is to evaluate the mental state and

personality of the candidates. Interviewers announce the questions and the candidates are required to give answers on site. The full score of this part is 20 points, the passing line is 16 points and it must be finished in 10 minutes.

The average score of the above 3 parts will be the final score of the whole assessment (the 3rd number after decimal point will be rounded off). Candidates will be ranked according to their final score, from highest to lowest. Those who fail in any one of the above 3 parts will lose the eligibility.

The Department of Tourism Management actively recruits qualified faculty through the above-mentioned procedures, and push forward the development of both academic level and professional skills.

Academic Coordination

Academic coordination is demonstrated in the following aspects:

Curriculum team activities—in the department of tourism management, teachers working on the same curriculum form a relatively independent curriculum team, each of these teams will hold meetings, be engaged in the teaching and non-teaching activities of the department, such as collective study of curriculum standard and teaching material, analysis of learning status, formulation of the teaching plan, decomposition the tasks of course preparation, review on the teaching outline, feedback of teaching practice information. Based on the collectively prepared teaching outline and learning status of each class, the teachers work out the teaching plan.

Departmental activities—the department of tourism management has definite stipulations about departmental activities, for example to hold scheduled staff meeting periodically to discuss the difficulties in work and corresponding solutions. For instance, in 2017, the department sent its faculty to attend miscellaneous training relating to department development and curriculum conception. Then the department invited those trained faculty to give a presentation on the training, to share the constructive ideas with the other staff. To encourage the faculty to improve themselves, all major/curriculum-related training held by legitimate organizations can be chosen by staff as self-improving program.

Mutual assistance between teachers and administrative staff—in the department of tourism management, teaching faculty and administrative staff cooperate to promote the progress of the students, the development of the department and their own development in career. This cooperation may demonstrate in the setting departmental vision, designing the students' cultivation programs and the arrangement and coordination in teaching schedule.

Program-related research activities—the tourism management department and its faculty boast intense passion for relevant research activities. Each of the faculty has attended in one of the above-mentioned research activities, 1/2 of the faculty were/are host of one research project, nearly 1/3 of the staff were/are in charge of research project (s) on the municipal level. Detailed information (copies of research application approval) is attached to this report.

College-enterprise interaction—college-enterprise interaction plays an important role in promoting teaching quality in Guangdong Polytechnic of Science and Technology, because it helps the teachers to cultivate students in accordance with the needs of the enterprises, which focus on the practical ability of their staff. The school authority sets up a special action group to guide and supervise the jointly cultivation of teachers and mutual recruitment of professionals by the school and the enterprises. The president being the group leader, all the deans being the members of the group, they work together to run the group. A series of regulations have been set especially for the building up of a team of teachers working part-time in enterprises, to negotiate and offer more opportunities for full-time faculty in the college to earn practical position experience in enterprises, to make sure that both full-time teaching faculty in school and part-time enterprise professionals have their legitimate income for the teaching job while they enjoy the salary from the enterprises. As this mode tells, the enterprise professionals and full-time teaching faculty learn from each other, the result is that enterprise professionals become better at teaching,

and the teachers in school gain precious practical position experience, thus enhance their ability for social contribution.

· During the college-enterprise interaction, a training process of professional teachers is set up, including the following methods : the two parties (college and enterprises) select specialized teachers and enterprise professionals to participate in professional training courses organized by relevant government departments.

· The college selects professional teachers to work periodically in a career-related position in partner enterprises or participate in on-the-job training organized by enterprises.

· Partner enterprises are contracted to provide training courses on practical skills and corporate culture for the college's professional teachers to promote their practical experience. The training is expected to promote professional teachers' practical skills up to the same level with those part-time professionals from the enterprises within 3 years.

· The college is contracted to provide training courses on teaching methodology and comprehensive qualifications for part-time teachers from the partner enterprises. The training is expected to promote their' teaching capability up to the same level with the full-time teachers on campus within 3 years.

· The college hold at least one seminar each semester between full-time on-campus teachers and part-time teachers from enterprises. Meetings of such kind are expected to offer opportunities for both to communicate on their reflection and difficulties on their adaptability in the new roles, and learn from each other.

· The college invites top enterprise experts to take part in the college's research projects, mainly providing instructions on the practical conduction of research.

Professional Performance

The faculty of Tourism Management Department, including 1 teaching assistant,15 lecturers, 4 associate professors and 3 professors have made wonderful achievements both in teaching and research fields.

In Teaching

The team has made good achievements in course teaching, 3 courses have been completed, more courses are listed as the key courses by the polytechnic. Besides, Miss Su Dan has got the third prize in the national education informatization competition. One teacher won the second president teaching prize in 2017 and one teacher won the third president teaching prize in 2017. Two teachers got prizes for most satisfactory course evaluated by students. Recently, the teaching group won the first prize awarded by the polytechnic.

In Research

In addition, the teaching staff have made wonderful performance in research. They have completed 3 state-level projects, 2 province-level projects, 6 city-level projects and 15 college-level projects. 16 textbooks have been published, 71 essays have been published in national key journals or international conferences. One teacher won the Zhuhai government prize for excellent scholastic achievement in 2011.

In Career-related Skill Competition

Currently the department has 23 full-time teachers, four of whom hold English and Chinese tour guide certificates, one has certificate of senior tourism counselor three earn certification of Tea Art Specialist (level II) , one certified air crew trainer, and one has certification of international exhibition clerk instructor.

Therefore, the qualified teaching team also excel in coaching the career skill competition, they have won 2 second prizes in the national college skill competition, 8 first prizes and 17 second prizes in provincial competition and more than 10 prizes in the competitions sponsored by Chinese Tourism Education Association. Besides, the students have won prizes awarded by the district and city bureau of tourism.

Continuous Knowledge Update

Training

The tourism management department boasts two types of faculty training :

Internal training, like the latest one in early 2017—tea art specialist training organized for professional teachers. This type of training is closely related to the establishment of bi-professional quality teaching faculty.

External training, which is carried out in accordance with colligate policies on faculty training , all eligible training programs will be funded by the college. According to the statistics, from 2015 to 2017, teachers of tourism management department participated in on-the-job training 58 times, the training content was mainly about promoting teaching skills. From 2011 to 2015, 18 papers were published in major journals, 8 research projects were established, carried out and completed, 24 training programs and social service projects were held.

The training record of the last three years shows that the on-the-job training for teachers are mainly focused on improving the teaching level, expanding program-related knowledge, and updating on the latest information of the tourism industry.

The selection of teachers' training programs depends on training course's relevancy to collegiate developing goals, which is verified by the management of the department. Training programs relating to the latest trend in tourism industry are more likely to be approved by the management.

Professional teachers actively involved various kinds of research projects at university-level, municipal, provincial and state-level, and took the initiative to participate in various informatization teaching competitions and have won excellent rankings.

Research Activities

Tourism management department attaches great importance to scientific research activities, actively announce various research application information, provides all kinds of resources to support their implementation. Language labs, training rooms are available for the faculty in need.

Most themes of the research activities in the department of tourism management are centered around three aspects: curriculum lectured by the faculty, demands of the public and cooperation projects with enterprises. There are various channels for the source of research information, and field researching and information exchanging activities are most frequently used means.

The tourism management department has an annual funding of 1,600,000 RMB in 2017 for its top—major—brand establishment project, which is dedicated to teaching activities and scientific research. The use of the fund will be approved only when the usage is for the purpose of the project progress.

Part V: The Management

Organizations

General organizational chart (Administration and Academics):

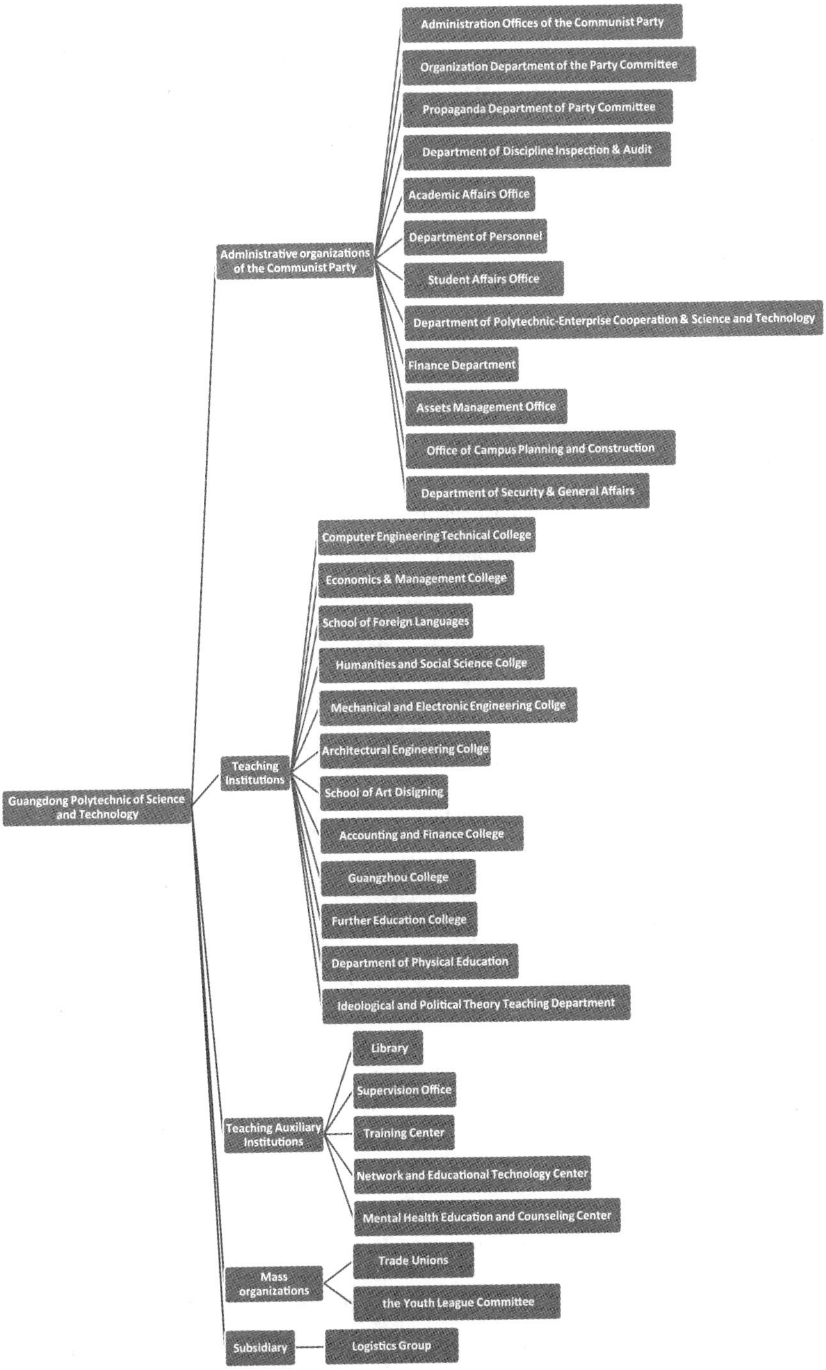

Administration Offices of the Communist Party

Organization Department of the Party Committee

Propaganda Department of Party Committee

Department of Discipline Inspection & Audit

Academic Affairs Office

Department of Personnel

Administrative organizations of the Communist Party

Student Affairs Office

Department of Polytechnic-Enterprise Cooperation & Science and Technology

Finance Department

Assets Management Office

Office of Campus Planning and Construction

Department of Security & General Affairs

Computer Engineering Technical College

Economics & Management College

School of Foreign Languages

Humanities and Social Science Collge

Mechanical and Electronic Engineering Collge

Architectural Engineering Collge

Teaching Institutions

School of Art Disigning

Accounting and Finance College

Guangzhou College

Further Education College

Department of Physical Education

Ideological and Political Theory Teaching Department

Guangdong Polytechnic of Science and Technology

Library

Supervision Office

Teaching Auxiliary Institutions

Training Center

Network and Educational Technology Center

Mental Health Education and Counseling Center

Trade Unions

Mass organizations

the Youth League Committee

Subsidiary

Logistics Group

Organization chart and job responsibilities

This specialty is based on the tourism advantages of the regions of Zhuhai, Hong Kong and Macao, and actively takes the approach of close cooperation among governments, the polytechnic, enterprises and the industry.

Cooperation between governments and the polytechnic

Teachers and students have frequently participated in activities such as the Guangdong International Tourism Culture Festival hosted by Guangdong Provincial Tourism Bureau, Zhuhai College Student Tourism Festival organized by Zhuhai Culture Sports and Tourism Bureau and the Travel Trade Fair as members of Zhuhai delegation, which not only provides the relevant governmental departments with various tourism services but also improves the tourism-based practical ability of the teachers and students. In addition, some teachers who are consulting experts of Zhuhai Culture Sports and Tourism Bureau have participated in the consultation and evaluation of the tourism projects of Zhuhai City for many times. Meanwhile, some leaders of Zhuhai Culture Sports and Tourism Bureau are members of the teaching steering committee for tourism management. They are involved in the professional construction and guidance.

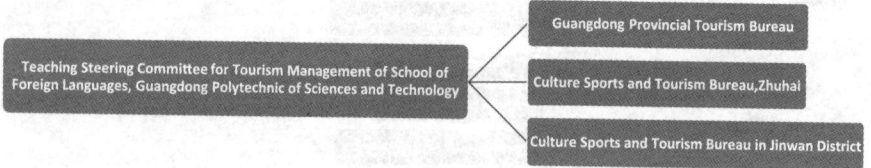

Cooperation between the polytechnic and the industry

As the college is a collective member of the council of Zhuhai Tourism Association and a Vice-President unit of Zhuhai Tourist Guide Association, all teachers and students of the program often participate in various activities and service work organized by Zhuhai Tourism Industry Association and the fellowship societies by the Tourist Guide Association of Guangdong, Hong Kong and Macao. It not only has tied up the relation with the tourism industry in Hong Kong and Macao as well as enterprises, but also facilitate students to practice and work in Hong Kong and Macao.

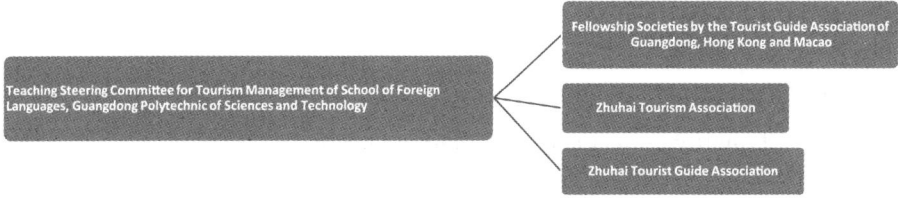

Cooperation between the polytechnic and enterprises

Since 2004, the polytechnic has successively cooperated with many famous scenic spots, hotels and travel agencies such as Zhuhai Imperial Hot Spring Resort, Dongguan Fengtai Garden Hotel, Zhuhai Bayview Hotel, Chimelong Holiday Resort, and China Travel Service, Gongbei Port, etc. The modes of cooperation mainly includes the following: senior managers of tourism enterprises become members of the professional construction committee; the polytechnic and enterprises have co-constructed off campus practice bases and jointly managed and assessed the interns; some backbones of tourism are hired as part-time teachers and take some training courses; some teachers are sent to enterprises for professional training; tourism enterprises sponsor and support the construction of the campus training rooms and the contest of tourist guide skills.

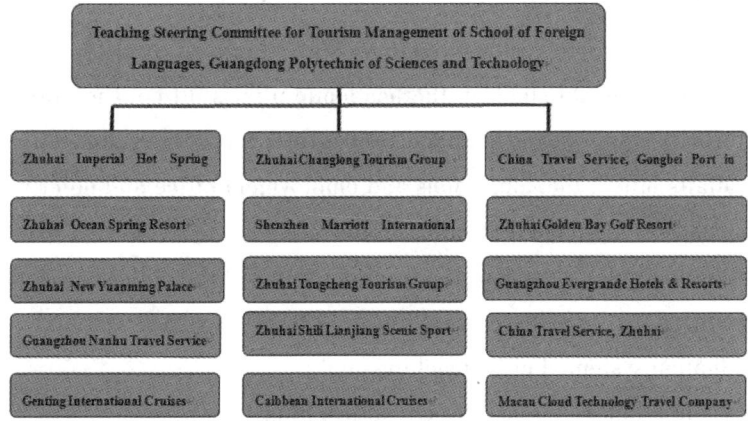

Questionnaire on working environment

Internship Appraisal of Graduates and Interns of 2016

Quality Assurance

Quality Plan

Overall quality project and its supporting manual.

Talent training project of Tourism Management in Guangdong Polytechnic of Sciences and Technology.

Questionnaire or evaluation system for internal and external stakeholders to understand the project.

Questionnaire and report on professional settings in 2016.

Documentary Evidences

Opinions on Strengthening the Talent Training in Higher Vocational Education（Ministry of Education, PRC. No. 2, 2000）.

Opinions on Improving the Teaching Quality of Higher Vocational Education（Ministry of Education, PRC. No. 16, 2006）.

Program of Teaching Quality Inspection and Improvement in the Academic Year of 2017–2018 in Guangdong Polytechnic of Sciences and Technology（Innovation and Enhance Office of Guangdong Polytechnic of Sciences and Technology, No. 9, 2017）.

Quality Monitoring

Quality Monitoring Index System : The teaching quality monitoring system is jointly established by the academic affairs office, the polytechnic and enterprise cooperation management office, the supervision office, the student affairs office, the admissions and employment office and other relevant departments. The main contents are as follows.

Evaluation index system of the teaching status of the college（faculty and department）.

Evaluation system of class teaching quality.

Evaluation index system of practical teaching.

Evaluation system of graduation thesis（graduation internship）.

Grading evaluation standard of on–campus teaching enterprises and off–campus teaching enterprises.

Report on the quality of employment of graduates.

Quality Monitoring Team

Supervisory Authority : The teaching quality monitoring organization branches two levels : polytechnic level and school (faculty or department) level. The former is composed of the polytechnic teaching committee, the academic affairs office, the supervision office, the student affairs office, the admissions and employment office, the polytechnic-enterprise cooperation management office (training center, offices) and other relevant departments. It is responsible for monitoring and evaluating the teaching status and teaching quality of the whole polytechnic and confirming the monitoring and evaluation results. The latter is made up of the school (faculty or department) teaching committee, teaching and research section and other relevant departments, which is responsible for monitoring and evaluating the teaching status and teaching quality of the school (faculty or department) , and reporting the monitoring and evaluation results to the relevant teaching quality monitoring organizations at the polytechnic level.

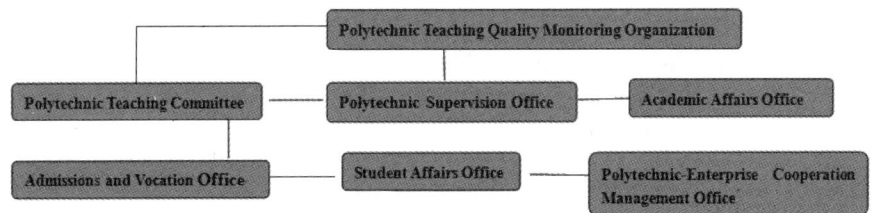

Monitoring Responsibilities

Responsibilities of the Polytechnic Teaching Committee : Under the leadership of the president, the polytechnic teaching committee is an important organization which studies the major issues, makes decisions, guides, plans, validates and supervises in the polytechnic teaching. Its main responsibilities in teaching quality monitoring are as follows.

To manage and guide broadly for the monitoring and evaluation of teaching quality in the polytechnic.

To urge and strengthen the teaching quality management both at the polytechnic level and school level in order to ensure the comprehensive improvement of the teaching quality.

Responsibilities of the Academic Affairs Office

To organize and make the teaching quality related standards or specifications of the polytechnic.

To formulate plans for basic teaching construction such as professional construction, curriculum construction and textbook construction, and put forward special evaluation plans.

To organize and work out the relevant assessment schemes and evaluation index systems, implementation methods and support documents required by the monitoring system.

To inspect, evaluate and supervise the operation and effect of the teaching process.

To formulate improvement measures and construction programs to cope with problems found in the monitoring and evaluation of teaching quality.

To investigate the teaching quality facing to students and provide feedback to relevant departments and teaching units.

Responsibilities of Polytechnic–Enterprise Cooperation Management Office

To formulate the basic construction plans of the school training rooms, training bases and "teaching enterprises", and be responsible for putting forward special evaluation plans.

To make the practical teaching of the school training rooms and training bases, the evaluation schemes of internships, and the framework plan for the evaluation of practical teaching of "teaching enterprises".

To track and supervise the internships.

To formulate improvement measures and construction programs in view of the problems found in the monitoring and evaluation of internships.

Responsibilities of the Polytechnic Supervision Office

To organize the relevant assessment schemes and evaluation index systems, implementation methods and supporting documents required by the quality monitoring system related to the teaching supervision.

To track and supervise the school teaching process.

To make an objective evaluation of the teaching quality and problems existing in teaching and learning, put forward suggestions for improvement, and give timely feedback to relevant departments in the form of teaching supervision information.

Responsibilities of Student Affairs Office

To formulate the evaluation plan for students' learning status and effect.

To put forward concrete measures to strengthen the management of education and the forming of study style to overcome the problems found in the monitoring and evaluation of the teaching quality such as the students' learning thoughts, learning attitude and study discipline.

To organize the assessment of students' learning status and effects.

To organize and conduct the research on the quality of freshmen.

To analyze the situation of talent demand.

To analyze the data of employment status.

To organize the follow-up survey of graduates.

Responsibilities of the Admissions and Employment Office

To analyze the data of employment status.

To organize the follow-up survey of graduates.

To organize surveys on the satisfaction of industry experts and employers.

To investigate the job suited rate.

Responsibilities of the School (Faculty and Department) Teaching Committee

To carry out the evaluations of teaching and learning according to the index system and evaluation criteria of the polytechnic teaching quality monitoring and evaluation.

To monitor the teaching quality of teachers in the school.

To assess students' learning status and effects in the school.

To analyze and study the problems found in the evaluation, and put forward measures for improvement.

To carry out other work under the leadership of the polytechnic teaching quality monitoring organization.

Responsibilities of Student Information Office

To make a timely comments and suggestions on the teaching management work such as teaching plans, teaching methods and means, teaching management, teaching conditions, teaching evaluation and teaching team, and to make regular feedback to the academic affairs office and the school.

To timely know the learning situation of students and reflect their information in various aspects including classes, experiments, internships, assignments and social practice.

Application of Quality Index and Its Result

MyCOS Students Quality Assessment Report. Relevant Information Reflecting the Norms of Global Ethics.

Employer

Did your institution/programme consider the principles of the Global Code of Ethics for Tourism in formulating the mission and the action plan?

The program is based in Zhuhai, a well-known tourist city in China. Zhuhai is located within Guangdong, Hong Kong and Macao Greater Bay Area which China is endeavoring to build. With the improvement of China's economic development, per capita disposable income continues to grow, and the public places higher demands on tourism. Prior to the establishment of the specialty, an in-depth study has been made concerning tourism needs of people of different income levels in the country. Combined with the characteristics of local economic development, especially the development of Zhuhai City's

"three highs and one special" industries concerned in the modern service industry requirements, the establishment of tourism management specialty is seen as an important means to resolve the contradiction between meeting the people' s growing needs for a better life and the imbalanced and insufficient development, and running a good and strong tourism management specialty is taken as a supporting force to serve local economic growth. In order to strive for excellent talent cultivation effect, tourism management specialty has designed talents training program according to the rules of global ethics in close connection with the social and economic development.

Does the institution/programme collaborate with the public/private sector in the implementation of the principles of the Global Code of Ethics for Tourism? If yes, please give examples.

In order to adapt to the new trend of the development of tourism industry and implement the guidelines of global ethics, a professional teaching council and a steering committee for tourism management have been established, which are composed of authoritative experts in the field of tourism in China. The list includes: Mr. Ke (Secretary–General of Zhuhai Tourism Association), Mr. Liu (Director of Zhuhai Sports and Tourism Bureau), Ms. Li (Personnel Supervisor of Zhuhai Bayview Hotel), Mr. Li (Manager of Zhuhai Haitian International Travel Service), Ms.Wang (Training Manager of Zhuhai Resort Hotel), Mr. Yang (Senior Manager of Gongbei Port China Travel Service). On the one hand, the establishment of professional teaching steering committee is conducive to the talent training objectives in line with the needs of local economic development in Guangdong Province and Zhuhai City. On the other hand, the participation of workers in enterprises can make the teaching process in schools more in line with the needs, so that the personnel training work can truly be implemented. At the same time, it cooperates with the local major tourism group Chime Long Group, foreign brands such as Zhuhai Marriott Hotel, Sheraton Zhuhai, JW Marriott Shenzhen, and the local leading travel service GZL, South Lake International Travel, Zhuhai Gongbei Port CTS, Shenzhen Baoan China Travel and other enterprises. Meanwhile it cooperates with Hong Kong Genting Cruise Group. The two sides have conducted a full-range cooperation on personnel training objectives, curriculum design and implementation, internship and practical training, employment orientation, student management, faculty and staffing, assessment and evaluation. On top of this, they have also conducted a series of practical exploration and tracking research. Now the first modern apprenticeship class students have graduated successfully. It is expected that in the future these students will better serve the enterprises with what they learned in class.

The Students

In the admission of students, does your institution/programme respect the equality of people (sex, race, religion, political view, etc.) ? Does your institution/programme promote the admission of the most vulnerable groups (persons with disabilities, ethnic minorities, indigenous people, etc.) ?

In addition to recruiting students in Guangdong Province, the Tourism Management program also enrols students from other provinces, including Xinjiang, Sichuan, Anhui, Henan, Hunan, Guizhou, Gansu, Shanxi, Shaanxi, and other undeveloped areas. The students are of Han, Uygur and Tujia ethnic groups. Besides ordinary high school students, Tourism Management will admit a certain percentage of secondary vocational students every year. In order to recruit more excellent secondary vocational students, each year before enrolment, the school will send teachers to secondary vocational schools which are excellent or with which it has cooperated to discuss issues concerned, seeking more cooperation and publicity in their schools and attracting more outstanding students by means of proper system and preaching. So far, we have reached 3 plus 2 training program agreement (3 years for secondary learning and 2 years for college learning) with a number of secondary vocational schools.

Does your institution/programme promote understanding and respect among students? Please give some examples.

At the beginning of school, the program director will give the students an entrance education, which includes professional profiles, course guiding, job

analysis, professional spirit and ethics, teaching team, and so on, to lay a good foundation for students to start college life. Meanwhile some graduates will be invited back to school to exchange with the freshmen. Moreover, some industry professionals will be invited to give the new students a professional cognitive education. During the 3-year college period, the school arranges irregular expert lectures, graduate forums, school symposiums and other activities for the students to choose according to their own professional needs, in order to assist students to be more professional and to provide them with more internship positions. The school also organizes special parties for ethnic minority students, sponsors various tea parties and fraternities to promote understanding among students from different regions and with different religious belief, thus strengthen the feelings among them.

Does your institution/programme promote the mobility of students?

Tourism Management program allows students to mobile freely. Students of other majors can be transferred to the program of tourism management, and vice versa.The program cooperates with the local major tourism group Chimelong Group, foreign brands such as Zhuhai Marriott Hotel, Sheraton Zhuhai, JW Marriott Shenzhen, and the local leading travel service GZL, South Lake International Travel Service, Zhuhai Gongbei Port CTS, Shenzhen Baoan China Travel Service and other enterprises. Meanwhile it cooperates with Hong Kong Genting Cruise Group.Students are arranged to exchange and practice in these enterprises, thus train qualified personnel for these enterprises. In 2016, the head of Japanese Hotel Group came to our school to select the social practice students to Japan. The students of 2016 modern apprenticeship class participated in the recognition internship and then a seminar was held on "the development of tourism business operation and tourism industry." As a result, Tourism Management opened up a new career training market.

Does your institution/programme evaluate students on knowledge, skills and values? Please give examples.

Faculty of tourism management give a comprehensive evaluation of students' academic performance, which includes the academic performance of students, the certificates or grades examination results, the participation in social organizations, the participation in skills competitions, the participation in extracurricular activities, etc. Different courses are evaluated in different ways. For academic evaluation of training courses, the students are mainly examined on skill mastery, which is usually reflected in the end-term skill tests and daily skill learning and practice. For theoretical courses, the students are comprehensively appraised mainly through the final exam and the daily performance. Theoretical course teachers design the questions in two forms : subjective questions and objective questions. The answer time allowed to the students is usually 90 minutes to two hours. The results of theoretical courses come from students' class attendance, class performance (including class discipline, class interaction, class discussions, etc.) , home assignments, etc. Through theoretical and practical training courses, students can develop good professional ethics and professionalism and master the tourism service and management skills.

According to Article 5 of the Global Code of Ethics for Tourism "Tourism professionals should carry out studies of the impact of their development projects on the environment and natural surroundings" . Do you ask the students of your institution/programme to carry out studies about tourism in your country/region or to be part of any cooperation for development activity?

Professional courses in Tourism Management Program require students to conduct studies on the impact of tourism on the natural environment and on green tourism. For example, in the Tourism Introduction, China Tourism Geography and other courses, the impact of tourism and sustainable development of tourism-related content are taught, and students are required to complete research and promotion activities on the sustainable development of tourism.

Does your Institution/Programme have programmes that strengthen ethic values on the students' behaviour? Please give examples.

The curriculum of Tourism Management Program includes courses that strengthen students' moral values such as honesty cultivation, mental health

education, military training and entrance education (including military theory), employment guidance, tourism laws and regulations, intercultural communication and tourism service etiquette.

Curriculum and Pedagogical System: How does the curriculum contain the principles of the Global Code of Ethics for Tourism: as a transversal issue in all subjects, as a specific subject about ethics or both?

The three-year courses of Tourism Management Program total 2,637 hours, 131 credits. From the perspective of vertical structure, they are divided into four modules of comprehensive quality courses (compulsory), comprehensive quality courses (elective), professional courses compulsory modules (including professional foundation, professional core and professional comprehensive practice) and professional development module. In the professional curriculum structure, general education courses and professional fundamental courses are set for first year, professional core courses, professional practice courses and professional development courses are set for the second and third year, by integrating global ethics guidelines into all professional courses. In the course of Tourism Introduction, many chapters concern the content of global ethical code; the course of Tour Guide Business include the content of respect of dignity, religion belief and customs of the tourists and obedience to laws; the course Hotel Front and Room Management emphasizes the people oriented and the humanistic care to tourists.

How does your institution/programme inform the students and professors about the principles of the Global Code of Ethics for Tourism (seminars, specific classes, brochure, etc.)?

Tourism Management Program often organizes lectures to preach global ethics norms to students and introduce global ethics norms to courses such as travel agency operations and management, tourism marketing, tour guiding and tour regulations. WeChat groups and QQ groups and other media also serve as platform to promote the tourism ethics norms.

What is the pedagogical method used to teach the principles of the Global Code of Ethics for Tourism to the students? Do you think the students might remember the principles and are they able to apply them once they leave the institution? How do you ensure that this knowledge is acquired?

A number of tourism management teachers applied the teaching concept of work process to curriculum reform and adopted a task-driven and project-oriented teaching approach to instil global ethical norms into students. According to the functions and qualities of tourism occupations, teachers design the curriculum content in the light of the actual conditions and characteristics of the tourism development in the Pearl River Delta Region. Global ethics norms were run through the whole teaching process, the teachers pay much attention to the training of student professional ethics, ability to explain, adaptability, group norms, psychological quality and so on. During the teaching process, teachers use the online Rain Class to teach. With this online class teachers can know in time whether the students have mastered the knowledge.

The Teachers

What is the admission process of your institution/programme regarding faculty? Does your institution/programme respect the equality of people (sex, race, religion, political view, etc.) ?

Currently there are 23 teachers in Tourism Management Program of Guangdong Polytechnic of Science and Technology, including 15 females and 8 males, all of them are citizens of the People's Republic of China. In the management process, three females Gu Yihua, Hu Xiaojing and Guo Weina hold important management positions. The existing 20 professional training rooms equipped with multimedia equipment can be used by all teachers for specialty construction and independent learning activities.

In a latest faculty recruitment of 2016, Tourism Management posted the recruitment conditions as below : with master's degree or above, lecturer and above, under 40 years with more than 2 years of teaching experience in the corresponding professional institutions of higher learning or more than 2 years of experience in the corresponding professional and technical work.

All conditions of employment are open and transparent, non-

discriminatory, including gender, race, religion and political orientation.

Does your institution/programme promote equity of gender among the Faculty members? Please give examples.

For Tourism Management Program there is a mutual cooperation and common development between professional teachers, whether they are male or female. In fact we have 14 female teachers and 9 male teachers. One of the vice deans Professor Gu Yihua is a female. Tourism Management sets specialty goals and takes them as a prerequisite to design student training programs. The training programs are taken as core to work out and coordinate the teaching plan and schedule. Tourism Management Program will also organize teachers to prepare lessons collectively, in which teachers are required to help each other and develop curriculum and teaching materials with partner enterprises.

Does your institution/programme promote understanding and respect among the faculty members as well as between them and the students and other staff members?

All the staffs and students respect each other, no matter their race, origin, gender, or religious belief. No crime has been committed; no hatred has been harbored.

Does your institution/programme promote the mobility of faculty abroad (to study or to be trained) ?

In line with the related school regulations, all teachers can choose formal, high-quality training institutions or units on their own to participate in training.The contents of the training can be applied for in accordance with their majors, the courses taught, the direction of scientific research and education reform carried out, and the ongoing course and specialty construction content.

Among them, Mr. Yang Yide was sent to Singapore in 2013 to study the advanced management at the Nanyang Polytechnic; the teachers Wan Fangqiu and Feng Shuling were invited to participate in "German Competence-Oriented Teaching System for Dual-System Vocational and Technical Education" in Germany from July to August 2016 (Guopei Rice Code : 38153013) .

Does your institution/programme have programmes that strengthen ethic values on the faculty and other staff members? Please give examples.

In order to reinforce the professional ethics of teachers and other employees first, the program requires that teachers engaged in the education industry must have the corresponding teaching certification. Second, going with the arrangements of the School Department for Continuing Education, teachers are required to actively participate in continuing education activities and encouraged to take part in related school training work.For example, in September 2017, the school organized backbone training classes for all teachers within the school, more than 50% of the teachers in the program attended.

Does the Faculty of your institution/programme carry out studies about tourism in your country/region?

The teachers carry out tourism research in the region through reporting subjects, publishing papers, developing textbooks in cooperation with enterprises and so on.

The Management

Does your institution/programme respect economic, social and cultural environment and transmit the same to the students, professors and local community? Please, give examples.

The teachers and students of Tourism Management Program respect the economic, social, and cultural environment. The school asked the students and teachers to read General Secretary Xi Jinping's speech, the 18th and 19th National Congress of the CPC reports. The 18th CPC National Congress report clearly put forward the "five in one" general layout for building socialism with Chinese characteristics. The overall layout of building socialism with Chinese characteristics has been expanded from the "three in one" and the "four in one" to the "five in one" for economic construction, political construction, cultural construction, social construction and ecological construction, and the overall layout of building socialism with Chinese characteristics has been further improved.

Does your institution/programme observe and respect the social and

cultural traditions of all peoples, including minorities and indigenous people? Does your programme promote their integration and teach students respect towards everyone?

Tourism Management abides by and respects the social and cultural traditions of all ethnic groups, including ethnic minorities and indigenous peoples. In the professional course The Rudiment of Tour Guide, there is a unit to introduce the ethnic minorities in China. When teachers introduce this section, they not only introduce the relevant knowledge to students, but also require students to respect everyone.

Does your institution/programme help other institutions/programmes of least developed destinations to create/update their tourism programmes using as reference the principles of the Global Code of Ethics for Tourism while developing their mission, action plan, curriculum, etc.?

In 2015, Tourism Management Program supported Xishuangbanna Vocational and Technical College in Yunnan and helped it complete its missions, action plans and course plans. It also sent professional teachers to train staffs in the undeveloped area.

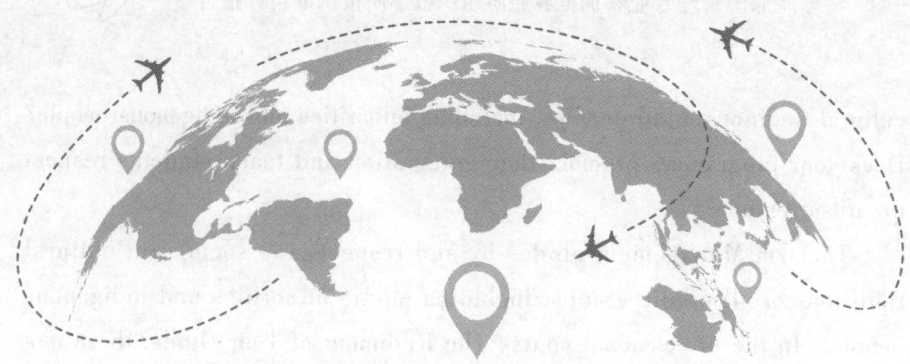

第四章　佐证材料总目录

PROCESS No 1

The Employers

表4-1

Public and Private Sector Objective The aim of this process is to verify that the programme has taken into consideration the views and needs of future employers : public and private sector. Given the above reason, this process will require evidence that the following measures/actions have been carried out : 1.1.Inclusion of the employers needs in defining the mission, action plan and curriculum content; 1.2.Continuous adaptation of the programme to new trends and hence to new requirements of the tourism sector employers

表4-2

0.1 INCLUSION OF THE EMPLOYERS NEEDS IN DEFINING THE MISSION, ACTION PLAN AND CURRICULUM CONTENT	
1.1 a) Mission	
Required Documentation	（please add in the following boxes, all your comments, documents reference numbers or any other information you deem necessary）
1.1.a)1)Record of meetings（with the corresponding minutes）where the programme's mission was defined	1.The founding files of the steering committee of the program established in 2014 and renewed in 2016. 材料1.旅游管理专业建设委员会成立纪要
1.1.a)2)Methodology used and reports showing the needs of external and internal actors（public / private sector and civil society）have been taken into consideration when defining the Programme's mission. *Please send at least the following documentation： –Three reports showing that reality（with corresponding updates). –SWOT Analysis（of the external environment)	2. The talent demand report in Guangdong-Hong kong-Macao Greater Bay Area 材料2.粤港澳大湾区人才需求报告 3. SWOT analysis 材料3.本专业SWOT分析
1.1.a)3)Documentation which clearly expresses（externally and internally）the Programme's mission statement.	4.the provincial key program. 材料4.广东省二类品牌专业项目申报书
1.1b) Action Plan	
Defining objectives 1.1.b)1)Documentation reflecting the strategic objectives and criteria followed to define the action plan. 1.1.b)2)Documentation of internal and external communication（to potential employers）where such action plan has been made known	5. the curriculum criteria for 2016 材料5.2016版人才培养方案 6. the yearly action plan for 2016—2018 材料6.品牌专业年度计划台账

1. 1b) Action Plan	
Implementation 1.1.b)3)Documentation where the resources to be allocated and the available budget to implement the programme are defined. 1.1.b)4)Financial documentation which reflects the budget allocated for the implementation of strategic objectives. 1.1.b)5) Documentation reflecting the methodology used for its implementation of the action plan（please indicate the team responsible）	7. The document showing the per capita funding by the government. 材料 7. 生均拨款数据、学校对旅游管理专业"创新强校"工程的经费投入。 8. The document showing the yearly budget for the program 2016–2018. 材料 8. 品牌专业财政拨款证明资料。 9. The document showing the methodology for its implementation. 材料 9. 品牌专业建设任务台账及其团队、方法等
Evaluation and Review 1.1.b)6) Satisfaction questionnaires/self evaluation questionnaires addressed to the internal and external actors. –Internal：students attending the programme, faculty and administrative staff involved in its development. –External：public, private and civil society. 1.1.b)7)Existence of progress reports （reality vs compliance with the objectives）	10. The questionnaire on the program, faculty and the management by the graduates. 材料 10. 学院针对毕业生就学院师资、教学、管理等的问卷调查。 11. The evaluation by some key companies including the Chimelong Group,the CTS Zhuhai Gongbei Port Company, etc. 材料 11. 学生就业所在企业对本专业的满意度调查。 12. quality improvement report by the school 材料 12. 学院质量改进报告
1.1 c) Curriculum content	
1.1.c)1)Documentation（market research or similar studies）which reflect the work skills needed by the sector regarding each sub–sector. 1.1.c)2)Documentation showing the correlation between these needs and the programme's curriculum content	13. The questionnaire showing the required professional skills the students should develop. 材料 13. 调查表显示学生应该具备的技能。 14. The documents showing the correlation between these needs and the Programme's curriculum content. 材料 14. 学生技能培养与课程内容的关联度

1.2 Continuous adaptation of the programme to new trends and requirements of the employers.	
1.2 a) Existence of monitoring mechanisms to assess needs	
1.2.a)1)Evidence on the existence of committees/ instruments/ coordination activities/ permanent cooperation between the Programme and employers (e.g. Advisory Councils). Existence of technical collaboration mechanisms between the programme and the employers (e.g. innovation circles, etc.)	15. The adviser committee offered advice both to the program and the employers. 材料15. 专业建设委员会向学院和企业提出的建议。 16. The collaboration agreement between the programme and the employers. 材料16. 学院与企业的合作协议
1.2 b) Adjustment actions	
1.2.b)1)Evidence showing the curriculum has been provided with a system that allows progressive assimilation of market needs. 1.2.b)2)Evidence on how the results of these continuous changes to the programme are measured	17. The modern apprenticeship schooling system. 材料17. 现代学徒制文件。 18. Progressive assimilation of courses : courses for international cruises. 材料18. 与国际邮轮合作的文件和开设相关课程的材料。 19. Report from the Chimelong Innovative Service School. 材料19. 长隆创新服务学院的文件。 20. The innovative contents of the new curriculum plan. 材料20. 2018新的人才培养方案的创新内容

PROCESS No. 2

The Student

表4-3

Objective
The alienabled efficient mechanisms for communication and coordination with the student (before, during and after graduation). It also seeks to assess students' performance and their satisfaction with the programme. Given the above reason, this process will require evidence that the following measures/actions have been carried out : 2.1.Communication and promotion of the programme (before and during the admission process). 2.2.Introduction of the student in the programme (post admission). 2.3.Meeting the students' needs–administrative, academic, student welfare and curriculum support (during the study). 2.4.Assessment of student's performance. 2.5.Evaluation of student satisfaction level regarding the programme and additional services. 2.6.Post–graduation follow–up of the students

表4-4

2.1 COMMUNICATION AND PROMOTION OF THE PROGRAMME (BEFORE AND DURING THE ADMISSION PROCESS)	
2.1.1 Communication and promotion plan (marketing plan, if applicable)	1. The latest 5 years enrolment plan. 材料 1. 学校近五年（2013—2018）高考前的招生计划
2.1.2 Documentation regarding pre-admission information where entry requirements, curriculum, faculty, administrative process and associated costs are specified	2.The latest 5 years prospectus. 材料 2. 近五年本专业招生简章宣传册（包含入学要求、课程、师资、管理以及相关费用等）
2.1.3 Promotional and communication material about events organized to make the programme known among students 2.1.4 Examples (evidence) of TEP marketing communication activities	3.Promotional and communication material in guangzhou, shenzhen and other cities. 材料 3. 招生宣传的活动材料（包括画册和网络），赴中职（深圳市福田区华强职业技术学校、惠州市商贸旅游高校职业技术学校）开展对接活动的材料
2.1.5 Documentation reflecting the evaluation and the results of such marketing communication activities	4.Documentation reflecting the evaluation and the results of such marketing communication activities. 材料 4. 赴中职学校对接招生宣传结果的评估材料

续　表

2.2 INTRODUCTION OF THE STUDENT IN THE PROGRAMME (POST ADMISSION)	
2.2.1 Documentation of post-admission information (student guides)	5.Documentation of post-admission information. 材料 5.学生录取后的告知文件或通知。
2.2.2 Final registry of admissions (enrolment)	6.Final registry of admissions. 材料 6.近五年旅游管理和旅游英语专业录取名册
2.2.3 Evidence of briefings given to first year students	7.Evidence of briefings given to first year students. 材料 7.对新生的专业介绍 PPT

2.3 ATTENTION GIVEN TO STUDENTS' NEEDS-ADMINISTRATIVE, ACADEMIC, SOCIAL WELFARE AND CURRICULUM SUPPORT	
Administrative 2.3.1 Evidence on the existence of personalized attention to the student. 2.3.2 Examples of the administrative offices' communications and opening hours (compatible with the students' schedules). 2.3.3 Administration procedures to handle academic records. 2.3.4 Documentation certifying that students can access their academic records	8.Evidence on the existence of personalized attention to the student. 材料 8.对学生个性化关注的材料。 9.Administrative offices' communications and opening hours. 材料 9.学生管理办公室开放和交流的证据。 10.Administration procedures to handle academic records. 材料 10.学生成绩评定的管理程序。 11.Documentation certifying that students can access their academic records. 材料 11.学生知晓成绩的文件
Academic/Curriculum support activities 2.3.5 Documentation on the mentoring system (on-line and face to face), as well as the following curriculum support activities: academic exchange programmes; internship agreements with the public and private sector	12.Documentation on the mentoring system. 材料 12.学徒制体系文件，包含下列支撑文件：学术交流活动；学徒制的实习协议；网上辅导和现场面授
Student Welfare 2.3.6 Evidence to prove the existence of a student welfare department/unit, as well as its functions	13.Evidence to prove the existence of a student welfare. 材料 13.学生福利证明文件（评选国家奖学金、贫困助学金、技能大赛奖学金、勤工俭学等材料）

2.4 ASSESSMENT OF THE STUDENT'S PERFORMANCE	
2.4.1 Evidence on the existence of mechanisms and tools that allow teachers to assess the student performance in a comprehensive manner	14.Evidence on the existence of mechanisms and tools that allow teachers to assess the student performance in a comprehensive manner. 材料 14. 教师评价学生的机制和手段（包括近五年旅游管理和旅游英语专业学生专升本名单及相关材料，近五年四六级考试、计算机考试、各种职业资格证获取的数据）
2.5 EVALUATION OF STUDENTS' SATISFACTION LEVEL REGARDING THE PROGRAMME AND ADDITIONAL SERVICES	
2.5.1 Attendance list to the various courses 2.5.2 Attendance policy	15.Attendance list to the various courses. 材料 15. 各门课程的出勤表。 16. Attendance policy. 材料 16. 学院考勤的规定
2.5.3 Statistics on the extent of absenteeism and desertion	17. Statistics on the extent of absenteeism and desertion. 材料 17. 近五年本专业学生缺勤和旷课的统计、请假情况统计
2.5.4 Existence of mechanisms and instruments that allow the student to evaluate teachers' performance in each subject, relevance of content taught, as well as teaching and evaluation methods	18. The indicators that allow the student to evaluate teachers' performance. 材料 18. 近五年本专业学生对教师评教的指标体系
2.6 FOLLOW-UP OF GRADUATED STUDENTS	
2.6.1 Documents attesting there is a follow-up after the student graduates. Please provide the following documentation : –Alumni database identifying the company / organization and job position occupied by graduate students (please also provide evidence of update frequency). –Documentation of existing alumni associations, if any	19. Follow-up information after the student graduates. 材料 19. 近五年对毕业生跟踪的相关数据，如所在单位、职位等

续 表

2.6 FOLLOW-UP OF GRADUATED STUDENTS	
2.6.2 Statistics on the graduates' labour market insertion（please specify such information for two subsequent graduated classes and in respect to positions corresponding to the education received）	20. Statistics on the graduates' labour market insertion（please specify such information for two subsequent graduated classes 2013 and 2014） 材料20. 近五年2013和2014级旅游管理专业毕业生就业统计表
2.6.3 Evidence assessing the public and private sector satisfaction regarding the Programme's alumni working for them	21. satisfaction investigation 材料21. 企业满意度数据和材料

PROCESS No. 3

The Curriculum and Pedagogical System

表4-5

Objective

The aim of this process is to verify the curriculum content coherence, that effective pedagogical methods are being used, and the existence of and accessibility to pedagogical resources.

Given the above reason, this process will require evidence that the following measures/actions have been carried out：

2.1 Review of the methodology used to develop the curriculum.

2.2 Review of curriculum content consistency and coherence among different subjects.

2.3 Effectiveness of the（theoretical/ practical）pedagogical methods used to implement the curriculum.

2.4 Existence, access and usefulness of facilities that support the curriculum

表4-6

3.1 METHODOLOGY USED TO FORMULATE THE CURRICULUM	
3.1.1 Curriculum.	1.Curriculum. 材料1.最新版旅游管理专业教学进程表
3.1.2 Documentation on the methodology used to create the curriculum. 3.1.3 Documentation evidencing the inclusion of national standards and guidelines for tourism educational programmes.	2.Documentation on the methodology used to create the curriculum. 材料2.形成课程表的方法 3.Documentation evidencing the inclusion of national standards and guidelines for tourism educational programmes. 材料3.涵盖国家标准和旅游教育指南的材料
3.1.4 Professional experience of those who have participated in the creation of the curriculum. *Please specify if those professionals belong to the programme's .internal or external environment.	4. Professional experience of those who have participated in the creation of the curriculum. 材料4.参与制订培养方案的企业人士经验总结（注明：这些专业人士是否构成本专业的内部和外部资源）
3.1.5 Evidence showing that the recommendations made by the team of experts involved in the formulation have been incorporated	5.Evidence showing that the recommendations made by the team of experts. 材料5.专家团队提出的建议；
3.1.6 Plan to support implementation of the curriculum（department and teacher focused)	6. Plan to support implementation of the curriculum. 材料6.实施课程方案的行动计划材料
3.2 CURRICULUM COHERENCE	
3.2.1 Syllabus of each one of the TEP course	7. Syllabus of each one of the TEP course 材料7.每门专业课程的教学大纲或课程标准
3.2.2 Evidence of the designed course sequence within the curriculum	8. Evidence of the designed course sequence within the curriculum. 材料8.每门课程预期达成的结果
3.3 EFFECTIVENESS OF THE PEDAGOGICAL METHOD	
3.3.1 Operational guidelines for the implementation of the pedagogical method	9.Operational guidelines for the implementation of the pedagogical method. 材料9.课程的教学方法指南
3.3.2 Evidence showing the coherence between the methodology used and the assimilation of the programme contents	10.Evidence showing the coherence between the methodology and the programme contents. 材料10.教学方法与课程内容相连贯的证据

续　表

3.3 EFFECTIVENESS OF THE PEDAGOGICAL METHOD	
3.3.4 Documents certifying the existence of coordination among areas of knowledge, in order to avoid overlapping contents in the various subjects that constitute the Programme.	12. Documents avoid overlapping contents. 材料 12. 避免课程之间内容重复的协调文件
3.3.5 Record of meetings where the pedagogical method has been defined or updated to incorporate the new technologies and meet demand needs (of the public and private sectors)	13. Record of meetings where information technology has been updated. 材料 13. 运用新技术更新教学方法的会议记录
3.3.6 Documentation（evidence）which shows the balance between practical and theoretical content of each subject in the Programme	14. Documentation which shows the balance between practical and theoretical content of each subject. 材料 14. 平衡各门课程理论与实践内容的文件和证据

3.4 EXISTENCE, ACCESS AND USEFULNESS OF THE CURRICULUM SUPPORT FACILITIES	
3.4 a) Infrastructure and pedagogical equipment	
3.4.a)1）Information on regularly used classrooms * Please provide : – Photographs. – Maximum capacity. – Number of students per programme. – Equipment and minimum support material in each classroom	15. Information on regularly used classrooms. 材料 15. 常规教室资料:照片、最大容量、每一届学生的人数、每个教室的设备和最低配置
3.4.a)2）Information on the training classrooms used * Please provide : – Photographs. – Maximum capacity. – Number of students per programme. – Facilities and minimum support equipment in each training classroom. – Regulations and manuals regarding the use of facilities	16. Information on the training classrooms. 材料 16. 实训室资料:照片、最大容量、每一届学生的人数、每个教室的设备和最低配置、使用手册和规章制度

3.4 EXISTENCE, ACCESS AND USEFULNESS OF THE CURRICULUM SUPPORT FACILITIES	
3.4 a) Infrastructure and pedagogical equipment	
3.4.a)3）Information regarding the tourism documentation centre * Please provide： –Photographs. –Database of existing publications/documents in the documentation centre. –Inventory of existing services（audio, video, etc.). –Documents certifying existing subscriptions to journals and specialized publications available at the centre	17. Information regarding the tourism documentation centre 材料17.旅游资料中心信息：照片、出版物、数据库、音像资料、期刊等
3.4.a)4)Information regarding computer support facilities Please provide inventory of equipment（with their corresponding features）available at the computer facilities. Please show evidence of the degree to which the available equipment is utilized	18. Information regarding computer support facilities 材料18.计算机资料：可以使用的电脑设备清单以及功能
3.4 b) Infrastructure and equipment for pedagogical support and additional services	
3.4.b)1)Information on sports facilities. * Please provide： – Photographs. – Details of activities available to students and associated costs	19.Information on sports facilities 材料19.运动设施：照片、举行活动的资料和有关费用
3.4.b)2)Information on catering facilities（restaurants and cafeterias) * Please provide： – Photographs. – Details of services available to students and associated costs	20.Information on catering facilities（restaurants and cafeterias) 材料20.餐厅设施：照片、使用资料和费用

3.4 c) Support measures for the safety and maintenance of pedagogical resources	
3.4.c)1）Support measures on safety of infrastructure and educational equipment associated to the Programme. – Action plan for emergency situations. – First aid courses	21. Support measures on safety of infrastructure and educational equipment. 材料 21. 本专业教学设施安全保证措施与应急处理措施
3.4.c)2）Measures on maintenance of infrastructure and educational equipment associated to the Programme	22. Measures on maintenance of infrastructure and educational equipment. 材料 22. 本专业教学设施保养和维护措施
3.4.c)3）Documentation on the implementation of corrective measures to support safety and maintenance of infrastructure and educational equipment associated to the Programme	23.Documentation on the implementation of corrective measures to support safety and maintenance of infrastructure and equipment. 材料 23. 本专业教学设施使用记录

PROCESS No. 4

The Faculty

表4-7

Objective
The aim of this process is to verify the existence of transparent mechanisms to select the faculty, as well as favourable work conditions that promote their professional development. Given the above reason, this process will require evidence the following measures/actions have been carried out : 3.1 A criteria for the selection of the faculty has been designed and followed. 3.2 Academic coordination of the faculty. 3.3 Faculty's performance evaluation. 3.4 Programmes to continuously update teachers' knowledge

表4-8

4.1 FACULTY SELECTION	
4.1.1 Basic criteria used in the faculty pre-selection	1.Criteria for faculty selection. 材料 1. 本专业师资选拔标准

续 表

4.1 FACULTY SELECTION	
4.1.2 Procedure followed for the selection of teachers recruited under permanent contracts： —Record indicating the members of the selection committee that assessed the candidates, as well as their profiles. —Report on the selection process. —Announcement of the end of the selection process	2.The detailed procedures for faculty selection 材料 2. 师资选拔的程序
4.1.3 Evidence showing working professionals participate in the students' education	3.Records showing the teachers' current teaching . 材料 3. 教师的教学任务书
4.2 ACADEMIC COORDINATION	
4.2.1 Organizational chart of the academic coordination area	4. Organizational chart of the program ,school, polytechnic in academic coordination. 材料 4. 本专业的组织机构图
4.2.2 Documentation reflecting the existence of regular meetings with the Programme faculty	5. Seminars on teaching and research . 材料 5. 各个教研室的教研活动记录
4.2.3 Documentation on monitoring and evaluation of the results of the academic coordination process	6. A series of documents on monitoring and evaluation of the academic coordination process. 材料 6. 教学质量监控和评价的系列文件
4.3 PROFESSIONAL PERFORMANCE	
4.3.1 Documentation showing the system used to assess and reward teacher's performance	7.A series of documents to assess and reward teacher's performance. 材料 7. 评价和奖励教师的系列文件（包括组织公开课、学生最满意课程、教学质量校长奖等）
4.3.2 Documentation on existing opportunities for improvement/promotion of faculty members	8. Documents used for improvement/promotion of faculty members. 材料 8. 提高教学水平的材料（包括信息化比赛、精品课程、微课程等）

4.4 CONTINUOUS KNOWLEDGE UPDATE	
4.4 a) Training	
4.4.a)1)Programmes oriented to facilitate that teachers can broaden their（internal and external）qualifications	9. A list of vocational certificates and dual qualifications. 材料9.教师资格证、职业资格证和双师素质证书
4.4.a)2)Supporting documents for training programmes and seminars undertaken by the faculty（please specify the above information for the past three years）	10. A list of training and seminar programs. 材料10.继续教育和培训清单
4.4.a)3)Criteria for the definition and selection of training programmes	11. Criteria for the definition and selection of training programmes. 材料11.选择培训项目的标准
4.4 b) Research Activities	
4.4.b)1)Research activities conducted by the faculty	12. A List of staff members research programs. 材料12.教师科研项目清单
4.4.b)2)Facilities given to the faculty to conduct their research	13.The facilities used for scientific researches. 材料13.为教师科研提供的条件（包括期刊网、电子图书等）
4.4.b)3)Collaborative agreements with other institutions to further the research	14. Collaborative agreements with other institutions. 材料14.与其他机构签订的科研合作协议
4.4.b)4)Evidence concerning the consistency of research topics with the employers needs.	15.Documents concerning the consistency of research topics with the employers needs. 材料15.满足企业需求的科研合作项目。
4.4.b)5)Evidence of employers active participation（through information given or other means）in the development of such research activities	16. Employers active participation in research activities. 材料16.企业参与科研的一览表
4.4.b)6)Documentation proving the existence of a budget or financing sources for research development	17. Documents proving the existence of a budget or financing sources. 材料17.科研项目的资助情况
4.4.b)7)Evidence showing the usefulness of research activities	18. Evidence showing the usefulness of research activities. 材料18.科研活动的实用性证明（包括培训后取得的社会效益和经济效益）

PROCESS No. 5

The Management

表4-9

Objective
The aim of this process is to verify the existence of an organizational structure as well as support tools to monitor the programme's quality.   Given the above reason, this process will require evidence the following measures/actions have been carried out :   4.1 Definition of an organizational chart with corresponding job descriptions.   4.2 Existence of a quality plan with the corresponding tools to support the progression analysis and assessment

表4-10

5.1 ORGANIZATION	
5.1.1 Institution's organizational chart	1. The school's and the polytechnic's organizational chart. 材料1. 学校与学院的组织结构图
5.1.2 Organizational chart and job position descriptions of those who constitute the Centre/School /Institute to which the programme is affiliated. * Please attach job description of the staff responsible for finances, administration, academic records, programme quality management, safety and maintenance, if centralized	2. The school's description of each position. 材料2. 学院负责财务、招生、教学、质量管理、实训安全等事务的人员名单以及职位描述
5.1.3 Work environment questionnaire	3.Work environment questionnaire. 材料3. 工作环境问卷调查
5.2 QUALITY ASSURANCE	
5.2 a) Quality Plan	
5.2.a)1)Comprehensive quality plan and its corresponding manuals.	4.Comprehensive quality plan and its corresponding manuals. 材料4. 质量管理计划以及相应手册
（Only applicable in case of having a quality plan）	

5. 2 QUALITY ASSURANCE	
5. 2 a) Quality Plan	
5.2.a)3) Documentation certifying the implementation of the quality plan Communications / documents / promotional material showing the existence of quality policies as well as the parameters to measure its efficacy	6. Regulations for teaching plans. 材料6.教学质量控制的系列文件（包括：教案编写规定、教学档案管理规定、教学日历编排规定、教学事故认定规定等）
5. 2 b) Monitoring	
5.2.b)1)List of indicators that allow monitoring（internally and externally）the results of the implementation of the quality plan	7. The list of indicators : the teaching status quality,regular teaching quality,training quality,internship quality and employment quality. 材料7.教学质量监控的指标体系
5.2.b)2)Team responsible for the monitoring and their corresponding action areas	8. The inspection team for the school and the polytechnic. 材料8.校级和院级的督导团队名单
5.2.b)3)Application of these indicators, and their corresponding results	9. Rewarding measures for "president prize" winners and "most satisfactory course" winners. 材料9.对教学质量校长奖和我最满意课程奖的奖励措施

ACCOMPLISHMENT of the GLOBAL CODE of ETHICS for TOURISM

表4-11

1. The Employers	
1.1 Evidence on how the principles of the Global Code of Ethics for Tourism had been considerate once formulating the mission and the action plan of the Programme	1. The principles of the Global Code of Ethics for Tourism have been applied in the relevant course designing. 材料1. 各个版本旅游专业人才培养方案中加强旅游伦理道德规范类课程的描述
1.2 Evidence on how your institution/ programme collaborate with the public/ private sector in the implementation of the principles of the Global Code of Ethics for Tourism	2. The collaborate agreement with Zhuhai General Association of Tourism on the implementation of the principles of the Global Code of Ethics for Tourism. 材料2. 学院与其他机构合作协议中关于遵守全球道德规范的条款
2. The Student	
2.1 Evidence on how your institution/ Programme respect the equality of people (sex, race, religion, political view, etc.) and promote the admission of the most vulnerable groups (persons with disabilities, ethnic minorities, indigenous people, etc.) during the admission process	3.Non-discrimination on how the Programme respect the equality of people (sex, race, religion, political view, etc.) . 材料3 .学院在录取过程中无性别、民族、政治信仰歧视的佐证材料（对招生简章、招生宣传册进行补充和说明）
2.2 Evidence on how your institution/ programme promote understanding and respect among students	4. The mutual respect among student clubs, dormitories, and daily activities. 材料4. 学生之间互相尊重理解的佐证（包括社团活动、与外校交流、短期服务等）
2.3 Evidence on how your institution/ programme promote the mobility abroad and other activities that could support the internationalization of your students	5. Evidence on the student internationalization 材料5. 促进学生国际化的举措和案例
2.4 Evidence on how your institution/ programme evaluate students on knowledge, skills and values	6. Evaluation on students' knowledge, skills and values. 材料6. 评价学生知识、技能和价值的材料（麦可斯报告）

2. The Student	
2.5 Evidence on studies/projects your students carry out to support international/regional/local development through tourism	7. Evidence on students carry out to support local development through tourism. 材料7. 学生通过旅游活动支持地区发展的案例。(学生参加粤港澳大湾区导游交流项目、航展、马戏节等材料)
2.6 Evidence on how your Institution/Programme promote the understanding of local reality among students	8. Evidence on how the Programme promotes the understanding of local reality among students. 材料8. 让学生认识和理解当地旅游现状的材料
2.7 Evidence on other actions/activities that had been taken place in your Institution/Programme for strengthen ethic values in the students' behaviour	9. Evidence on strengthening students ethic values. 材料9. 在学生日常行为中增强道德观念的案例(学生管理守则、学生综合素质选修课学习等)
3. The Curriculum and Pedagogical System	
3.1a)Evidence on how does the curriculum includes the principles of the Global Code of Ethics for Tourism. 3.1b)Evidence on how your institution/programme informs the students and professors about the principles of the Global Code of Ethics for Tourism(seminars, specific classes, brochure, etc.)	10.Evidence on how the curriculum includes the principles of the Global Code of Ethics for Tourism. 材料10. 课程如何涵盖全球旅游道德规范。 11.Evidence on how the students and professors carry out the principles of the Global Code of Ethics for Tourism. 材料11. 本专业学生和教师如何遵守全球旅游道德规范
3.2 a)Evidence on the pedagogical method used to teach the principles of the Global Code of Ethics for Tourism to the students. 3.2b)Evidence on how do you ensure that this knowledge is acquired	12. Evidence on the pedagogical method used to teach the principles of the Global Code of Ethics for Tourism to the student 材料12. 教师讲授全球旅游道德规范的方法。 13.Evidence on how this knowledge is acquired. 材料13. 如何保证这类知识的获得

续　表

4. The Faculty	
4.1 Evidence on how your Institution/Programme respect the equality of people (sex, race, religion, political view, etc.) and promote the admission of the most vulnerable groups (persons with disabilities, ethnic minorities, indigenous people, etc.) during the admission process of Faculty	14. Evidence on how the Programme respect the equality of people (sex, race, religion, political view, etc.). 材料 14. 学院如何尊重性别、民族、政治信仰的不同等
4.2 Evidence on how your Institution/Programme have programmes that strengthen ethic values in the Faculty and other staff members? Please give examples	15. Evidence on how the Party committee and teachers union have strengthened ethic values in the Faculty. 材料 15. 党支部和分工会在教职工中强化道德规范的案例
4.3 Evidence on how your institution/programme promote understanding and respect among Faculty members as well as between them and the students and other staff members	16. Evidence on how the programme promote understanding and respect among Faculty members and students. 材料 16. 如何让教职工之间和教师与学生之间增强理解与尊重
4.4 Evidence on how your Institution/Programme promote the mobility of Faculty abroad (to study or to be trained)	17. Evidence on how the Programme promotes the mobility of Faculty abroad for training. 材料 17. 教师出国培训的案例
4.5a) Evidence on how your Institution/Programme carry out studies about tourism in your country/region/local level 4.5b) Evidence on existing mechanisms to assure this knowledge is transfer to students	18. List of programs that teachers carry out the tourism-related research. 材料 18. 教师开展旅游研究项目的一览表，保障知识传授给学生的机制
5. The Management	
5.1 Evidence on how your institution/programme respect economic, social and cultural environment and transmit the same to the students, professors and local community	19. Evidence on how the programme respect economic, social and cultural environment and transmit the same to the students, professors and local community. 材料 19. 学院尊重当地经济社会文化环境并要求学生、教师做到的措施

5. The Management	
5.2 Evidence on how your Institution/ Programme observes and respects the social and cultural traditions of all peoples in your host town	20. Evidence on how the Programme observes and respects the social and cultural traditions of all peoples in zhuhai. 材料 20. 学院参加本市各区组织的文化、体育、旅游等活动的材料
5.3 Evidence on how your institution/ Programme support other institutions/ Programmes of least developed countries to create/update their tourism programmes using the principles of the Global Code of Ethics for Tourism as a reference while developing their mission, action plan, curriculum, etc	21. Evidence on how the Programme support other Institutions of least developed regions to create/ update their tourism programmes using the principles of the Global Code of Ethics for Tourism as a reference while developing their mission, action plan, curriculum, etc. 材料 21. 学院践行全球道德规范支持其他机构，特别是欠发达地区机构开发课程、制订课程计划方面的材料

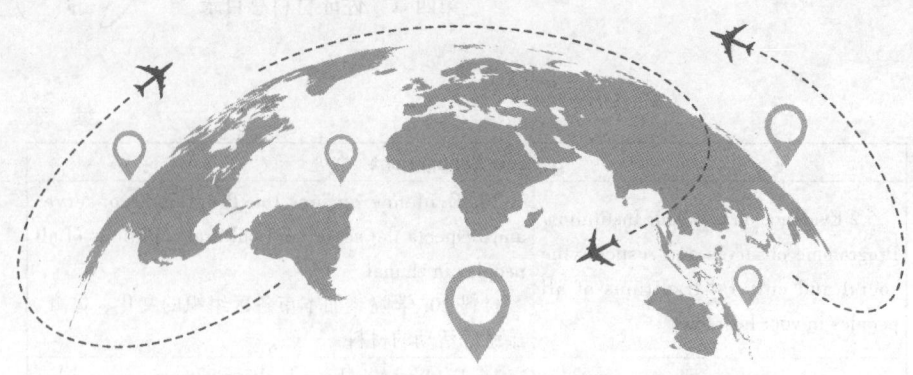

第五章 现场评估的日程安排

Agenda for the UNWTO-TedQual Audit

现场评估日程表

Day 1

表5-1

Time	Place (to be Completed by the Programme)	Assigned persons (to be Completed by the Programme)	Objectives/Subject
08：30 - 09：30	Polytechnic meeting room 学校会议室	The president, dean and the staff members of the program	Introduction to the in-situ audit process given to the team assigned by the programme. Explanation of the details related to the programme to be audited. Information on the review of documents and their location, and how the interviews will be conducted and their time-frame. 学院院长向认证专家进行自评汇报，专家向领导和教师说明认证的要点以及访谈的时间安排

续　表

Time	Place (to be Completed by the Programme)	Assigned persons (to be Completed by the Programme)	Objectives/Subject
09：30－10：30	Polytechnic meeting room 学校会议室	Vice president, teaching affairs director,student affairs director, director of enrolment, employment, training center library and public PE affairs. 与分管教学校长、教务处长、学生工作处长、招生就业处长、实训中心主任、图书馆馆长、公共体育部负责人座谈	Visual audit of the infrastructure/facilities of the institution/programme, focusing on the following areas：management/planning, student support offices (administration, employment, internships, interchanges etc.), library, computer and language labs, sports facilities, etc. 重点介绍为本专业提供的设施和条件
11：00－12：00	Polytechnic meeting room 学校会议室	Dean ,vice dean and program director and program manager. 与院长、负责国际交流的副院长、专业主任、项目负责人等访谈	Interview with the Director of the Programme, Director, of the Department/College/School which the Programme belongs to, Director of undergraduate and graduate degree respectively, responsible for the international relations office /department /unit and international programmes of the Institution. 从各自角度谈本专业的过去、现在和未来规划
12：00－13：00	Ding-room 餐厅		Lunch
13：00－14：00	Hotel		Lunch break
14：00－16：00	Off –campus training base		Visit Off –campus training bases. 参观校外实训基地，了解毕业生工作状况

Day 2

表5-2

Time	Place	Assigned Persons	Subject
08：30－10：00	School reference room 学院资料室	Interpreter	Continuation of the documental audit
10：00－12：00	Training Building 实训楼	Teaching staff	Appreciate the tea show and hotel service show 观摩茶艺与餐厅服务展示
12；00－13：00	Dining－room 餐厅		Lunch.
13：00－14：00	Hotel		Lunch break
14：30－15：30	Reference room 资料室	students	Interview with students
15：30－16.：30	Reference room 资料室	Alumni	Interview with alumni
16：30－17：30	Reference room 资料室	Interpreter	Interview with the staff members of the program

Day 3

表5-3

Time	Place	Assigned Persons	Subject
08：30－9：30	Campus	2 students	Tour around the campus visiting the canteen and library
9：30－10：00	Reference room 资料室	Interpreter	Continuation of the documental audit
10.00－12：00	Polytechnic meeting room 学校会议室	representatives of the enterprises. 与私有、公有企业代表座谈	Interview with representatives of the private and public sectors
12：00－13：00	Dining－room		Lunch
13：00－14：30	Hotel		Lunch break
15：00－17：00	Reference room 资料室	Interpreter	Continuation of the documental audit
17：00－18：00	Polytechnic meeting room 学校会议室	The president, dean and the staff members of the program. 学院领导和本专业全体教师	General conclusions of the audit process

参考文献

[1] 姜大源．世界职业教育课程改革的基本走势及其启示——职业教育课程开发漫谈[J]．中国职业技术教育，2008（27）：7–13.

[2] 布卢姆．教育目标分类学：第一分册 认知领域[M]上．海：华东师范大学出版社，1986.

[3] 严中华．职业教育课程开发与实施[M]．北京：清华大学出版社，2009.

[4] 严中华．国外职业教育先进理念解读——学习成果导向职业教育课程开发理论与实践[M]．北京：清华大学出版社，2017.

[5] 徐国庆．职业教育课程、教学与教师[J]．职业技术教育，2017（3）：63.

[6] 刘晶晶．职业院校教学管理：理念、模式与机制——基于全国职业院校教学管理与加强样本分析[J]．中国职业技术教育，2020（28）：73–78.

附录1 论文：高职旅游专业课程思政与 UNWTO 全球旅游道德规范融合的路径与实践

摘 要：世界旅游组织教学质量认证（UNWTO-TedQual）中对"全球旅游道德规范"有着明确的具体要求，这些要求与旅游专业课程思政的要求有一些共通之处，根据广东科学技术职业学院的实践，其融合实施的路径主要有四个方面：净化教师思想灵魂、量化学生考核指标、活化思政题材要素、强化课外实践实训。

关键词：旅游课程思政；全球旅游道德规范；世旅组织认证标准；融合路径

中图分类号：G641　文献标识码：A

Exploration on the Path of Integration of Tourism Curriculum Ideology and Global Tourism Ethics

Abstract：Teaching quality certification of the world tourism organization （UNWTO-TedQual）in the global tourism ethics has a clear specific requirements, these requirements and the demands of the tourism professional courses have some in common. According to the practice of Guangdong Polytechnic of Science and Technology, the integration of implementation path mainly has four aspects：to purify teachers thought and character, make quantitative assessment of student character index, activate ideological

elements and strengthen extracurricular practice.

Key words：Global tourism ethics；World Tourism Organization certification standards；Tourism curriculum ideology；integrated path

一、旅游专业实施课程思政的必要性

（一）实施课程思政是旅游教育发展的需要

旅游教育首先要本土化。本土化教育需要扎根中国，为国家旅游事业的高质量发展培养旅游高素质、技能型人才。2016年12月，习近平总书记在全国高校思想政治工作会议上强调，要用好课堂教学这个主渠道，思想政治理论课要坚持在改进中加强，各类课程与思想政治理论课同向同行，形成协同效应。课程思政正是贯彻落实习近平新时代中国特色社会主义思想、党的十九大精神以及社会主义核心价值观等重要精神和理念的一项举措。首先课程思政要在学科教学中融入思想道德教育，使学生的思想素养不断升华，思想境界不断提高，这对学生的个人品质和综合素质的提升起着重要作用。其次，课程思政也要国际化。国际化是旅游专业长久发展的必然选择。一方面，吸收和借鉴国外先进的办学理念和模式，提高旅游人才培养质量；另一方面通过开展国际交流合作、在国外开办分校、与国外院校互认学分、国内学生赴海外实践、与国外院校交换留学生等手段提高我国旅游教育的国际地位，增强我国的国际旅游教育话语权。在各种交流过程中，必然存在不同的思想观念和价值取向。这些冲突和融合为旅游专业学生提供了难得的机遇，同时对他们的道德水平和政治定力提出了新的挑战。面对这一现状，专业课程教授者和学习者要主动融入旅游专业，学习相关旅游专业知识，培养跨文化交流能力，找准切入点，帮助学生根据自己专业所学，提升其在国际交流合作中的交流和应变能力，使其坚持中国特色社会主义道路自信、理论自信、制度自信、文化自信，增加政治定力，讲好中国故事。

（二）实施课程思政是旅游产业发展的需要

以广东省为例，2018全年广东省接待入境过夜游客3 748.06万人次，

比上年增长 2.8%。国际旅游外汇收入 205.12 亿美元，增长 4.4%。整体看来，2013—2018 年广东省入境旅游市场基本保持稳定增长趋势，2018 年入境过夜游客超 3 700 万人，旅游外汇收入突破 200 亿美元，皆为近十年来最高值。尤其是近年来随着粤港澳大湾区建设的持续推进，经香港和澳门进入广东省乃至整个中国的外国旅游者不断增加，这意味着需要大量具备旅游专业知识、英语表达能力良好、具备较强责任意识和较高职业素养的专门性人才。英语类课程作为旅游专业的必修课程，既有工具性，又有人文性，其教学内容涵盖科学素养、人文素养、中国文化以及价值观念等多种话题。其工具性可以提高旅游专业学生的英语口语能力，从而向世界游客讲好美丽中国的故事；其人文性肩负培养旅游专业学生职业核心素养以及"民间外交使者"的责任。对涉外旅游的从业人员进行爱国主义教育和职业操守教育势在必行。

（三）实施课程思政是旅游专业学生成长的需要

大学时期是学生心智成长、世界观建立的重要阶段。旅游专业作为向旅游业输送人才的大本营，在育人方面承担着重要作用，要主动将思想品德教育和爱国主义教育融入教学中去，不断挖掘教学中各种思政教育资源，为旅游行业输送更多德才兼备的人才。

二、旅游专业实施课程思政的有效性

（一）主要课程教学内容与思政教育目标的一致性

旅游专业必修课程的教学内容含有大量的思政教育元素。如，《全国导游基础知识》的核心内容就涵盖了中国历史神话、文学诗词、小说戏剧、科技发明、楼阁建筑、书画艺术等众多尊重自然、改造世界的杰出人物和典型案例，是进行革命传统教育和爱国主义教育的优秀素材。英语课程不仅具有工具性，也具有人文性。ESP 英语课程所涉及的内容广泛、丰富，以笔者主编的旅游文化英语教材《旅游英语教程》为例，该教材的主题与思政教育不谋而合。

表1　旅游英语课程教学内容与思政目标的一致性

主题	内容	思政目标
Chinese festivals	Spring Festival and Mid-autumn Festival	熟悉中国传统节日，培养爱国爱家情操
Chinese gardens	Suzhou Classic Gardens	熟悉苏州古典园林的造园理念，培养尊重自然、道法自然的观念
Martial arts	Shaolin Temple	了解中华武术文化，培养强身健体的良好习惯，增强国防意识
Chinese tea culture	Tea Ceremony	了解中国茶文化，培养静和美的品格
Chinese cuisine	Top 8 local cuisines	了解中国主要菜系，培养鉴赏、烹饪中式菜肴的能力
Chinese local opera	Beijing Opera	熟悉中国戏剧，培养对说、舞、斗、唱等的审美能力。

（二）主要课程思政教育目标与世界旅游组织教学质量认证的一致性

教育质量认证（UNWTO-TedQual）是由联合国世界旅游组织颁发的唯一具有国际标准的旅游教育、培训及研究项目的质量认证。该认证以学生为中心，对办学定位、人才培养目标与雇主需求之间的关系，教师参与学生培养、课程建设等内容，课程设置与开发的合理性、科学性、系统性等内容，学院对教师和学生进行管理的科学性和有效性等方面进行全面评估。

（1）雇主（The Employers）视角：评价本专业（项目）如何满足雇主（用人单位）的期望和要求以及适应旅游行业新的挑战。

（2）学生（The Students）视角：评价本专业（项目）学生在校期间和毕业之后如何在学术贡献和技能发展方面更新知识。

（3）课程体系（The Curriculum and Pedagogic System）：评估本专业（项目）课程体系的一贯性与科学性。

（4）师资（The Faculty）视角：评估本专业（项目）确定的师资招募机制以及教师发展对本专业的贡献。

（5）管理（The Management）视角：评估学院组织结构和管理体系，使得教学质量、管理质量持续优化。

（6）全球旅游道德规范（The Implementation of the Global Ethics for Tourism）：评估本专业师生在遵守旅游道德、坚持旅游扶贫、从事旅游培训等方面的执行情况。

表2 世旅组织教学质量认证评价要求与课程思政教育要求的一致性

序号	ACCOMPLISHMENT of the GLOBAL CODE of ETHICSFOR TOURISM （教学机构在落实全球旅游道德规范中所取得的成就）	课程思政教育要求
1	Evidence on how the principles of the Global Code of Ethics for Tourism had been considerate once formulating the mission and the action plan of the Programme	人才培养方案中所有课程（包含英语课程）加强旅游伦理道德规范的描述
2	Evidence on how your institution/programme collaborate with the public/private sector in the implementation of the principles of the Global Code of Ethics for Tourism	学校与其他机构合作协议（如合作编写的教材）中关于遵守全球旅游道德规范的表述
3	Evidence on how your institution/programme promote the mobility abroad and other activities that could support the internationalization of your students	促进学生国际化的举措和案例
4	Evidence on studies/projects your students carry out to support international/regional/local development through tourism	学生通过旅游活动支持地区发展的案例
5	Evidence on how your Institution/Programme promote the understanding of local reality among students	让学生认识和了解当地旅游现状的案例
6	Evidence on other actions/activities that had been taken place in your Institution/Programme for strengthen ethic values in the students' behaviour	在学生日常行为中增强道德观念的案例
7	Evidence on how does the curriculum includes the principles of the Global Code of Ethics for Tourism Evidence on how the students and professors carry out the principles of the Global Code of Ethics for Tourism	课程如何涵盖全球旅游道德规范本，专业学生和教师如何遵守全球旅游道德规范
8	Evidence on how your institution/programme respect economic, social and cultural environment and transmit the same to the students, professors and local community	学院尊重当地经济社会文化环境并要求学生、教师做到的措施
9	Evidence on how your institution/programme observes and respects the social and cultural traditions of all peoples in your host town	教师和学生遵守当地社会和文化习俗的证明
10	Evidence on how your institution/programme support other institutions/programmes of least developed countries to create/update their tourism programmes using the principles of the Global Code of Ethics for Tourism as a reference while developing their mission, action plan, curriculum, etc.	师生运用这些规范扶持欠发达地区学校开发旅游项目的证明

三、旅游专业实施课程思政的路径与实践

（一）净化教师思想灵魂

习近平总书记强调，要把培育和践行社会主义核心价值观融入教书育人全过程，毫无疑问，广大教师是第一责任人。具体包括三方面：

1.提高教师职业道德素养

专业教师既要保持学术的专业性，又要保持思想的专一性。在新时代新要求下，旅游专业教师更需要强化思想政治意识，只有坚定政治立场才能保证课程融入思政教育。课程思政的实施，关键在于教师。在课程思政建设过程中，专业课教师任务艰巨，思政课教师要发挥指引作用。让教师定期走进企业学习锻炼，同时加强各学科教师思想观念与能力的融合。高度重视对专业课教师思想政治理论水平的提升，适当开展马克思主义理论教育，并安排专业课教师前往红色教育基地接受实践研修和思想洗礼，还要加强其对哲学社会科学理论的学习，提升专业课教师自身人文素质。学校通过安排知名专家讲座、交流研讨等形式帮助教师找到符合课程思政特点的课程改革方法和途径。

教师深入学生班级，每位教师兼任 20 名学生的"职业导师"。教师要站在学生的角度去考虑问题，不把学生当成与教师界限分明的受教者，教师是单纯的授业者。师者，所以传道授业解惑也。只有善良正直、诚实守信、尊重他人、为人师表的教师通过言传身教，才能传递给学生正能量，指引学生前行，促使学生"亲其师，信其道"，实现教育和教学真正的有机统一。让金牌导游、金牌服务员走进课堂，现身说法，为教师讲述他们长期从事旅游行业的经验。

2.提高教师职业能力素质

要真正实现"授业+传道+解惑"，教师不仅需要端正的品行，更需要扎实的专业功底、科学的思维方式和用专业知识解答学生思政之惑、职业之惑的能力。旅游专业教师不仅要具有广泛的专业知识，而且要不断关注旅游产业的新业态，学习旅游行业的新知识，掌握旅游行业的新技能，并随时研究如何在教学中成功融入思政教育，帮助旅游专业学生在未来的就业岗位中用"英语+旅游""互联网+旅游""旅游+教育""旅游＋创新"谋取旅游行业的新岗位，从而使其获得更大发展。

（二）量化学生的思政考核指标

目前，很多旅游专业课程采用形成性评价与终结性评价相结合的形式来考核学生。形成性评价根据学生课前、课中、课后环节的参与度、完成度和阶段性考核进行评分。广东科学技术职业学院的旅游专业课程将形成性评价内容分为两个模块：一方面考核学生的知识和能力，包括导游讲解能力、酒店服务能力、计算机操作能力、市场营销能力等基本技能，考核的主体包括任课教师评价，其他教师评价，学生互评，自我评价；另一方面考核学生思政情感要素，从专业学习的认知变化、态度变化、情感变化、动机变化、兴趣变化、效率变化等方面去评价。终结性评价鼓励教师创新考试内容，在书面考试（如旅行社经营与管理、地方导游基础知识、旅游地理学等）中融合旅游行业的职业素养内容；在口语考试中（如模拟导游、导游英语等）以考核学生的中文、英文讲解为主。

表3　学生每月思政教育考核表

序号	思想言论上	行为举止上
1	是否写过入党申请书	是否有过见义勇为的表现
2	是否在公开场合（包括社交媒体）发表过激言论	是否有嘲笑、讽刺、歧视他人或社会的行为
3	是否想过帮助过室友或同学	是否有帮助过室友或同学的举动
4	是否想过主动打扫一次课室	是否主动打扫过一次课室
5	是否在思想上尊敬老师	是否有过为老师分忧的举动
6	是否使用过不文明的语言	是否有过不文明的行为
7	是否想过要参加志愿者活动	是否实际参与过志愿者活动
8	是否想过要帮扶困难地区	是否真正帮扶过有需要的孩子或老人
9	是否想过参与旅游扶贫	是否参与过旅游扶贫
10	是否想过用专业知识服务社会	是否参与过用专业知识服务社会的项目（包括周末兼职、锻炼等）

此表每周通过学生自评、班干部评价、宿管员评价、教师评价，每项1分，总分10分，最终形成对该学生的评价，并将分值换算计入学生综合素质学分。

（三）活化课程思政教学素材

随着课程改革的不断深入，时代对旅游专业教师的教材选取和把握能力要求越来越高。教师一方面必须以教材为依托，透过语言的表象剖析其所传达的文化和人文精神，结合旅游专业，教育学生爱国爱家、爱岗敬业、明辨美丑；提高思想觉悟，培养道德品质，树立健康的人生观、价值观和世界观。另一方面，教师必须站在学生的角度，选取并挖掘符合时代特点的思政元素，根据学生的年龄特点和心理状态，灵活运用思政元素。广东科学技术职业学院旅游学院要求全体教师利用课前五分钟时间讲讲岭南风土人情、人物故事，用林则徐虎门销烟击退英军、容闳留学耶鲁报效祖国、孙中山推翻帝制主张共和、广州72烈士为国捐躯等革命先烈的英勇事迹培养学生的爱国情操，用岭南四大园林的精巧设计和曲径通幽培养学生的审美趣味，用广州开通近代史上首个通商口岸、中国进出口商品交易会（简称"广交会"）被誉为中国第一会展激发学生学好英语建设祖国的热情。

（四）强化学生实习实践能力

1. 发挥第二课堂作用

充分发挥学生参与第二课堂的积极性和创造性，开展有益于学生身心健康的各种活动，为学生创造良好的育人氛围，如"世界心理卫生日""世界读书日""国际博物馆日""中国旅游日"等各项活动。学生在参与活动的过程中其自身能力和素质也在不断增强，如能够学会与人沟通、融洽相处等，这些能力和素质在学生即将从事的旅游行业工作中能够起到重要的作用。导游协会、非常英语、摩子鱼、模特队等社团组织开展了主题鲜明的导游讲解、英语演讲、英语辩论、心理情景剧表演、模仿秀等活动。学生将旅游专业特色与社团活动相结合，使得活动丰富多彩、精彩纷呈。辩论会增强了学生的反应能力和语言表达能力，拓展了学生的思维和视野；戏剧社模拟职场与生活，主题多样，展现了职场服务礼仪和规范，增强了学生的自尊意识和自信心理，为其日后走上旅游行业工作岗位奠定了基础。

2. 融入企业深入锻炼

参与企业实训对学生眼界的拓展和职业能力的提升十分有益。根据合作企业的季节性需求，学校可以不定期地组织学生到当地旅游景点、涉外酒店、旅行社等实习基地开展实训。广东科学技术职业学院充分利用中国航展、国际马戏节、广交会以及长隆海洋度假区等节事活动让学生进行实地演练。学生们制定好海岛游、红色景点游、休闲游等多种路线，学生导游带着老师游客用中英文讲解各景点的人文风情、历史渊源，完成整个游览过程后由教师和景点讲解人员共同参评。按照学院要求，每个学生必须参加企业顶岗实习 6 个月以上。参与校外实习，不仅能诊断出学生是否掌握景点的旅游知识和相关的业务技能，还能让学生在具体的演练实训中切实地体验当地文化，了解当地发展历史和现状，增强其爱国爱乡之情。

四、结语

在新媒体如此发达的时代，旅游专业课程思政既符合中国特色社会主义理论对高职教育的要求，也契合世旅组织教学质量认证的要求。净化教师思想品质、量化学生考核内容、活化思政教育题材、强化学生课外实践等措施必将成为旅游专业课程思政的主要路径。

参考文献

[1] 曾俊秀.大学英语课程思政建设的价值、原则与路径[J].宁波教育学院学报，2020（2）：13-16.

[2] 王丹丹，职业教育"课程思政"研究现状与展望[J].中国职业技术教育，2020（5）：46-51.

[3] 谢雨萍，建设一流专业背景下旅游管理专业课程思政建设初探——以桂林旅游学院旅游管理专业为例[J].湖北开放职业学院学报，2020，10（71-73）：2.

[4] 张燕燕，旅游类高职院校大学英语课程思政路径探究——以江苏旅游职业学院旅游专业为例[J]，河北旅游职业学院学报，2020，25（1）：5.

附录 2　论文："三教"改革背景下导游英语课程的革新实践

摘要：旅游行业亟须大量的高素质旅游英语人才，而旅游专业学生的英语水平却有待提高。作为英语导游考证核心课程的"导游英语"由于多种因素也需要提高教学质量。广东科学技术职业学院从优化课程设计、泛化职业理念、精选教材内容、强化 VR 技术、活化教学模式、深化项目实践等方面进行了成功的探索。

关键词：三教改革；导游英语；变革；策略

中图分类号：G718　文献标识码：A

On the Innovation Strategy of English Course for Tour Guides under the Background of Education Reform

Abstract: The tourism industry is in urgent need of a large number of high-quality tourism-related English talents, but the English proficiency of tourism majors is not satisfactory; As one of the core courses of English tour guide certificate,English for tour guides is in an awkward situation due to many factors. How to break out of the awkward situation and make it develop healthily? Guangdong Polytechnic of Science and Technology has successfully explored the countermeasures to break through the awkwardness from the aspects of optimizing course design, widening the hospitality concept , handpicking textbook content, strengthening VR technology, activating teaching mode, deepening the practical project,etc.

Key words :education reform of three elements; English course for tour guides; innovation strategy

一、高职院校导游英语课程

（一）认证体系简介

高职院校英语导游人才培养作为地方性的高校，其旅游相关职业主要是服务地方经济发展、为地方旅游业培养专业涉外导游人才。所以，作为地处粤港澳大湾区的高职院校，应以服务粤港澳大湾区旅游行业为重点，以促进区域经济发展为目标进行专业设置，设定人才培养方案，走产学研深度融合的道路来优化旅游英语课程的实践教学体系，从而实现专业人才培养目标，凸显地区经济发展特色。近几年粤港澳大湾区高校中旅游管理专业毕业生就业情况调查结果显示，约有 65% 的学生从事旅游相关工作，但仅有部分学生可以真正在工作中发挥其专业特长，学以致用。无论是珠海本地的旅游市场还是粤港澳大湾区旅游市场上仍急需高技能英语导游人才。因此，我校培养的英语导游人才与粤港澳大湾区旅游市场需求还存在一定的差距，尚不能满足地方市场的需求。据有关方面统计，目前广东省开设的旅游管理专业的高职院校多达 43 所，但开设导游英语课程的学校仅仅 11 所，只占 25%。其原因大致有以下内容。

（1）课程设计不合理。目前因为疫情影响等原因，一些旅游院校取消了旅游英语专业，英语导游人才的培养主要依托旅游管理专业。而旅游管理专业所开的课程必然以旅游类专业课程为主，英语类课程通常只有旅游英语一门，理论性较强，且课时较少，只有 36 个课时。因专业限制，无法开设较多的英语课程，这样的课时量几乎无法培养学生对英语知识灵活运用和跨文化交际的能力。

（2）教师结构不够合理。由于高校人才体制管理的原因，中级导游（如果没有其他职称）无法等同于中级职称，高级导游当然也无法享受高级职称待遇。这样势必影响了高校对专业导游（特别是金牌导游）师资的引进；而校内教师即便考取了高级导游资格证书，由于没有实践经历，

在指导学生实践方面大多是纸上谈兵，教师中缺乏具有实践经验的英语导游，具备英语导游现场考官资格的教师更是不多。现阶段该专业教师一般有两种情况：第一种情况是教师具备专业知识，但是英语水平有限；另一种情况是教师英语水平较高，但是专业水平较低。这些都对英语导游专业教学和人才培养质量产生消极的影响。

（3）教材编写不尽如人意。这一问题主要体现为缺乏具有针对性和地方属性的教材。多数院校旅游管理专业的旅游英语课程，使用的是旅游英语通用教材。其一，教材以各大著名景点的英文介绍为主要内容，理论知识较多，且侧重语法，在课时较少的情况下教师在教授过程中只能如蜻蜓点水一般，基本无法培养学生的听说读写译能力，导致学生学到的英语知识与旅游行业需求有些错位。其二，教材并不具备一定的地方特色。这些全国通用教材无法关注粤港澳大湾区的旅游景点、旅游文化，学生对英语知识点也知之甚少，无法实现对学生实际能力的培养，导致毕业生具备的能力与区域旅游市场对人才的需求存在差距。

（4）学生兴趣不够浓厚。目前很多高职高专院校，其生源高考分数在 200 分左右，可见其文化基础较差，且多数学生英语基础薄弱。加之近两年受新冠肺炎疫情的影响，旅游行业遭受重创，使得原本招生较为困难的旅游专业更是雪上加霜。一些学生只好退而求其次进入本专业学习。客观上薄弱的基础和主观上的迫不得已势必导致学生学习的困难和兴趣的降低。一方面，高中学习中主要以语法、笔试为主，大学的英语学习除了理论知识，还需加强其口语锻炼，开口讲英语对从未有过口语练习的一些学生而言很困难难；另一方面，学生在学习英语的过程中屡屡受挫，见不到成效，会导致其在学习中失去兴趣，形成失败的消极心理。这些原因使得英语旅游人才的培养难见成效。

二、高职院校导游英语课程变革之道

（一）优化课程结构体系

要制定合理的人才培养模式，依据市场对人才的需求科学地设置课程，充分融合旅游专业课程和英语课程。在实际的英语课程教学中，这两类知识点是密不可分、相互融合的。在教授英语课程时，教师想要达

到良好的教学效果，需将旅游的工作流程、工作技能等专业知识结合起来，通过模拟实际的工作过程锻炼学生听说读等语言知识的运用能力。因此，笔者建议一些将培养目标定位于导游的旅游院校开设导游专业并增设涉外导游方向，这样便可区别于其他方向的旅游管理人才培养。这样在课时分配上，可以向英语课程倾斜，真正形成以旅游类课程为主线，以英语语言应用能力培养为目的的课程设置模式（鉴于中文导游类的很多课程在中职阶段已经完成，将高职阶段的导游专业向英语方向倾斜正是旅游高职院校的基本特色和重要使命）。

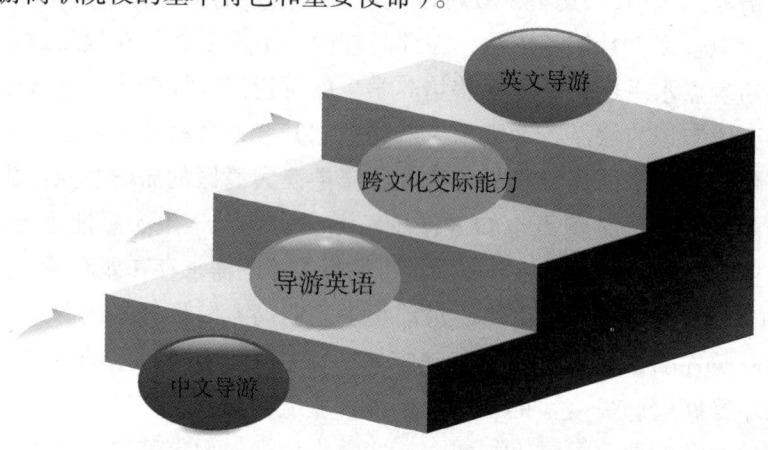

图 1　从中文导游到英文导游

各院校可以借鉴美国学历资格框架（Degree Qualifications Profile，DQP）的课程开发理念，优化并完善相应的课程标准。DQP 是以学生为中心、以成果为导向，教学设计和实施始终围绕学生的学习成果展开，主要关注以下四个方面：①学生需要完成的预期学习成果是什么；②为什么是这些学习成果；③如何帮助学生完成这些学习成果；④如何检测学生完成了这些学习成果。DQP 列出了三个学历层次、五个学习领域的 24 个具体学习成果参照点，这与 1998 年我国劳动和社会保障部（2008年撤销，成立人力资源和社会保障部）《国家技能振兴战略》中提出的"八大职业核心能力"基本一致，即自我学习、信息处理、数字应用、与人交流、与人合作、解决问题、创新革新和外语应用的能力。这为我国的高职院校设计课程预期学习成果提供了较具体的参照指标，对我国的高等职业教育改革具有一定的借鉴作用。

广东科学技术职业学院从 2017 年开始探索 DQP 框架下的教学改革，主要包括三个阶段：第一阶段是 DQP 有关理论的学习与探讨；第二阶段是专业规范、课程规范和考核方式的制定；第三阶段是对 DQP 课程规范的教学实践。其中，专业规范是按照 DQP 的五个维度的具体指标，以专业预期学习成果（Program Outcome，POC）和课程预期学习成果（Subject Outcome，SOC）来表达和细化每个专业的人才培养目标、规格，以此为依据确定每门课程的学时和学分。课程规范是在 DQP 指引下，学校、教师和学生三个平等主体间达成的适用于课程设计和实施的指导性文件。课程规范包括课程基本信息、课程总体目标设计、课程预期学习成果、教学内容、教学方式与手段、考核方式、教学资源七个部分。课程规范的制定和完善有助于本专业教师着眼课程定位目标，以预期学习成果为导向，提高教学水平，最终改进专业规范和实现对人才培养方案的优化。

表1　课程标准导引图

序号	结构	作用
1	课程基本信息	使学生了解本课程学分、学期分配、课程定位与作用
2	课程总体目标（POC）	支撑专业规范中的 POC，课程结束后学生能掌握的专业技能
3	课程预期学习成果（SOC）	学生在课程结束后需要完成的显性学习成果
4	教学内容	根据 POC 和 SOC 设计的教学内容
5	教学方式与手段	根据 SOC 采用的教学方式和手段
6	考核方式	对课程学习成果及效果的考核与评价，包括考核方式与评价标准
7	教学资源	学习本课程的教材、软件、硬件等资源

课程总目标：

（1）能够举例说明中西方文化差异在旅游行业中的具体实例。

（2）能够用旅游英语术语描述英文导游从入境接待、沿途讲解、酒店入住、餐饮服务、景点讲解、康乐服务、应急处置、欢送道别等一系列工作流程。

（3）能够用英文熟练讲解 1～2 个主要旅游景区。

（4）能够完成在机场、酒店、餐厅、景点等不同场合的沟通任务（如在处理客人投诉时能有效进行沟通）。

（5）能够用英语完成中国文化某一主题（包含民间风俗、传统节日、服装服饰、建筑园林等）的讲解，具备语言、文化、礼仪等多个领域的知识与技能。

（二）泛化旅游服务理念

虽然英语导游的基本职能在于为外国旅游者进行英语导游服务。但随着旅游行业从观光游览式旅游到休闲度假式旅游的转变，从跟团出游到自由旅行的转变，传统意义上的英语导游也要做出相应的转变。不少英语导游发挥自身英语应用能力较强的优势，有的在国际酒店从事前厅接待、销售服务等工作；有的在国际邮轮上从事接待和服务工作；有的在国际会展业中大显身手，从事翻译工作。这些都是与英文导游密切相关的岗位。目前一些转型的英文导游纷纷在一些海外社交媒体上建立自己的账号，发布自己的视频和文字讲解等，为吸引海外游客做足了功课。教师可以收集和采用这些案例丰富自己的教学内容，以拓宽学生的视野。

（三）精选教材教学内容

一本适合的教材是课堂教学成功与否的关键，也是实现课程所要达成目标的关键。鉴于目前很难找到适合粤港澳大湾区旅游市场的导游英语教材，广东科学技术职业学院与相关合作企业共同开发教材，其内容既包含对广州主要旅游景点的介绍，也包括珠海长隆国际海洋度假区的服务规范。编写教材时既要考虑学生的英语基础，又要注重教材的实用性和系统性，力求特色鲜明，还需具有一定的趣味性，突出岭南文化特色，将岭南地区旅游景点、岭南建筑、岭南人文、粤菜文化、特区文化、休闲娱乐、港澳风情等内容纳入教材，为粤港澳大湾区旅游业的发展服务。具有地方特色的教材，一方面，可以使学生的学习更具针对性和实用性，同时传承弘扬了地方文化。另一方面，学生在有一定的文化背景基础之上，学习相对应的英语知识也会更加轻松、更加自觉、更加投入，学习效率也会大大提高。

（四）强化 VR 技术手段

鉴于线下课堂的局限性和教学成本的考虑，很多学生无法接触旅游

的真实场景、真实对象，因此 VR 技术是目前体验式教学中最直接最高效的手段。目前，广东科学技术职业学院与广州数家科技公司开发出了旅游景区 100 套、突发情景 100 例，将这些 VR 情景在课堂里一一展示，让学生寻求解决之道，既增加了课堂的情境性，又激发了学生的学习兴趣，并突出了英语导游解决问题的实用性。

（五）活化教学互动模式

著名教育家郭思乐教授提出生本教育理念，他认为，生本教育是以"一切为了学生，高度尊重学生，全面依靠学生"为宗旨的教育，是真正做到以学生为学习的主人，为学生好学而设计的教育。生本教育要求教师关注学生，因材施教，把为教师的好教而设计的教育转向为学生的好学而设计的教育，从而使学生积极、主动、活泼、健康发展。

教师可以在课前开展 5 分钟英语趣配音、课中开展"剥豆豆"游戏抢答、课后 10 分钟开展观摩旅游城市英文宣传片等活动，由易到难，让所有学生能够开口说英语，激发其学习英语的兴趣。教师还可以在课中进行任务式教学、情景模拟教学、开展互动讨论、头脑风暴等，以教材内容为依托，以学生为学习主体创设学习情境，让学生自己活动起来，通过微课、慕课、翻转课堂等多种新媒体技术录制的课程以及基于云课堂、雨课堂等多种形式的讨论互动方式解决问题、巩固知识。尤其是通过与广东省金牌导游工作室或其他技能大师工作室的合作，在课内外与金牌英语导游实时互动，了解业界最新发展趋势和动态，使得学生学有目标、做有方向。课程采用理实一体化教室，让学生在"游玩"中体验、在体验中学习、在学习中提高。

（六）深化教学实践项目

常言道，实践出真知。只有通过实践，教师才能发现教学的不足，学生才会体会到书到用时方恨少。院校可以充分利用粤港澳大湾区会展资源丰富、节事赛事频繁的优势，将旅游与会展融为一体，让学生实时实地体验外事外贸服务接待工作。学生经过了无数次 VR 模拟实训，但在与外国客商或游客正面接触可能依然会紧张。有的学生在第一次广交会上从事为期 20 天的接待工作，开始时兴奋好奇、过程中紧张忙碌、结束后略有遗憾。不少学生的遗憾是对参展商的需求了解不够全面，或对顾客的问询答复不够流畅，或对自己的知识储备深感不足，这些遗憾都将化作学生第二次认真接待外国客人时的动力。

三、结论

随着出入境旅游业的蓬勃发展（虽然新冠肺炎疫情对其影响较大，但复苏中的旅游市场仍然蕴藏着巨大的潜力），市场对于英语旅游人才的需求越来越旺盛，对人才的要求标准也越来越高。广东科学技术职业学院旅游学院身处粤港澳大湾区，其旅游专业有着 20 余年的历史，但近三年以来专业教学改革力度之大、专业课程探索之深、校企融合之广前所未有。旅游学院肩负着旅游管理和旅游英语人才培养的重要使命，特别是要与港澳地区产业相融合。2018 年，广东科学技术职业学院旅游学院成为广东省内率先通过世界旅游组织教学质量认证（ UNWTO-TedQual ）的学院。同时，广东科学技术职业学院旅游学院根据大湾区旅游市场的需求在优化课程体系、泛化服务理念、精选教材内容、强化 VR 技术、活化教学模式、强化实践项目等方面进行了有益的改革与尝试，使得课程既有趣味性和观赏性，又有实用性和针对性，提高了学生学习导游英语的积极性和主动性，增强了学生专业素养和英语运用能力，提高了学生报考英语导游证的积极性和通过率，培养出了一批深受业界好评的旅游人才（尤其是旅游英语人才），进而为粤港澳大湾区旅游业的发展做出了应有的贡献。

参考文献

[1] 严中华 . 国外职业教育核心理念解读 [M]. 北京：清华大学出版社，2017.

[2] 李德煜 . 以英语导游证为导向，培养旅游英语应用型人才 [J]. 文教资料，2019（25）：113-114.

[3] 吴涤 . 基于 ESP 需求分析的高职高专英语导游实训课教学研究 [J]. 现代职业教育，2020（17）：98-99.

[4] 祝钦 . 地方高职院校英语导游人才培养探究——以湖北工业作业技术学院为例，[J].2019（3）：27-29.

后 记

　　2015年5月一个偶然的机会，笔者有幸以参观者的身份实地了解了浙江旅游职业学院和成都职业技术学院申报的世界旅游组织教学质量认证项目，实地感受了两所学校在当地的影响力与知名度。2017年7月，笔者参加了中山大学旅游学院主办的认证培训会议，于是便萌发了参与世界旅游组织教学质量认证的念头。这是一项浩大的工程，从2017年9月正式递交申请以来，课题组焚膏继晷、夜以继日地努力工作，牺牲了大量的休息时间，花费了无数的精力和心血，先后撰写了长达12万字的自评报告，收集、整理并翻译了100万字的佐证材料，终于在2019年5月获得正式通过。

　　在项目申报和建设的过程中有幸得到了广东科学技术职业学院的万方秋、马玉波、蒋桂红、唐春英、郭卫娜、杨易、冯淑玲、段金梅、周程明、陈小兵、万承刚、顾忆华、苏丹、甘佳讯、李任欣、李嘉伟、赖玺婷、胡晓晶、吴迪、许雷、刘中梁、徐晓丽、张彤、康梅林、杨宏伟等老师，以及广东省拱北口岸中国旅行社有限公司、珠海长隆国际海洋度假区、广东省导游协会、珠海市文体旅游局、珠海市旅游总会、珠海中金湾区文体旅游局等单位的热情支持。感谢诸君在百忙之中提供的协助，使得项目顺利通过；更要感谢吴肖淮教授的大力支持，让我们一鼓作气将这一成果公开出版。

　　由于时间、精力和学识所限，书中难免存在不足之处，敬请批评指正！

著作者：杨义德 朱瀚 魏微

2022年10月